AF791540

Missing V

Veronika Dolar · Teresa Perry
Editors

Missing Voices in Economics

Addressing the Gender Gap

palgrave
macmillan

Editors
Veronika Dolar
Department of Economics
Pace University
New York, NY, USA

Teresa Perry
Department of Economics
California State University San Bernardino
San Bernardino, CA, USA

ISBN 978-3-031-97179-2 ISBN 978-3-031-97180-8 (eBook)
https://doi.org/10.1007/978-3-031-97180-8

© The Editor(s) (if applicable) and The Author(s), under exclusive license to Springer Nature Switzerland AG 2026

This work is subject to copyright. All rights are solely and exclusively licensed by the Publisher, whether the whole or part of the material is concerned, specifically the rights of translation, reprinting, reuse of illustrations, recitation, broadcasting, reproduction on microfilms or in any other physical way, and transmission or information storage and retrieval, electronic adaptation, computer software, or by similar or dissimilar methodology now known or hereafter developed.
The use of general descriptive names, registered names, trademarks, service marks, etc. in this publication does not imply, even in the absence of a specific statement, that such names are exempt from the relevant protective laws and regulations and therefore free for general use.
The publisher, the authors and the editors are safe to assume that the advice and information in this book are believed to be true and accurate at the date of publication. Neither the publisher nor the authors or the editors give a warranty, expressed or implied, with respect to the material contained herein or for any errors or omissions that may have been made. The publisher remains neutral with regard to jurisdictional claims in published maps and institutional affiliations.

This Palgrave Macmillan imprint is published by the registered company Springer Nature Switzerland AG
The registered company address is: Gewerbestrasse 11, 6330 Cham, Switzerland

If disposing of this product, please recycle the paper.

Preface

Women in Economics

In March 2021, to celebrate Women's History Month, I wrote an article titled "The gender gap in economics is huge—it's even worse than tech." In this piece, I highlighted a reality too often ignored: Economics, as an academic discipline, is one of the worst fields for women. Through existing research and data, I showed how pervasive sexism, underrepresentation, and stagnant progress have held women back in ways more severe than even in the traditionally male-dominated STEM fields. Despite the increasing visibility of women in leadership roles across various sectors, economics lags far behind. Fewer than 15% of full professors in economics are women, and this percentage has remained unchanged for more than two decades.

My article brought to light systemic issues: a glaring lack of role models, the entrenched sexism in economics departments, and the hostile environments that make it difficult for women to thrive or even persist in the field. Women economists often face patronizing or hostile questioning when presenting their research—something men are less likely to encounter. It's a barrier that goes beyond simple underrepresentation and reflects a deep-rooted, gendered power dynamic in the discipline.

A 2019 American Economic Association survey revealed a stark reality: nearly half of women in economics reported gender discrimination, including exclusion from key professional opportunities and backlash for speaking about sexism. New evidence reinforces these concerns.

A forthcoming American Economic Review paper, Gender Differences in Economics Seminars, shows that women presenting research are interrupted more often—and more negatively—than men, even after accounting for presenter, paper, and audience characteristics (Dupas et al., forthcoming). These interruptions are more likely to cut women off mid-sentence and undermine their authority. The study also finds that female audience members engage more with female presenters, highlighting the importance of visible role models. Together, this research underscores how the profession's lack of diversity not only harms women's careers but also limits the discipline's creativity, rigor, and policy relevance.

Within minutes of the article being published on the Conversation platform,[1] I encountered a striking example of the very sexism I had written about. I received a comment from a reader that read:

> Another nose-counting article to support a predetermined outcome. Prof. Doker should be ashamed of herself for this blatant example of post hoc, ergo propter hoc logic. I'm sure that there are virtually no leading economists of mixed Irish Eskimo extraction either. What exactly does this prove? The fact that she has discovered fewer women in Economics leadership roles in no way leads to the conclusions she has drawn. Women in general may not be attracted to this field in greater numbers. Perhaps Prof. Doker has personal experience of the exclusion policies which she is citing. If so, she should act on these experiences and seek legal or financial remedies. That she is a woman who is already a regular faculty member in a State University weakens her argument considerably.

Aside from misspelling my name, the comment did precisely what I had argued was part of the problem: It dismissed my argument, made personal attacks, and reduced my professional insights to mere "nose-counting." The commentator suggested that I should be "ashamed" of myself. But why should I feel ashamed for exposing inequities that continue to harm so many women? Rather than engaging with the data, the evidence, or the systemic issues I highlighted, the focus was on undermining me as an individual. This is the kind of hostility that women in economics often

[1] The Conversation is an independent, nonprofit online media outlet that provides news and analysis written by academic experts and researchers. It aims to bridge the gap between academia and the general public by offering accessible, evidence-based articles on a wide range of topics, including science, politics, culture, and economics.

face: not a reasoned critique of our work, but an attack on our right to speak at all.

Despite the initial hostility, what followed was largely an outpouring of support and meaningful discussion. The article was widely shared on social media, picked up by national and international outlets, and even translated into French and Italian. What surprised me even more, however, were the emails I received from women all over the world—women who saw their own experiences reflected in my writing. These personal stories underscored just how deeply ingrained these issues are and how little space exists for women to share their struggles openly.

One email in particular has stayed with me. It came from a woman pursuing a PhD in economics. She recounted a disheartening experience in a reading class where two male professors told her that the job market was tougher for white male students, dismissing her concerns about gender and race affecting job prospects. When she attempted to share her own experience of having to "prove herself more than required," her professors insisted that academia was free of a gender gap. Their remarks left her frustrated and demotivated. It took her nearly a year to process the event, and when she read my article, she finally felt a sense of validation and solidarity.

What struck me most about her message—and many others like it—was how women in economics are often gaslighted into believing that their struggles are unique, isolated experiences rather than symptoms of a widespread, systemic issue. These women begin to doubt themselves, thinking that perhaps it is only their personal circumstances, or a lack of individual ability, that is responsible for their challenges. This gaslighting creates a vicious cycle of self-doubt, where women internalize the discrimination they face rather than recognizing it as part of a larger, pervasive problem.

The silence that surrounds these experiences only compounds the problem. We do not talk about them enough. When women feel alone in their struggles, the collective issue goes unaddressed, and no solutions are sought. By not sharing our stories, we allow the system to persist unchallenged, perpetuating an environment where sexism can thrive. This is why writing this book became so important—to give voice to these experiences and break the isolation.

Her story, like many others I received, reminded me just how critical this conversation is. It is easy for male economists, who often live in a bubble of privilege, to deny or dismiss the gender gap. But for women, especially those from underrepresented backgrounds, the challenges are very real. We face barriers not just of merit, but of perception. We lack the role models and institutional support that our male counterparts often take for granted, and this absence makes our struggles even more difficult to overcome.

In the following chapters, *Missing Voices in Economics* seeks to break the long-standing silence surrounding the experiences of women in economics by combining and exploring three critical spheres of analysis. The first sphere is the absence of women and the concept of gender in mainstream economic analysis and models, as discussed by scholars like Ferber and Nelson (1993, 2003). The second addresses the neglected contributions of women economists to the evolution of economic thought, an area highlighted by Kuiper (2022) and Chassonnery-Zaïgouche et al. (2022). Finally, the third focuses on the persistently low presence of women in the economics discipline, particularly in top academic positions, as noted by Lundberg and Stearns (2019) and Ginther and Kahn (2021). By combining these three areas of inquiry, this book not only exposes the barriers women face but also empowers those who feel isolated in their struggles, offering a broader perspective on the structural inequities that persist in the field.

The first sphere highlights the exclusion of women and gender considerations in economic models, a gap that has long narrowed the scope of economic thought. Economic policies that fail to account for gender differences perpetuate a limited understanding of the economy. By centering gender in economic analysis, as Ferber and Nelson have advocated, we can create models and policies that better reflect the lived realities of all people, not just a subset of the population.

The second sphere examines the overlooked contributions of women economists to the development of economic theory. Kuiper (2022) and Chassonnery-Zaïgouche et al. (2022) have documented how the work of women economists has often been marginalized, their contributions ignored or forgotten. This book aims to restore their rightful place in the history of economic thought, highlighting their groundbreaking ideas and showing how their insights have shaped the field, even if they were not always recognized for it.

The third sphere addresses the underrepresentation of women in the economics profession, especially in top academic and policymaking roles. As Lundberg and Stearns (2019) and Ginther and Kahn (2021) have shown, despite some progress, women remain woefully underrepresented in influential positions within the field. This lack of representation creates a cycle where fewer women have access to mentorship, opportunities, and platforms to share their research. This book calls attention to this imbalance and advocates for structural changes to ensure that more women are able to rise to the highest levels of academia and policymaking.

By combining these three spheres of analysis, this book examines the barriers women face in economics and the urgent need for systemic change. It is more than a collection of personal stories or an analysis of gender disparities; it is a call to action. *Missing Voices in Economics* brings together diverse experiences to highlight not just the challenges but also the resilience and contributions of women in the field. It insists that diversity is not a token gesture, but an essential component of shaping a more inclusive, dynamic, and forward-thinking discipline.

This book brings together a rich and diverse set of perspectives on the intersection of gender and economics, offering a critical examination of how systemic barriers have shaped the experiences of women in the field. In "Missing Voices, Missing Perspectives, Missing Women, Missing Reality—Gender in Economics," Marlene Kim sets the stage by discussing the long-standing exclusion of gender perspectives from mainstream economic analysis. Laura Beltran's chapter builds on this by exploring how external factors, such as institutional norms and departmental cultures, affect gender equity in U.S. economics departments. Similarly, Giulia Zacchia and Izaskun Zuazu analyze gender differences in research areas among top economists, raising essential questions about how the discipline itself is gendered.

The book also broadens its scope internationally, with Marcella Corsi and Giulia Zacchia examining institutional discrimination in Italian universities, while Asma Hyder addresses gender diversity in South Asian academic spaces. The chapters by Ariane Agunsoye and Jacqueline Strenio, and Sarah F. Small and Teresa Perry, delve into how the undergraduate economics curriculum can be a pivotal point for attracting and retaining more women in the field, particularly through courses on gender economics. Justine Dombrowski's "Transing the Gendered Lens in Economics" offers a groundbreaking approach to rethinking the discipline through a non-binary lens, while Olivia Young's chapter reclaims the work of Florence Edler, shedding light on women's overlooked contributions to economic history. Finally, Irene Sotiropoulou's exploration of economic critique in folktales uncovers the voices of marginalized women who used storytelling to challenge patriarchal economic norms. Each chapter contributes to a fuller understanding of how gender intersects with economics, both historically and in contemporary practice.

While this book centers on the missing voices of women in economics, it's crucial to acknowledge that many other marginalized voices are similarly underrepresented in the field. For instance, Black economists make up less than 4% of all PhD economists in the USA, a stark reminder that race, in addition to gender, remains a significant barrier to full participation in the discipline. Hispanic and Indigenous scholars are also severely underrepresented, as are economists from the LGBTQ+ community and those from lower socioeconomic backgrounds. These gaps reflect a broader systemic issue that goes beyond individual experiences of exclusion to point to deep-seated inequities within the profession itself. The lack of diversity means we lose out on the full range of insights, experiences, and solutions that these groups could bring to economic thought and policymaking.

Addressing the exclusion of these voices is not just about fairness or representation; it's about enhancing the quality and relevance of economics as a discipline. Research consistently shows that diverse teams produce better outcomes, as they are able to approach problems from multiple angles and create more innovative solutions. In economics, this kind of diversity is especially critical. When entire groups are left out of the conversation, the resulting analyses and policies are less likely to be inclusive or effective for the populations they are meant to serve. For example, policies designed without input from underrepresented communities may inadvertently perpetuate inequality rather than addressing it. By bringing more women, people of color, LGBTQ+ individuals, and others into the fold, we ensure that economics becomes not just a tool for understanding the world as it is, but for shaping a world that is more just and equitable.

This book is only one element of the conversation. While it highlights the experiences of women in economics, the hope is that it sparks a broader movement toward addressing the missing voices of all marginalized groups in the field. The challenges women face are often compounded by other intersecting identities—race, ethnicity, sexuality, and class—which means that the solutions must be equally multifaceted. Future work must go beyond a gendered lens to incorporate the full range of underrepresented perspectives, ensuring that the discipline evolves in a way that is truly inclusive.

Glenwood Landing, USA
April 2025

Veronika Dolar

References

Chassonnery-Zaïgouche, C., E. L. Forget, and J. D. Singleton. 2022. Women and Economics: New Historical Perspectives. *History of Political Economy* 54(S1):1–15.

Dupas, P., A. Handlan, A. S. Modestino, M. Niederle, M. Seré, H. Sheng, J. Wolfers, and the Seminar Dynamics Collective. Forthcoming. Gender Differences in Economics Seminars. *American Economic Review.*

Ferber, M. A., and J. A. Nelson. 1993. *Beyond Economic Man: Feminist Theory and Economics.* Chicago: University of Chicago.

Ginther, D. K., and S. Kahn. 2021. Women in Academic Economics: Have We Made Progress? *AEA Papers and Proceedings* 111:138–142.

Kuiper, E. 2022. *A Herstory of Economics.* Hoboken: Wiley.

Lundberg, Shelly, and Jenna Stearns. 2019. Women in Economics: Stalled Progress. *Journal of Economic Perspectives* 33(1):3–22.

Contents

Missing Voices, Missing Perspectives, Missing Women, Missing Reality—Gender in Economics 1
Marlene Kim

Exploring the Role of External Characteristics on Gender Equity: A Study of Economics Departments in the United States 37
Laura Beltran Figueroa

Is Economics What Women Economists Do? Gender Differences in Fields of Research Among Top Economists 57
Giulia Zacchia and Izaskun Zuazu

Institutional Discrimination: An Analysis of Women in Economics in Italian Universities 75
Giulia Zacchia and Marcella Corsi

Gender Diversity in Economics in South Asian Academic Spaces 97
Asma Hyder

Diversity, Equity, and Inclusion in the Undergraduate Economics Curriculum: A Patch for the Leaky Pipeline of Women in Economics? 113
Ariane Agunsoye and Jacqueline Strenio

Place and Space for Feminist Economists? The Development and Maintenance of Feminist Economics Graduate Training in the United States 135
Sarah F. Small and Teresa Perry

Can Gender Economics Courses Attract More Undergraduate Women to Economics Departments? 155
Teresa Perry and Sarah F. Small

Trans*ing the Economic Lens 173
Justine Dombrowski

Florence Edler: The "Indispensable Collaborator" of Raymond De Roover 197
Olivia M. Young

Doing the "Bad Job" to Make a Living and Expose Men: Economic Critique Voiced in Folktales by Marginalised Women 215
Irene Sotiropoulou

Conclusion 247
Teresa Perry

Index 255

Editors and Contributors

About the Editors

Veronika Dolar is Associate Professor in the Economics Department at Pace University, where she teaches courses including introductory microeconomics, introductory macroeconomics, health economics, economics of poverty, economics of income distribution, and economics of gender, race, and class. Her research focuses on health economics, labor economics, and economic education, and she has been widely published in these areas in numerous peer-reviewed journals. In addition to her academic work, Dr. Dolar writes articles on economic topics for the general public, which have been featured in various national and international news outlets. She raised in Yugoslavia during the war, and she has a remarkable background; English is her third language. Dolar obtained her international baccalaureate in Italy at the United World College of the Adriatic and went on to graduate summa cum laude from Western University. She earned a PhD from the University of Minnesota. She is a co-author of the widely used textbooks ECON Micro and ECON Macro (Cengage), which integrate empirical perspectives and critical approaches to traditional economic models.

Teresa Perry is an Assistant Professor in the Department of Economics at California State University San Bernardino. She holds a PhD in Economics from Colorado State University. Her research focuses on the political economy of health, interdisciplinary approaches to studying substance use and addiction in economics, and feminist economics. She is particularly interested in how capitalism and institutional power shape the lived experiences of women and other marginalized groups.

Contributors

Ariane Agunsoye is an Assistant Professor of Economics at Goldsmiths, University of London. She is also on the steering committee of D-Econ, a network of economists who aim to promote inclusiveness in economics, and on the management committee of the Association for Heterodox Economics. Prior to joining Goldsmiths, she was a visiting lecturer in Germany and worked several years in the private sector. Her current research interests are centered on the impact of financialization on everyday life. In particular, she is interested in exploring gender inequalities in times of asset-based welfare and in interdisciplinary approaches in studying financialization, combining social theory, finance, cultural, and political economy.

Laura Beltran-Figueroa is a Postdoctoral Researcher at the Center for Women and Work, Rutgers University. She holds a PhD in Economics from the University of Utah and previously served as a Fellow at Voices for Utah Children. Her research centers on public policy and feminist economics, with a particular focus on labor market inequalities, child care accessibility, and social benefit programs. She employs both quantitative and qualitative methods to examine how economic structures and workplace policies affect the lives of women, immigrants, and low-income families, aiming to inform more equitable policy solutions that address systemic barriers to economic security.

Marcella Corsi, received PhD in Economics from the University of Manchester (UK). She teaches political economy (undergraduate level) and gender economics (postgraduate level) at "Sapienza" University of Rome. Her research activity mainly focuses on issues related to social inclusion, social protection and income distribution. In the past, she has carried out several research projects (e.g. about financial exclusion and microfinance, women empowerment, social inclusion and migration) at international level. She has worked as a consultant for OECD, European Parliament and European Commission, and several Italian institutions.

Since March 2017 she is editor of the International Review of Sociology, member of the editorial board of the web-magazine inGenere.it and coordinator of Minerva–Laboratory on diversity and gender inequality.

Justine Dombrowski is a (barely) 20-something trans-researcher, living with their partner and pups in dusty the southwest. They are in the sunset stages of their academics, finishing their MEd and PhD in Economics soon. Justine intends on engaging in participatory study, as well as to make every subject they touch more complex and nuanced. They have interests in education, surveillance, and gender economics, and they hope to teach and do research with students in the near future.

Asma Hyder is a Professor and Dean of the School of Economics and Social Sciences at IBA, Karachi. She received the Fulbright J. William Award for International Understanding and did her post-doctorate from the University of Pennsylvania, USA. She has been a Visiting Research Fellow at the University of Sussex, London School of Economics and Political Science, UK and Carleton University, Canada. Her research interest focuses on development, health, the social sector in general, labor market issues and well-being. Her major contribution to literature is the empirical investigation of households' behavior toward labor market decisions and child welfare during climatic and negative economic shocks in developing and poorest societies of the world.

Marlene Kim is Professor of Economics at the University of Massachusetts, Boston. A labor economist, she specializes in race and gender discrimination in employment and the working poor. She is the recipient of the first Rhonda Williams Prize and has published widely in journals and books, including editing Race and Economic Opportunity in the Twenty-First Century (Routledge, 2007). She serves on the editorial boards of Industrial Relations, the Review of Radical Political Economics, and Feminist Economics. Her current research examines race and gender discrimination, especially the intersection of race and gender in the earnings of women of color. She holds a PhD in Economics from the University of California, Berkeley.

Sarah F. Small is an Assistant Professor in the Department of Economics at the University of Utah. She holds a PhD in Economics from Colorado State University and was previously a Visiting Scholar at the Center for the History of Political Economy at Duke University and a Postdoctoral Researcher at the Center for Women and Work at Rutgers University. Her research focuses on intrahousehold bargaining, occupational crowding, history of feminist economic thought, and feminist methodology and pedagogy.

Irene Sotiropoulou is a lawyer and heterodox economist. She is the author of *Machines Against Measures* (2023). She specializes in ecological, feminist, solidarity and non-capitalist economics, heterodox theories and practices about money and finance, non-monetary economics, and small production and distribution modes. Her economics research has been awarded fellowships by the GEM-IWG/GEM-Europe and World Social Science (UNESCO) Fellowship programs and a Newton Mobility Grant by the British Academy.

Jacqueline Strenio is Assistant Professor of Economics at Norwich University in Vermont. Her research and teaching interests are in feminist economics, health, public policy, and pedagogy. Her current research focuses on violence against women and girls. She holds a Higher Education Teaching Specialist (HETS) designation and is committed to implementing more effective, research-backed practices in her classrooms and encouraging diversity in economics education more broadly. She has published on the necessity of plurality and innovation in economics education. She earned her MS and PhD in Economics from the University of Utah and a BA in Economics from the University of Colorado, Boulder.

Olivia M. Young is a third year PhD student in the History Department at the University of Chicago, whose research focuses on early modern Western Sephardim in Western Europe and North Africa, and their roles as agents of community reconstitution, political economic theorists, informal and semi-formal diplomats, and political actors, as well as the history of political economy and cross-cultural relations more broadly. She has previously taken degrees at the London School of Economics (BA in History with Russian Language) and Yale University (MA in History) and maintains a special interest in the underappreciated role which female scholars have played in the development of her specialty.

Giulia Zacchia is Associate Professor of Economics in the Department of Statistics, Sapienza University of Rome. She collaborates with the Minerva–Laboratory on gender diversity and inequalities (https://web.uniroma1.it/labminerva/en [web.uniroma1.it]). Her research interests include social and financial inclusion, feminist economics, and gender gaps in labor markets and academia. Her current research project focuses on identifying women's contributions to the development of economic thought, and she seeks to address the lack of knowledge about who the pioneering women in economics were in Italy.

Izaskun Zuazu is a Postdoctoral Researcher in the Institute for Socio-Economics, University of Duisburg (Germany). She holds a PhD in Economics from the Econometrics and Statistics Department, University of the Basque Country (Spain). She was a Visiting Scholar at the Toulouse School of Economics and in the Politics Department of New York University. She worked as a Postdoctoral Fellow for the Statistics Department at Sapienza University of Rome. Zuazu's research is focused on political economy, labor economics, and macroeconomics from a gender perspective. She is currently working on automation and women in manufacturing, and the intersection between gender and labor market status in political ideology. Her work appears in *European Journal of Political Economy*, *Empirical Economics*, *Kyklos*, and more.

List of Figures

Exploring the Role of External Characteristics on Gender Equity: A Study of Economics Departments in the United States

Fig. 1	Upset plot with institutional characteristics of top economics departments	45
Fig. 2	Field categorization among women professors	47
Fig. 3	Distribution of research interests among women	48

Is Economics What Women Economists Do? Gender Differences in Fields of Research Among Top Economists

Fig. 1	Main field of women and men top economists 1983–2017 (share). *Data source*: own elaboration based on the database constructed from RePEc (1983–2017 averages)	63
Fig. 2	Main field of women and men top economists by year (share). *Data source*: own elaboration based on the database constructed from RePEc. Note: Data collapsed into five-year bins for smoothness, i.e., the 2013 bin contains data from 2013 to 2017	63
Fig. 3	Women and men top economists in selected fields by year (share). *Data source*: own elaboration based on the database constructed from RePEc	65
Fig. 4	Evolution of gender segregation by field of research among top economists. *Data source*: own elaboration based on the database constructed from RePEc	67

Fig. 5 Gender economics and feminist economics ad fields of research (%). *Data source*: own elaboration based on the database constructed from RePEc 68

Institutional Discrimination: An Analysis of Women in Economics in Italian Universities

Fig. 1 PhD research area (%). *Source*: survey distributed to members of the Italian Economic Society in 2013–185 respondents 81
Fig. 2 Distribution of research topics (JEL Code) chosen for the PhD thesis (%). *Source*: survey distributed to members of the Italian Economic Society in 2013–185 respondents 83
Fig. 3 Distribution by domestic and care workload within the household. *Source*: survey distributed to members of the Italian Economic Society in 2013–185 respondents 87
Fig. 4 Distribution by work time spent on research. *Source*: survey distributed to members of the Italian Economic Society in 2013–185 respondents 88
Fig. 5 Thematic segregation index by age group. *Source*: survey distributed to members of the Italian Economic Society in 2013–185 respondents 90

List of Tables

Missing Voices, Missing Perspectives, Missing Women, Missing Reality—Gender in Economics

Table 1 Female representation (percent female) in the economics profession, 2022 3
Table 2 Experiences of discrimination and unfair treatment as a student 7
Table 3 Academic economists experiencing discrimination or unfair treatment regarding... 9
Table 4 Non-academia: Have you personally experienced discrimination or unfair treatment with regard to... 13
Table 5 Outcomes by gender 18
Table 6 Experiences of economists 18

Exploring the Role of External Characteristics on Gender Equity: A Study of Economics Departments in the United States

Table 1 Descriptive statistics for the sample of faculty in top economics departments 46
Table 2 Regressions depicting the relationship between gender distribution among economics faculty and external factors 51

Institutional Discrimination: An Analysis of Women in Economics in Italian Universities

Table 1 Average number of publications per year over the last 5 years 84
Table 2 Number of publications per year in the last 5 years in relation to time spent on research 89

Can Gender Economics Courses Attract More Undergraduate Women to Economics Departments?

Table 1 Top 5 Majors in the gender in the economy course 160
Table 2 Summary statistics 161
Table 3 Percentage of students that take another economics course 163
Table 4 Effect of gender in the economy on taking a future economics course 165
Table 5 Intersectional analysis of the effect of gender in the economy on taking a future economics course 166
Table 6 Effect of a race, inequality, and discrimination course on taking a future economics course 167

Conclusion

Table 1 Degrees awarded to women by year and discipline 248

Missing Voices, Missing Perspectives, Missing Women, Missing Reality—Gender in Economics

Marlene Kim

1 Introduction

Economics has a gender problem. Women remain a minority in the profession and have difficulties advancing. Compared to 13% of male economists, 30% of female economists believe they have been discriminated against or treated unfairly (Allgood et al. 2019). Even top officials of the profession acknowledge that "many members of the profession have suffered harassment and discrimination during their careers, including both overt acts of abuse and more subtle forms of marginalization" and that "this is unacceptable" (Blanchard et al. 2019). Unfortunately, as this chapter shows, such behaviors are not unusual: Women experience more discrimination, unfair treatment, biased evaluations of their work, and less mentoring and support compared to their male counterparts.

This chapter surveys the problems women face in the profession of economics. I draw from research on this topic, including from the American Economic Association's (AEA's) survey of its members (Allgood

M. Kim (✉)
University of Massachusetts, Boston, USA
e-mail: Marlene.Kim@umb.edu

© The Author(s), under exclusive license to Springer Nature Switzerland AG 2026

V. Dolar and T. Perry (eds.), *Missing Voices in Economics*,
https://doi.org/10.1007/978-3-031-97180-8_1

et al. 2019; henceforth “climate survey”). I also draw from my research on this subject (Kim 2023a, 2023b), which involved interviewing approximately forty women in the economics profession.[1] Finally, I draw from my own experience as a female economist in this very male profession over thirty years. I close with recommendations and remedies for reducing these problems. Because the problems are many, including hostility, sexual harassment, and the very theory of economics itself, radical changes are needed to uproot the problems of deep sexism in the profession. These reforms include not only relatively costless and traditional initiatives, such as providing information about economics to undergraduate students and mentoring for graduate students and junior scholars, but also overhauling the very theory, instruction, and practices to increase inclusivity and to reshape economic theory and research to reflect the realities of women. Doing so would improve the profession and economic policies that can contribute to healthy and robust world economies.

2 The Problem of Gender in the Profession of Economics

In the US, women remain a minority in the economics profession (Committee on the Status of Women in the Economics Profession (CSWEP) 2023), and progress toward greater representation has stalled (CSWEP 2022; Lundberg and Stearn 2019; Avilova and Golden 2020). Economics is arguably worse than other fields that require mathematics, including science, technology, engineering, and math (STEM). Female faculty comprise just one-quarter of economists. Worse, the higher the position and rank and the more prestigious the school, the fewer women.

[1] These studies include Kim (2023a and 2023b). I interviewed twenty women for Kim (2023a) and about twenty for Kim (2023b), using a snowball methodology, which entailed contacting people I knew and asking if they knew of others I should interview about gender and economics. For Kim (2024), I interviewed women during 2020 via Skype. For Kim (2024), I interviewed women during 2022 and in early 2023 using the same methodology. For this latter study, I also posted on the listserv for the International Association for Feminist Economics (IAFFE), stating interest in interviewing women about gender and economics. I presented preliminary findings at the IAFFE conference and at the Allied Social Science Association conferences in 2022 and 2023 and asked for more interviewees during these presentations. I use material from these that have already been published, but I also use statements from interviews that I conducted for this study that had not been previously used or published. Some interviewees wished to remain anonymous.

Women are more likely to work in non-tenure-track positions: They comprise 37% of these faculty. In contrast, they comprise 24% of tenure-track faculty (see Table 1). More women serve in departments without PhD programs than in departments with them—36% compared to 26%, respectively (see Table 1). Even among departments with PhD programs, fewer women work in the top 20 departments, and fewer yet, among those at departments in the top 10 schools (22% and 20%, respectively).

The rank of faculty matters. Women populate Assistant Professor levels to a greater extent than they do Associate Professor positions, and to a greater extent still than Full Professorship. For example, in departments with doctoral programs, women comprise 34% of Assistant Professors, 28% of Associate Professors, and 18% of Full Professors. These proportions are higher for women in departments without PhD programs (42%, 38%, and 28%, respectively). Note that the same pattern of declining proportions of women persists the higher the rank along the tenure track.

Table 1 Female representation (percent female) in the economics profession, 2022

	Percent Female in Economics Departments by Type of Program			
	Departments with Doctoral Programs			*Departments w/o PhD Programs*
	All	*Top 10*	*Top 20*	
1. Faculty				
Type of Faculty				
a. All Faculty	26.3	19.7	21.6	35.7
b. All Tenure Track	23.9	16.7	18.8	35.1
c. All Non-Tenure Track	37.2	6.8	38.8	38.4
Rank of Faculty				
d. Full Professor	17.5	14.0	15.0	28.1
e. Associate Professor	27.6	21.3	22.9	37.7
f. Assistant Professor	33.7	24.1	26.7	42.4
2. Students				
g. PhDs Granted	31.9	24.4	24.3	N/A
h. 1st year PhD	37.1	38.8	37.0	N/A
i. Econ Majors Graduated	34.0	41.8	40.0	38.8
j. Senior Majors	35.7	39.6	39.4	37.4

Source: Table 1, CSWEP 2023

Although these data derive only from the US, the patterns seen of fewer women the higher the rank and at the top institutions endure in Europe.[2]

Elite schools in the US employ even fewer women: Among the top 10(20) schools, only 14(15)% of Full Professors are women, 21(23)% of Associate Professors are women, and 24(27)% of Assistant Professors are female (see Table 1). This means that only eight women are Associate Professors in the top ten departments and only 21 in the top twenty! (CSWEP 2023). These top 20 schools produce the majority of faculty who teach in PhD-granting departments.[3] Research indicates that greater shares of female faculty in economics departments are correlated with more female graduate students and higher chances of female graduate student success (possibly because of the existence of role models and mentors) (see Boustan and Langan, 2019; Bostwick and Weinberg, 2020). Thus, this dearth of women as faculty can impede the progress and success of female graduate students and limit the ability to diversify the field.

The pipeline to tenure-track positions remains constricted: Only 32% of those receiving PhDs in economics are women (see Table 1). A higher proportion, around 37–38%, populate the number of first-year PhD students. This indicates that women continue to fail to complete their PhD programs to a greater extent than male students. Either more women than men are dropping out of these programs, failing their first-year exams, or are failing for other reasons.

Interestingly, the pattern of elitism and female representation is somewhat attenuated in the top 10 and 20 schools for undergraduates: The proportion of women who are senior majors and who graduate with econ majors are at roughly the same levels as each other (in the top 10 and 20 programs) and higher than that of other (not top 20) schools. Acceptance of first-year female PhD students is either the same or higher than the schools below the top 20. This indicates that either these top 20 schools may be succeeding in efforts to attract women or that women are more

[2] In fact, social norms of gender equity may be at play, with Nordic countries and France enjoying higher gender equity because economics was considered a "female" occupation there (Auriol et. al. 2020). Data from the climate survey, in Kim 2023a and 2023b, are international in scope.

[3] According to CSWEP (2023), there are a total of 8 female associate professors in the top ten departments, and a total of 21 in the "top twenty." Unfortunately, this report does not describe which schools are in the top 10 and top 20, and school names are anonymous in the publicly available data.

likely to attend these elite schools if they are also accepted among schools that are not among the top 20. However, these same women disproportionately fail to complete their PhDs: Women comprise 24% of graduating PhD students in the top 10 or 20 schools, compared to 32% in schools below the top 20. Thus, although entering at higher rates, women drop out and fail to complete their PhDs at higher rates in these elite schools compared to less elite universities and also compared to men.

Why do women drop out or fail to complete their PhD degrees at higher rates than men? As this chapter will show, in part, women are perceived differently than men and are thus treated differently: They report failing to gain the same support as men in graduate school—both academically and financially. They also are perceived and treated differently throughout their careers: They fail to achieve the same levels of acceptance, recognition, credit, support and rewards as men from advisors, colleagues, mentors, and the profession itself. The outcome is that women disproportionately work in the lowest ranked schools and positions in the economics profession. Although the percentage of female assistant professors has reached a new high (CSWEP 2023), unless the profession improves, history shows that they will drop out, fail to receive tenure, or move to a different field. This chapter investigates these phenomena. There are remedies to increase the proportion of women in the economics profession that have been successfully established in some programs and in other disciplines that the field of economics can widely adopt. This will benefit the profession and the world, as more women will be able to contribute their knowledge to solve economic problems and improve economies.

2.1 Gendered Treatment as Students

Women report discrimination or unfair treatment at much higher rates than men in the economics profession during every step of their careers, beginning as early as graduate students—and sometimes as undergraduate students. Women may not be as encouraged by undergraduate advisors or faculty. This author was never encouraged to enter graduate school, and in fact, I was discouraged as an undergraduate. "Don't get a Ph.D. All you do is research," one economics faculty member told me, assuming that I would not like research—although in fact, I do! Later, in graduate school in economics, I discovered that another economics professor told a graduate student to read my undergraduate senior honor's thesis to inform her dissertation (I attended the same undergraduate and graduate school) and that this professor said that she "couldn't believe an undergraduate student did this work." This other professor never told me this nor encouraged me to enter graduate school, either.

My experiences, although 30 years ago, do not appear to be outliers. As the climate survey found, as students, "women and POC [people of color] may not be overtly treated poorly, but they are not encouraged and supported as are white men" (Anonymous in Allgood et al. 2019). This is eminently true in graduate schools in economics. One graduate student's experience exemplifies the lack of encouragement and interest toward female students. During her first year of graduate school:

> I got [a high score on a core exam]...my husband did not do particularly well in the course...But ...the professor who was teaching the course reached out to my husband and tried to encourage him to go into [the field] and didn't say anything to me. (Anonymous in Boustan and Langan 2019)

This student attributes the gendered preference toward her husband as implicit bias. Such bias has important implications that affect success in graduate school and in one's career, such as co-authorships and access to advisors. Many female students report difficulties finding advisors in graduate school. One student reports:

> When it came time to choose an advisor, I had substantial issues finding one. Also I was less likely to be promoted to 'coauthor' from RA than my male classmates, even for the same work. (Anonymous in Allgood et al. 2019)

Even the best female graduate students are not rewarded as are male students. A graduate student in an elite university revealed that her economics department used core exams to weed out graduate students so that only a few passed. She was one of three who passed, and the only woman. The others, both men, were hired in the summer as RAs; she was not[4] (Anonymous in Kim 2023b). Findings from the AEA's climate survey corroborate these stories: More women than men feel that they

[4] Oddly, my own graduate program had a scholarship intended for a female graduate student but had not awarded it to anyone for several years. Thus, even when available to women, it wasn't even awarded! A fellow graduate student told me that the department

Table 2 Experiences of discrimination and unfair treatment as a student

	Male	*Female*
During your time as a student, have you personally experienced discrimination or unfair treatment with regard to...		
Access to research assistantships	0.07	0.18
Access to advisors	0.06	0.20
Access to quality advising	0.07	0.23
Job market	0.15	0.36

Source: Allgood et al., *AEA Professional Climate Survey,* Table 4

have experienced discrimination and unfair treatment while a student, and in terms of quality advising, access to advisors, research assistantships, and on the job market (see Table 2). This gender differential may explain (in part) the higher dropout rate of women in graduate schools and the comparatively fewer numbers of women as assistant professors and in any tenure-track position compared to men.

Insider–outsider dynamics may explain these phenomena, with those on the inside, who are mostly men, mentoring, advising, and grooming those who are on the inside (i.e., other men), while relatively ignoring women, who are relegated to the outside (Chen and Li 2009). However, homophily bias may explain this as well: People generally favor and support those who are like themselves. Thus, managers groom those from the same social and economic circles as themselves, as well as from the same gender and professional categories (Kanter, 1977).[5] In this way, male economists are more likely to tap and support male students. As one woman said about her elite department, "My advisor lavished support on another student, a man," rather than her, even though he was her advisor. "Mentoring is informal: [professors] pick people who are like themselves, choosing [students] who look 'suitable'" (Anonymous for Kim 2023b).

informed her of this and awarded it to her one year. I and certainly other women could have benefitted from this award in previous, unawarded, years.

[5] Kanter (1977) was one of the first to describe this phenomenon regarding working women. Kim (2023a, 2023b, and 2026) describes the dynamics of homophily bias by gender.

2.2 *Networking and Conferences*

Academia is difficult. Once on the tenure track, mentoring, networks, attending conferences, and receiving feedback on one's work are critical. Women have a more difficult time accessing these. Women have smaller networks compared to men, when larger networks are shown to be beneficial (Ductor et al. 2020). This smaller network may be due to bias. Compared to similarly qualified men, female economists are less likely to receive credit for their work when working with senior male professors (Sarsons 2017). For this reason, junior women are advised to work with other junior women, so that they receive credit for their research contributions (Erten in Kim 2023b). Obviously, this workaround is problematic because it eliminates successful and well-known senior male colleagues from mentoring and co-authoring with junior women. By co-authoring with only other junior women, junior women are limited to those who are not yet successful and well known. Men don't face this problem: They can co-author with senior men and benefit from their networks, mentoring, reputations, and success. As Table 3 shows, women are more likely to report discrimination or unfair treatment regarding access to potential co-authors.

Women are less likely to be accepted into conferences compared to similarly qualified men, and this differential is entirely driven by men. Women evaluate men and women similarly who submit abstracts of research papers that they propose to present. However, men favor male over female authors and are more likely to accept men to present their work at conferences (Hospido and Sanz 2020). This is unfortunate, as conferences allow participants to extend their networks and future collaborations, gain visibility, receive critical feedback on research, and hear current research. Conferences provide opportunities to become acquainted with and interact with fellow economists. Conference participants are more likely to co-author research articles with other participants, and their articles are more likely to be cited compared to non-participants (Hospido and Sanz 2020).

Furthermore, compared to men, women are more likely to report discrimination or unfair treatment regarding access to time and funding in order to attend conferences and seminars (see Table 3). They also report failing to receive information and support about research leaves and conferences. Women are more likely to cite more discrimination or

Table 3 Academic economists experiencing discrimination or unfair treatment regarding...

	All	*Male*	*Female*
Promotion decisions	0.16	0.11	0.27
Compensation	0.20	0.12	0.37
Teaching assignments	0.15	0.09	0.28
Service obligations	0.19	0.09	0.43
Access to time and funding to attend conferences and seminars	0.10	0.07	0.16
Access to graduate student researchers	0.08	0.05	0.15
Course evaluations	0.20	0.08	0.47
Publishing decisions	0.22	0.18	0.31
Funding decisions	0.14	0.12	0.20
Sabbatical time	0.05	0.04	0.09
Access to potential co-authors	0.10	0.06	0.21
Invitations to participate in research conferences, associations, and networks	0.19	0.14	0.32

Reported in each cell is the share of respondents that report having personally experienced discrimination or unfair treatment in these aspects of work over the last ten years (if in the field of economics for more than 10 years) or during their time in the field of economics (if in the field of economics for less than 10 years)
Source: Allgood et al., *AEA Professional Climate Survey*, Table 5B

unfair treatment regarding invitations to participate in research conferences, associations, and networks: One-third of women report difficulties receiving these invitations compared to 14% of men (Table 3). As one senior woman at an elite university said, "My male colleagues are part of associations. I'm not getting these invitations [to join], [but] my [male] colleagues are getting these invitations" (Anonymous, for Kim 2023b).

2.3 *Teaching and Teaching Evaluations*

Almost half (47%) of the women surveyed by the AEA reported that they experienced discrimination or unfair treatment regarding course evaluations. In contrast, only 8% of men claimed that this was a problem (see Table 3). This is consistent with research that finds that women receive worse student course evaluations than men. For example, one male and one female instructor co-taught an online undergraduate course where each was responsible for teaching separate groups of students. Without informing them, they swapped some of their students and coordinated teaching and grading so that they graded at the same time and taught in the same way. Yet students gave lower teaching scores to the perceived female instructor, even on objective criteria such as how prompt the instructor was in grading (Boring, 2020).

Students can be more difficult to female faculty in the classroom. One female professor was assigned to teach a required graduate course in economic history that many students resented having to take. Students were angry that they had to learn and critique feudalism, so they made the professor miserable:

> I was young, I was female and I was teaching a course they really didn't want to take and they just unloaded. Because I was young and female, they felt they could unload all of their anger about the course on me....I don't think they would have done that to a male faculty member...It was pretty awful. It was the women graduate students who explained that to me. (Olney 2020)

In addition, decisions on course assignments and curriculum requirements can be gendered. Forty-three percent of women (compared to 7% of men) believed that they had experienced discrimination or unfair treatment regarding teaching assignments (see Table 3). One professor complained that a course she taught was removed from one of the economics tracks (Hopkins 2022).

2.4 *Service*

In the climate survey, 43% of women compared to 9% of men reported discrimination or unfair treatment regarding service obligations (see Table 3). This is consistent with much research that shows that women perform more service than men and that service is not counted much or at all in promotions and tenure (Allgood et al., 2019; Guarino and Borden, 2017; O'Meara et al., 2017). In addition, there's a hidden service: "Women come to you and ask if they should wear their wedding ring. They come to other women to ask these questions. My colleagues send students to me, especially women and people of color." In addition, perceptions of service are different for women than for men. As this same professor explains, "When men do extra service, they're seen as these great citizens and contributors to the public good. When women do it, it's more likely to be seen as detracting from their research" (Chen 2022).

2.5 *Research and Resources for Research*

Women face higher hurdles than men when publishing their research: Theirs must be of higher quality. Although editors appear to go along with referee comments and recommendations, both male and female referees (who read academic work and suggest if the work should be rejected, revised for publication, or published in academic journals) are biased against women (Card et al., 2020; Hengel, 2020).[6] Thus, women must spend more time conducting and writing up their research and thus produce quantitatively less but better-quality research compared to men. In addition, women receive less credit for their research accomplishments: When women co-author with a senior man, readers assume that the senior male performed most of the work (Sarsons, 2017). This assumption is not made when a male economist co-authors with a senior man, however.

Funding and access to graduate students to help with one's research is critical. Yet women are more likely than men to report more difficulties with these (see Table 3). One senior woman noted that she was more productive but received less research money. Another, that the senior faculty actively discouraged graduate students from working with her (Anonymous for and in Kim 2023b). To my knowledge, no one has conducted quantitative studies on research support, but given that women have more service obligations, are less likely to publish, and are less likely to receive conference invitations, it would not be surprising if quantitative studies confirm these survey results: that women receive inferior research support.[7]

[6] In the sciences, moreover, women are less likely than men to be credited as co-authors! See Ross et al. (2022).

[7] Research on grant funding is mixed. Some research finds that women are less likely to be awarded grants. See, for example, van der Lee and Ellemers (2019). Other research, however, fails to find a gender difference: Ceci et al. (2014). Still other research finds some gender differences depending on the academic field—and unfortunately, economics is not listed separately from the social sciences. See Sugimoto and Lariviere (2023).

2.6 *Promotions*

In academia, research, service, and teaching govern tenure decisions. With fewer publications, biased teaching evaluations, and more service work, which is often counted less than research, it is no surprise that women are less likely to climb the academic career ladder. They are less likely to receive tenure and thus promotion from Assistant to Associate Professor compared to similar men.[8] Additionally, even with similar records as their male peers, women are also less likely to be promoted from associate professor to full professor—the highest rank (Kleemans and Thornton 2023). A now-senior woman faced gender bias with these two different promotions: For her first promotion when trying to obtain tenure, she was simply told by a colleague that "if I were a man, I would have gotten tenure." When she went up for promotion to full professor at a different university, her male senior colleagues told her to wait to submit her materials because her research and service were "just average" and "she wasn't ready" for this promotion, but she researched the last person who was successfully promoted to full professor, and "compared to this man, [she] had exceeded him on all metrics" (Anonymous in Kim 2023b).

Interestingly, the climate survey suggests that many women are aware that they face unfair treatment with promotions and other matters. As Table 3 shows, 27% of women believe they experienced unfair treatment or discrimination regarding promotion decisions (compared to 11% of men). Over one-third of women believe they faced discrimination or unfair treatment regarding their compensation (compared to 12% of men). One-third of women believe they experienced discrimination or unfair treatment regarding publishing decisions (in comparison, 18% of men feel this way). Thirty-one percent believe they experienced discrimination or unfair treatment regarding funding decisions, compared to 18% of men. Many women are not fooled.

[8] For decades, women had lower tenure rates than men even with the same characteristics or research portfolios. And although this is still true today, in one dataset, only at the most elite schools was the gender difference in tenure insignificant. Most schools, however, still have a tenure gap by gender. See Khan (2020).

Table 4 Non-academia: Have you personally experienced discrimination or unfair treatment with regard to...

	All	*Male*	*Female*
Promotion decisions	0.18	0.14	0.31
Compensation	0.17	0.11	0.32
Professional development opportunities	0.17	0.12	0.29
Publishing decisions	0.18	0.15	0.24

Source: Allgood et al., *AEA Professional Climate Survey*, Table 6

2.7 Non-Academic Careers

These patterns are similar in non-academic jobs. For example, at the European Central Bank (ECB), a large gender promotion gap existed for years: Women were 36% less likely to be promoted compared to men after 10 years of working. This gender difference was eliminated only after the ECB publicly issued a statement supporting diversity and implemented measures to achieve greater gender balance (Hospido et al. 2020). Although it is heartening that commitment to gender diversity can eliminate problems, this is only one institution. As Table 4 shows, one-third of female economists working in non-academic jobs believe they experienced discrimination or unfair treatment regarding promotion decisions. In comparison, 14% of men felt this way.

In addition, the climate survey indicates that one-third of female non-academic economists felt they had personally experienced discrimination or unfair treatment in compensation (compared to 11% of men). Over double the number of women (29%) compared to men (12%) felt they had personally experienced discrimination or unfair treatment regarding professional development opportunities. One-quarter of women reported experiencing discrimination or unfair treatment regarding publishing decisions; in contrast, 18% of men reported this (see Table 4). Thus, unfortunately, disparate treatment is reported by women in both academic and non-academic careers.

2.8 **Perceptions of Women and Their Work**

Many women felt that they were perceived differently simply because they were women and that they were evaluated differently as a result. This difference extended to their work. As one senior woman said, "Women's work is still devalued. When you go up for tenure, the work can be devalued. It's not seen as important as the work men do" (Brown 2020). Indeed, many women I interviewed agreed (Kim 2023a, 2023b). The previous vignette, "If I were a man, I would have gotten tenure," exemplifies this. A similar exchange happened to a non-academic economist, who was made fun of. Her male colleague explained, "You were the only woman there, and they teased just you. If you had been a guy, they wouldn't have done that" (Anonymous in Kim 2023b). Another non-academic economist also received disparate treatment:

> If I came up with an idea—it was automatically bad and he rejected it, or it was like I didn't speak. Or my colleagues would see the ideas as if they were their own. Either it was bad, or it was invisible. He was rejecting the work because I had done it, not because it was bad work. After I calculated the cost for a complicated project, he said, "We've got to do better than this." (Anonymous in Kim 2023b)

Even at the senior levels, bias persists. One interviewee recalled a meeting when there were two outgoing board members present: "The chair thanked the man because he brought intellectual rigor to the association, and the woman because her smile lit up the room.

The woman is not an expert, but the man is, even though they hold the same position" (Anonymous in Kim 2023b).

Women are less likely to be perceived as competent and intellectual compared to men, probably contributing to the gender differentials in publishing their research and in tenure and promotions (Kim 2023b). Women are also more likely to be seen as sexual. Alice Wu (2018) analyzed the content of an online economics forum, Economics Job Market Rumors, which was mostly for graduate students and those looking for jobs in economics to obtain information, such as hiring outcomes and if a particular school had scheduled interviews with job candidates. Posts are anonymous. Wu identified the words that were most strongly associated with discussions of men and women. She found that female economists and professors were viewed sexually and less professionally than their male colleagues. Posts focused on physical appearances or personal information: Words like "breast," "attractive," "hot," "beautiful," and "vagina" were commonly used. In contrast, the words that described men were more likely to be academic or professional, regarding their work or their job: The most common words used to describe men included "advisor," "supervisor," "Nobel," and "macroeconomics" (Wu 2018).

2.9 Sexual Harassment of Women

Unfortunately, characterizing women as sexual and by their appearance and physical attributes reflects gender bias and a mindset that has resulted in much sexual harassment in the profession. Twenty-three percent of women in economics have experienced sexual harassment (Allgood et al. 2019). At a job interview luncheon, one woman recounted that faculty members cracked "whorehouse jokes," and that when the department head drove her back to the airport, he "reached over and grabbed my breasts" (CSWEP 2018). Other stories are similar:

> At a dinner honoring a distinguished colleague, the guest of honor sat across the table from me, winking and grinning (and drinking heavily)….[H]e announced…."I don't really know who you are, but I like the looks of you." As the dinner adjourned, he came over to me to ask for "just a little kiss," while my senior colleagues looked on…. (CSWEP 2018)
>
> At a reception honoring my department head's advisor, we posed for a department photo with the honoree. I was placed next to him in the photo. While posing for the photo, he reached over and grabbed my butt. He also kissed me on the mouth when saying goodbye after dinner. (CSWEP 2018)
>
> I was responsible for driving seminar speakers to dinner and back to their hotels. On two separate occasions, a guest speaker grabbed me and forced a kiss on me prior to exiting the car. (CSWEP 2018)

Unfortunately, graduate students also experience sexual harassment. One student explained that a professor in her PhD program "pushed me against the wall of a building and forcefully kissed me and touched me" (CSWEP 2018). Another graduate student who was a teaching assistant for a professor said that during a meeting with him, "he put his hand on my thigh" (CSWEP 2018). One graduate student in this author's PhD program was told by her advisor to have sex with him if she expected to graduate with a PhD. She didn't want to do this, but she felt she had no choice (Kim 2023a). At another university, a professor recalled a conversation in a hotel elevator after attending a gala conference dinner: A male professor riding in the elevator with his graduate student waved the keys to his hotel room at this female graduate student and said, "Now we can talk about your PhD" (Anonymous for Kim 2023b). A graduate student who was "just starting to go to conferences" reported that she experienced "multiple incidences of men twenty years [her] senior hitting on [her] or making inappropriate passes" (CSWEP 2018).

Most instances of sexual harassment are unreported (CSWEP 2018). Those who do report these, or faculty who try to help women undergoing these problems, are penalized (Kim 2023b). In addition, women avoid attending social events at the Allied Social Science Association (ASSA) meetings to avoid this behavior (CSWEP 2018). One female economist explains:

> I think men don't realize the negative externality of using the pool of junior female economists as a dating pool—it might seem like not a big deal to flirt with a student or a junior faculty member when an individual man does it, but when every man makes that choice, the climate of going to conferences and informally networking is very uncomfortable for young women in economics. I have personally avoided participating in networking and informal social events because of the discomfort of having people flirt with me or hit on me when I think we're discussing research. (Anonymous in Allgood et al. 2019)

These behaviors continue to affect graduate students and even undergraduate students (Kim 2023b). Thirty years ago, this author witnessed three male professors dating three different female graduate students in the same economics graduate program. A male professor who was not among these three didn't think anything was amiss, since the relationships were consensual. However, it sexualizes the department and leads to an uncomfortable environment for all women and even for male graduate students, who would rightly wonder if they had less access to information and help than was available to those in relationships with economics professors.

Today, most universities have disclosure requirements and processes that prevent conflicts of interest. Yet having three male professors date their graduate students in one program sexualizes the program and would lead to discomfort if others, both men and women, feel they had less access to information, mentoring, and tutoring. When I told the previous story to another professor I know who was not in this department (or in economics), he believed that this behavior was acceptable because "Where else would you meet people you have much in common with and whom you're interested in?".

The answer lies in the previous negative externality example and the following: I was recently informed about a male economist who is established in the field and showed interest in a graduate student at a professional event's reception. This woman did not attend this reception the following year. Although this may not be sexual harassment per se, it reinforces the sense that women exist, not for their intellect, but for their sexual and social desirability. This can undermine their professional self-esteem and eschew them from socializing at economics meetings and outings—as it already does for some women—limiting their ability to network and succeed in the profession.

2.10 *Excluded, Not Valued, Not Respected*

Women are less likely than men to be included socially (see Tables 5 and 6). Sixty-five percent of women feel socially excluded at a meeting or event in economics, compared to 40% of men. Faculty report being excluded from meetings, committees, and social events where department decisions are being made. One senior woman I interviewed said that she was "systematically kept off every committee," and that she had "no say on department decision-making." The guys "scheme together" while socializing and making departmental decisions during those social outings (Anonymous in Kim 2023b). Others relate that:

> When the women began to ask to join committees and to see committee minutes, the committees first stopped keeping minutes, and then stopped meeting altogether. We understood that some decisions were made in the men's bathroom. (CSWEP 2018)

For some, this can harm their tenure cases:

> All of the male faculty members in my department go to lunch on a regular basis. Although I have asked to be invited, normally, they do not invite me. In one of my annual reviews, I was told that I was not a good departmental citizen because I didn't go to lunch enough! (Anonymous, CSWEP 2018)

Graduate students report social exclusion as well:

Table 5 Outcomes by gender

	All	*Male*	*Female*
Satisfied with the overall climate			
Within the field of economics	0.34	0.40	0.20
At my institution/place of employment	0.56	0.61	0.46
Valued			
Within the field of economics	0.40	0.46	0.25
At my institution/place of employment	0.63	0.67	0.52
Always feel included socially			
Within the field of economics	0.37	0.43	0.21
At my institution/place of employment	0.63	0.67	0.52
Always feel included intellectually			
Within the field of economics	0.42	0.48	0.27
At my institution/place of employment	0.64	0.69	0.53
Work that I do is valued			
Within the field of economics	0.40	0.43	0.33
At my institution/place of employment	0.63	0.65	0.56
I think i have a great deal of power			
Within the field of economics	0.07	0.08	0.05
At my institution/place of employment	0.24	0.25	0.20
My ideas and opinions are often ignored			
Within the field of economics	0.21	0.20	0.23
At my institution/place of employment	0.13	0.12	0.14

Source: Allgood et al., *AEA Professional Climate Survey*, Table 2. Questions are slightly edited to fit in the first column above

Table 6 Experiences of economists

	All	*Male*	*Female*
Have you ever experienced any of the following?			
Felt socially excluded at a meeting or event in the field	0.47	0.40	0.65
Felt disrespected by your economist colleagues	0.45	0.38	0.62
Felt that your work was not taken as seriously as that of your economist colleagues	0.51	0.43	0.69
Felt that the subject or methodology of your research was not taken as seriously as that of your economist colleagues	0.46	0.40	0.59

Source: Allgood et al., *AEA Professional Climate Survey*, Table 8

> Early in graduate school ...I was excluded from some social activities outside of the office where my male classmates and the male faculty formed some early informal bonds. Nobody thought to include me—I'm a woman. (Anonymous, in Allgood et al. 2018)

Whether due to insider–outsider or homophily dynamics, social exclusion is harmful. For graduate students, it harms their ability to find mentors and advisors (Allgood et al. 2019). This may be one cause of why more women drop out of PhD programs or fail to complete these. For faculty, social exclusion limits their ability to find mentors and co-authors and to network. It affects their promotions and their careers.

In addition, compared to men, women are less likely to feel included intellectually in economics, and they are less likely to feel that the work they do is valued (see Table 5). Only one-fourth of women (compared to nearly half of men) feel valued in the field of economics (see Table 5). A whopping 62% of women feel disrespected by their economist colleagues; in comparison, 38% of men feel this way (see Table 6). This could take the form of a "simple lack of respect for one's opinions at faculty meetings" (Anonymous, in Allgood et al. 2019). More than two-thirds of women—69%—feel that their work is not taken as seriously as that of their economist colleagues (compared to 43% of men). A majority of women, 59% (this compares to 40% of men), feel that the subject matter or the methodology they employ in their research was not taken as seriously as that of their colleagues (see Table 6).

These findings are supported by my interviews, where many women reported feeling disrespected and not valued (Kim 2023b). One woman said that her colleagues characterized her publications as terrible—that "she only published 'crap papers'" (Anonymous for Kim 2023b). Others explained that they were held to different tenure standards—their interdisciplinary publications didn't count, but male colleagues' interdisciplinary publications did count (Kim 2023b). As women, they were ignored. One senior woman complained that when her "male counterparts wrote an email, everyone responds. If I write an email, I have to write three follow-ups and I still have to walk down to their office to get them to reply" (Anonymous in Kim 2023b). In another department that had only two women, the male colleagues couldn't recognize one woman from the other, often calling them by the other woman's name, even though "one of us has long hair; the other has short hair" (Hopkins 2022).

In a toxic cocktail of sexual harassment and not feeling valued, included, or respected, it's no wonder that few women—only one out of five—are satisfied with the overall climate in economics (in comparison, two out of five men are satisfied; see Table 5). Very few—only 5% of women—feel that they have a great deal of power in the profession. Almost a quarter feel that their ideas and opinions are often ignored. The comparable responses from men are 8 and 20%, respectively—still quite low, but higher than women's (see Table 5).

2.11 Economic Seminars

Economic seminars are aggressively masculine and confrontational, where it's more a sport than an intellectual activity, with men being "concerned more with showing how clever they are" instead of listening (Anonymous, for Kim 2023b; Allgood et al. 2019). Worse, "this is especially the case when the presenters are ...female" (Allgood et al. 2019). Research confirms that female presenters in economic seminars are more likely to be interrupted and are asked more hostile and patronizing questions than male presenters (Dupas et al. 2021). Many female economists I interviewed recollected horrific reactions to their or others' research when presenting to a primarily male audience. They had difficulty discussing their work because of hostility to their ideas, research, or presentation (Kim 2023a, 2023b). For example, at a job market seminar, one woman was showing how the percentage of women in an occupation has an independent, negative effect that lowers pay in female jobs. "The men started laughing, making fun of my equations" (Hartmann in Kim 2023a). At another university, another female economist described witnessing a different woman giving a job market talk as a "public humiliation" (Anonymous for Kim 2023b).

At yet another economics seminar at an elite university, when a junior faculty member said that she was going to argue to subsidize childcare similarly to how economists argue that education should be subsidized, her colleagues "started screaming to each other and to me about how outrageous this was" (Strober, in Kim 2023a). Finally, one woman giving a seminar at a top ten Ivy League economics department said:

> They didn't let me get past the first slide because the title had "discrimination" in it, and I mentioned that I was testing the Gary Becker Hypothesis.

> They attacked me....they wouldn't believe my work. It was horrible. I hated it. I haven't been back since. (Rodgers in Kim 2023b)

Is it any wonder that only 16% of women feel that their gender is respected? Remarkably, most men fail to perceive the gendered treatment and perceptions of women: 51% of male economists feel that women are respected in economics—far more than that reported by women (Allgood et al. 2019).

2.12 The Problem of the Content and Theory in Economics

Theories in mainstream economics explain that gender differentials in pay, work hours, and occupations are caused by preferences and choice (such as risk adversity), different skills of women vis a vis men (less likely to initiate or be adept at bargaining), and different productivities (less productive at paid work; more productive at unpaid work) that explain the status quo (Kim 2024). Thus, students are told that women are paid less than men because their marginal product of labor is lower (Kim 2023a, 2023b, 2024). Female students understandably reject these theories: They are likely to pursue other fields in the social sciences that adhere to tenets and theories that explain gender inequality in ways that conform to their perceptions of the world and how gender and inequality manifest. Furthermore, depictions in economics textbooks exclude women. Three-quarters of the people mentioned in textbooks—both real people and those who were imagined in examples—are male (Stevenson and Zlotnick 2018). The dearth of representation of women is likely to further imply that the field of economics is not for them.

In addition, although it is now possible to research gender, one must use the correct methodology (mathematics, high-level statistics), and not mention that there is discrimination (Kim 2023a, 2023b). One senior economist explained: "The word 'discrimination' has almost disappeared. It's the wage gap and unexplained factors or women being less competitive or household responsibilities—anything other than discrimination. Comparable worth discussions have disappeared" (Nelson 2020).

Publishing in heterodox, feminist, or women's studies journals is frowned upon and may not count for tenure; publishing feminist work even in high-level economics journals may not count, either (Kim 2023a, 2023b). One professor published in top economics journals, including the *American Economic Review* (the top economics journal), but when members of the department actually read her work when she went up for tenure, "they couldn't wait to get rid" of her (Nelson, in Kim 2023a).

Failure to use mainstream theories and find conclusions other than that of mainstream economics—that gender differences are the result of preferences, less productivity, or skills—receive rejections from editors of prominent journals:

> If you write a paper about gender, unless you show that it's the woman's fault, nobody's interested, and it's the same with race. If you have a paper on gender, there's always some preference story: it's because we're risk-averse. I had a paper rejected and they said on one part of the paper that women can't deal with failure, and on another part of the paper they said women are too aggressive and persistent. How can you be both more persistent and aggressive and more averse to failure at the same time? They just make up stories about women's preferences and it's impossible to defend against that, because you can't measure them, so there's always some omitted variable related to women's preferences that they use to reject your papers. If anyone is risk averse it's journal editors. It's not the women, it's the journal editors. (Anonymous for Kim 2023b).

Thus, research using other theories or finding other conclusions outside of the mainstream is less likely to be accepted and published, especially in mainstream economics journals (Kim 2023a, 2023b). Even work published in top journals can be discounted or not counted for tenure or promotions if the traditional explanations are not used and traditional conclusions are not found (Kim 2023a, 2023b). Consequently, women face even more difficulties becoming published, tenured, and promoted. This dynamic—that women can't publish or that they fail to perform the work—perpetuates mainstream economic ideology that gender differences are driven by the supply side: Women can't attain the records that men can more easily reach.

2.13 *Problems with Gender Don't Exist: Women Can't Complain*

Another major barrier with gender inequity is that women can't complain about them, suggest alternatives, mention problems, or even say the word "gender" or "women"—this is too threatening to the status quo: A professor at an elite university noticed that the only women on the seminar list were their own graduate students, so she said that it would be great if they invited more women. "My department chair completely freaked out and cc'd the Dean, saying that I was accusing the seminar organizers of discrimination, when I was just saying that we should invite more women; we should try" (Anonymous for Kim 2023b). She had to spend a lot of time on emails clarifying her intent. About a year later, the same department head "suggested that they should invite more women to the seminar series and advertise the fact that they were inviting more women":

> When I suggested it, it was a big deal, but now he thinks it would be good to get on this gender bandwagon and show how great the university is in terms of diversity: So why don't we advertise that we're inviting more women to our seminar series? If he says it, it's okay, but if I say it, then I'm a bitch. (Anonymous for Kim 2023b)

Of course, even if topics are outside of gender issues, because women have less credibility, respect, and purchase, they must make suggestions very gently. These suggestions have to be conducted without undermining authority because they have to perform their gender roles as subservient and less knowledgeable:

> If you have a complaint at work, you are nagging. If women are upset, they are emotional. "She must have her period." If a man is upset, he must be passionate. Women are not supposed to complain; you are supposed to do your job quietly. If you complain, you are annoying or unreasonable (Anonymous, for Kim 2023b).

This poses two problems: First, women cannot raise problems, and if they do so, they must be particularly careful not to offend men or the powers that be. Second, women who voice problems are punished. They are isolated, ostracized, ridiculed, denied tenure or promotion, and/or labeled as bad apples (Kim 2023b). Hence the problems continue.

2.14 Women Leave the Field of Economics

What happens when women are treated like this? When they are disrespected, not valued, ignored, sexually harassed, and must hew to theoretical models or conclusions that they don't believe? When they face difficulties publishing and finding mentors and support? Senior women, junior women, and graduate students leave the profession and go elsewhere: into sociology, women's and gender studies, other fields, universities, and departments (Kim 2023b). Few feminist economists' tenure homes are in economics: Many have to be employed in other fields or departments that value them and their work (Kim 2023a, 2023b). However, these other fields and departments (outside of business departments or schools) pay less than economics (Rodgers 2022)! This may be one mechanism by which the gender pay gap in economics manifests.

Thus, the explanation for why women are underrepresented in economics, hold lower completion rates in graduate school, and are underrepresented at every stage in their careers, at PhD-granting schools, at more prestigious universities, and at higher level ranks and positions is that they are treated differently, evaluated differently, less likely to be mentored and supported, and have a more difficult time publishing and performing their work in this profession. Resolving these problems would bring progress toward women's representation in economics.

3 Remedies

Many recommendations have been suggested to improve gender equity in economics, and many best practices are widely available (see Bayer et al. 2019). I delineate here many of the suggestions I have mentioned elsewhere (Kim 2023b, 2024), which are adapted for gender and expanded. Most important is a commitment to gender equity at the top of the organization and awareness of gender bias from senior faculty and top administrators (Kim 2024; Hospido et al. 2020; Boustan and Langan 2019). A lack of commitment to gender equity is probably why most organizations and universities fail.

Given that women receive less mentoring in graduate schools and as junior professors, mentoring programs are essential: They make a difference (Erten 2022; Kim 2023b; Hospido et al., 2020; Boustein and Langan 2019; Ginther et al. 2020). Formal mentoring programs increase the number of research publications for mentees, including in top-tier journals, and increased tenure rates in the top 50 economics departments (Ginther et al. 2020). Many of the women I interviewed discussed mentors having an enormous impact on them. Notable feminist economists sparked interest in some of these women to enter the field of economics (Anonymous interviews for Kim, 2023a, 2023b). An undergraduate economics major returned to graduate studies in economics only after a mentor took an interest in and encouraged her to write and present a paper at an economics conference (Nunes 2022).

Role models are also critical. They can provide encouragement for graduate and undergraduate students as well as to other faculty members. Role models who look like you, have similar backgrounds, and show that you can succeed can provide confidence to students so they can flourish in the profession (Porter and Serra 2020). As one graduate student said, "Every semester we always had one female teaching us in the core first-year classes." She felt that "I can do this and be a woman," after interacting with these role models (Boustan and Langan 2019). The same is true for undergraduate female students. They are more likely to major in economics after hearing successful female economics alumni discuss their careers (Porter and Serra 2020; Buckles 2020).

Undergraduates know little about the economics profession, including what type of careers one can have with an economics degree. Nor are they aware that one can study issues like economic development in less-developed countries, health care, inequality, and gender and race. Increasing knowledge of the field can encourage women to enter it. Simply providing information to undergraduate students about the economics major and career prospects increases the likelihood of closing the gender gap in economics majors (Li 2018). When women who received above-average scores in an introductory economics course learned about career prospects with an economics degree and were encouraged to major in economics, they were more likely to pursue an economics major (research shows that men don't need this encouragement, but that it does make a difference for women), thus closing the gender gap in economics majors (Li 2018; Buckles 2020).

Having more female faculty inspires graduate students to succeed and is associated with better retention and completion rates for female graduate students (Boustan and Langan 2019). This is likely because increasing female faculty changes the climate for women, while also elevating the number of female role models and mentors available. Having high levels of female graduate students in one's cohort also improves the climate for graduate students and their PhD completion rate. Thus, gender equity initiatives at faculty and graduate student levels can promote retention and success rates of women in graduate school (Boustan and Langan 2019; Porter and Serra 2020; Buckles 2020).

So how can departments, universities, and institutions raise the number of female faculty and graduate students in their programs?

3.1 What Can Departments, Universities, and Organizations Do to Increase Female Representation?

Departments can embrace practices that work. They can implement mentoring programs for faculty and graduate students. They can encourage those who perform well in introductory economics courses to major in economics and provide information about majoring in economics (Li 2018). They can also invite successful alumni who are female role models to discuss their careers in economics and expected earnings (Porter and Serra 2020). A commitment to success in hiring women on the faculty is important (Boustan and Langan 2019), but further changes are often needed. Individual departments can examine their procedures and requirements for graduate student admissions, and hiring, tenure, and promotions for faculty, scrutinizing these for gender bias.

For example, Stanford University examined problems in the graduate student pipeline for women and found that requiring real analysis didn't predict success in the profession and that it reduced the number of female applicants, so they eliminated this requirement. This change subsequently increased the number of female graduate students applying to and being accepted into the economics program (Bernheim 2023).[9] They also implemented a formal mentoring program, where female senior graduate students mentor female junior graduate students. Finally, they cracked down on abusive and undesirable behavior from male graduate students. Their representation of women increased rapidly to 40% (Bernheim 2023).

Other departments and universities can replicate this and extend it to other procedures. Amazon has examined its HR policies and procedures and made these more inclusive (Chen in Kim 2023b). Universities and departments can do the same. Universities and institutions can conduct salary audits by gender and make corrections to these periodically (not by reducing, but only increasing salaries). They can also require department chairs to justify pay disparities in excess of 10% for the same rank,

[9] Notably, the late Elinor Ostrom, only one of three women to receive a (shared) Nobel Prize in economics, had a PhD in political science at UCLA because economics would not allow her into their PhD program since she had not taken trigonometry. This math requirement was clearly not essential for her to work in economics and for her shared Nobel in 2009.

years of experience, and other metrics that they choose. If these cannot be justified, they need to be remediated (Chen 2022).

3.2 *Hiring, Admissions, and Promotions*

Departments, universities, and institutions can blind applicants (for job positions and graduate school) by race/gender/institution. When hiring with institutions blinded, departments can read and rate the job market papers before they read the letters of recommendation. This rates people on their work, not their institution, increases interviews from lower-ranked institutions, and provides a pool of more diverse candidates by gender and by race (Anonymous in Kim 2023b).

Departments and universities can also mandate gender equity training for chairs and hiring committee members to reduce bias. Bard College requires the latter. This increases the proportion of women hired and accepted, and the job offer rates for women (Buckles 2020). AI can be programmed to be less biased than people and can conduct initial screenings for hiring, which can increase the pool of female applicants, and the proportion of women hired (Avery et al. 2023). Having external observers for the hiring process can ensure equal treatment and identify and correct for any bias and inconsistencies.

Departments and institutions can examine their tenure and promotion criteria for bias and consider changing these policies. For promotions and tenure cases, they can allow for external observation of the deliberations to ensure that they are consistent and that implicit biases don't creep in, or they can allow for the candidate to have an advocate in the room who doesn't vote but advocates for their case. This can increase information and advocacy for women when these are lacking (Chen in Kim 2024).

Departments should hire women (and people of color) in numbers: Much research suggests hiring (or admitting into graduate programs) women as a group to ensure success. This way, women are not seen as just "the one" female colleague and are treated differently. Instead, they are seen and treated as one of many colleagues (Kanter 1977, 1980). Those who succeed in economics were often part of a cohort that had enough women so that they could provide support for each other and were not seen as "different" (Erten 2022; Kim 2023a).

Departments can change the climate in their seminars so that these are collegial and helpful, where constructive comments are offered, and graduate students can present their work. This improves female graduate student completion rates (Boustan and Langan 2019). They can open up the journals and the type of work that is counted for tenure, promotions, and merit pay, ensuring that work that is relevant to women and women's experiences is counted.

3.3 *Economic Theory, Pedagogy, Content*

The content of economics needs change: in its theories, instruction, curriculum, research, and textbooks. Women need to be represented and see themselves in the examples used, and the theory and curriculum should not be gender-biased nor hostile to gender. Women should not be described as risk averse when this is not true (Nelson 2017). They should not be assumed to have more productivity in unpaid work and less in paid work compared to men. Instead, the concepts of patriarchy and gender bias should be included throughout the curriculum—not just in one course. This requires incorporating theories and ideas outside of economics that allow for discrimination and differential treatment to exist by race, gender, and other demographic groups in the curriculum, instruction, textbooks, and research. Economic theory needs to incorporate theories outside of economics since these explain economic behavior and differentials that affect women, girls, and gender with gender-friendly concepts and theories, unlike those in economics.

3.4 *What the Profession Can Do*

3.4.1 *Gather Data*

The AEA can gather demographic data on Allied Social Science Association (ASSA) participation by counting men and women by gender and race who present papers, participate in panels, chair sessions, and discuss papers. They can then report these statistics annually. If there is a lack of diversity, they can take the initiative to implement a system (see below) to allow more papers to be presented by women and people of color. There are many more submissions than slots available: There is no reason for all white male panels to exist, especially for panels about gender and race.

3.4.2 *Include More Sessions at the ASSA Meetings for Heterodox and Feminist Research*

Since heterodox and feminist organizations are more likely to include and incorporate women, gender, and feminist inquiry to a greater extent than more mainstream economic organizations, the AEA should allocate more slots at the ASSA meetings to the International Association for Feminist Economics (IAFFE) and heterodox groups that have more female and underrepresented minority members (Rodgers in Kim 2024). This will help diverse groups present their work and thus help their careers. For the same reasons, ensure 1–2 guaranteed panels for IAFFE for papers in the proceedings and heterodox organizations (Rodgers in Kim 2024).

3.4.3 *The AEA and ASSA can Implement Affirmative Action for Women and People of Color on their AEA Panels and in the Proceedings*

These organizations can give extra points to women and people of color for paper proposals so that at the margin, more diverse panels will be included in sessions. To encourage diversity at the ASSA meetings and to encourage research that addresses members of underrepresented groups, when the AEA counts the number of people presenting papers and in the audience at ASSA sessions, women can count as more than one person (Kim 2024).

3.4.4 *Provide Travel Grants to Attend the ASSA Meetings for People from the Global South*

Offering travel grants to people who lack institutional funding and for graduate students to attend the ASSA meeting will help diversity the ASSA meetings.

3.4.5 *Sexual Harassment and Gender Equity Training*

The AEA should mandate sexual harassment or gender equity/DEI training (or both) in all AEA sessions for chairs and participants (including discussants) if their universities do not require either of these. This will help educate participants about bias, inclusion, and sexual harassment. Departments and universities can require the same (Kim 2024).

3.4.6 *The AEA and Its Affiliates Can Implement Codes of Conduct and/or Procedures During Sessions at the ASSA Meetings*

Since people interrupt women more than men, the ASSA and AEA can prohibit questions (except perhaps clarifying questions) until the end of the session. It can enforce having collegial discussions instead of attacks on women when giving talks that present different ideas or theories. It should also consider what the Union for Radical Political Economics (URPE) used to do in its sessions: Every other person chosen to speak or comment from the audience should be a woman. Alternating with people of color is also encouraged. Economics departments can implement similar procedures and rules.

3.4.7 The AEA Should Reinstate Double-Blind Reviewing for Its Journal Articles

If work by women is less likely to be valued and published, double-blind reviewing is essential. Although people can try to find the author's identity online, this entails some work, and not everyone will try to do this. Furthermore, as is the case now, journal editors should *not* have the right to review National Bureau of Economic Research (NBER) research papers before they are submitted for publication, given these biases (Allgood et al. 2019).

3.4.8 The AEA Journals Should Recommend Citations in the Order of Contribution

Rather than in alphabetical order, given that junior women are unlikely to receive credit for their research contributions, authorship should be listed by contribution. Asterisks can explain if equal contributions were made. Other journals can follow this practice.

3.4.9 The AEA Should Implement an Open and Transparent Process for AEA Officers, Committee Memberships, and Journal Editors

Rather than just having a nominating committee, this process should be inclusive, including an open call, and allowing for self-nominations (Chen 2022; Rodgers 2022). Expanding the universities that house the AEA journals and editors of these journals to break the monopoly of the 3–5 universities that house them can also enhance transparency (Rodgers 2022). The top schools should not be the de facto editors of top journals (Chen 2022). Including women and underrepresented minorities as editors, associate editors, and on the editorial boards is another critical piece of this call to action.

3.4.10 Funders and Grants

The EU is distributing $95 billion in grants for research in the STEM fields. The funded grants must examine gender, and if they don't, they should explain why the research cannot examine this. Institutions (including higher education, non-profit, and government institutions) must implement a gender equity plan to apply. These plans must evaluate their institutions regarding how they can increase equity by gender across the institution, including for staff, faculty, researchers, and students. They also must address and remedy all aspects of gender, including compensation, promotions, obtaining grants, research assistance, differential treatment, and the working environment (Horizon Europe 2022).

This initiative has resulted in worthwhile change. For instance, in Ireland, crash dummies for testing car safety are now the size and weight of the average *person* rather than the average *man* (Horizon Europe 2022). Although economics is excluded as a STEM field, it can be included. The same requirements for funding opportunities can be instituted for STEM and economics in the US for the National Science Foundation (NSF) and funding from other US government agencies. Progressive funders can require a gender lens as well. For example, one progressive funder in the EU is also mandating that grant recipients address diversity (Anonymous for Kim 2023b).

Progressive funders in the US and elsewhere can do likewise. Funders and granting agencies can boost topics on gender, mandate gender equity plans for institutions applying for funding as the EU is stipulating, and require examining gender in the research, similar to the EU directives.

4 Conclusion

Women continue to represent a minority in the field of economics. They experience difficulties during every stage of their career path. As graduate students, they are less likely to receive mentoring, advising, and financial support. As Assistant Professors and beyond, they are subject to differential treatment in evaluating their work and publishing decisions and feel less valued, respected, and included compared to their male colleagues. The content of economics—the theory and what is taught in schools—fails to consider and represent women and women's lives and experiences. Efforts to include these in feminist and heterodox work are often not published, counted for tenure, or otherwise disregarded. Many women in a discipline hostile to the fact that women face more difficulties compared to men either cannot make it in the field or leave (Kim 2023a, 2023b). There is no mystery as to why women are underrepresented in economics and among higher-ranked schools, and why the leaky pipeline (where women are decreasingly represented the higher the rank in their careers) continues. Economics treats women adversely; moreover, at its core—its very theory—is hostile to women.

This need not be the case. Many other professions, including in the social sciences and STEM, have made progress on these issues by adopting many of the remedies described, but economics has not. The result is very little progress in the field and low numbers of women in the profession. Economics remains a laggard (Lundberg 2020a, 2020b).

Why is this a problem? It's a problem because women's voices are missing. Missing are the talent and insight of half the population, solving economic problems and contributing to solutions. We are failing to heed these articulations and listen to half the world's people and their problems and solutions—and women differ from men in these. Women are more likely to favor policies that produce more equitable income distributions. They are more likely than men to believe that men and women face different job opportunities, that humane labor standards in countries should be linked with openness to imports from that country, and that government regulation is not excessive in the economy. Finally, research shows that diversity leads to better outcomes since different perspectives are considered, and group dynamics and decision-making change for the better the higher the proportion of women (Dolar 2021; Bayer and Rouse 2016).

The fact that most male economists fail to perceive the gender bias in the profession means that they are unlikely to resolve this problem as well as gender bias in the economy and the world. There are many solutions and best practices that have worked in STEM, in other disciplines in the US, and in some economics departments in the US. Other departments, the economics profession, the US, and the world can follow.

References

Allgood, Sam, Lee Badgett, Amanda Bayer, Marianne Bertrand, Sandra E. Black, Nick Bloom, and Lisa D. Cook. 2019. Committee on Equity, Diversity and Professional Conduct. AEA Professional Climate Survey: Final Report.

Auriol, Emmanuelle, Guido Friebel, and Sascha Wilhelm. 2020. Women in European Economics. In *Women in Economics*, ed. Shelly Lundberg, 26–30. London: Centre for Economic Policy.

Avery, Mallory, Andreas Leibbrandt, and Joseph Vecci. 2023. *Does Artificial Intelligence Help or Hurt Gender Diversity? Evidence from Two Field Experiments on Recruitment in Tech.* New York: Mimeo.

Avilova, Tatyana, and Claudia Goldin. 2020. What Can UWE Do for Economics? In *Women in Economics*, ed. Shelly Lundberg, 43–50. London: Centre for Economic Policy.

Bayer, Amanda, Şebnem Kalemli-Özcan, Rohini Pande, Cecilia Elena Rouse, Anthony A. Smith Jr., Juan Carlos Suárez Serrato, and David W. Wilcox. 2019. *Best Practices for Economists: Building a More Diverse, Inclusive, and Productive Profession.* American Economic Association. Accessed at https://www.aeaweb.org/resources/best-practices.

Bayer, Amanda, and Cecelia Rouse. 2016. Diversity in the Economics Profession: A New Attack on an Old Problem. *Journal of Economic Perspectives* 30(4):221–241.

Bernheim, Douglas. 2003. *Presentation at CSWEP's Solutions/Innovative Ideas for Addressing DEI Issues.* New Orleans: Allied Social Science Association.

Blanchard, Olivier, Ben Bernanke, and Janet Yellen. 2019. *A Message from the AEA Leadership on the Professional Climate in Economics.* March 18, 2019.

Boring, Anne. 2020. Gender Bias in Student Evaluations of Teaching. In *Women in Economics*, ed. Shelly Lundberg, 118–122. London: Centre for Economic Policy.

Botswick, Valerie K., and Bruce A. Weinberg. 2020. Peer Effects in Graduate Programmes. In *Women in Economics*, ed. Shelly Lundberg, 65–71. London: Centre for Economic Policy.

Boustan, Leah, and Andrew Langan. 2019. "Variation in women's success across PhD programs in economics. *Journal of Economic Perspectives* 33(1):57–64.

Brown, Clair. 2020. Interview with the Author by Zoom. November 18.

Buckles, Kasey. 2020. Proven Strategies for Making Economics Work for Women. In *Women in Economics*, ed. Shelly Lundberg, 131–135. London: Centre for Economic Policy.

Card, David, Stefano Della Vigna, Patricia Funk, and Nagore Iriberri. 2020. Are Referees and Editors in Economics Gender Neutral? *Quarterly Journal of Economics* 135(1):269–327.

Ceci, Stephen J., Donna K. Ginther, Shulamit Kahn, and Wendy M. Williams. 2014. Women in Academic Science: A Changing Landscape. *Psychological Science in the Public Interest* 15(3):75–141.

Chen, Joyce. 2022. Interview with the Author via Zoom. June 2.

Chen, Yan, and Sherry Xin Li. 2009. Group Identity and Social Preferences. *American Economic Review* 99(1):431–457.

Committee on the Status of Women in the Economics Profession. 2018 Focus: Dealing with Sexual Harassment. Learning from the Experiences of CSWEP Members. *CSWEP News* 1:5–6.

Committee on the Status of Women in the Economics Profession. 2022. CSWEP: Survey and annual report.

Committee on the Status of Women in the Economics Profession. 2023. CSWEP: Survey and annual report.

Dolar, Veronika. 2021. The Gender Gap in Economics is Huge—It's Even Worse Than Tech. *The Conversation*. March 12.

Ductor, Lorenzo, Sanjeev Goyal, and Anja Prummer. 2020. Gender and Collaboration. In *Women in Economics*, ed. Shelly Lundberg, 74–78. London: Centre for Economic Policy Research.

Dupas, Pascaline, Alicia Sasser Modestino, Muriel Niederle, Justin Wolfers, and the Seminar Dynamics Collective. Gender and the Dynamics of Economics Seminars. NBER Working Paper 28494. Cambridge: NBER.

Erten, Bilge. 2022. Interview with author via zoom. June 1.

Ginther, Donna K., and Shulamit Kahn. 2014. Academic Women's Careers in the Social Science. In *The Economics of Economists: Institutional Setting, Individual Incentives, and Future Prospects*, ed. Alessandro Lanteri and Jack Vromen, 285–315. Cambridge: Cambridge University Press.

Ginther, Donna K., Janet M. Currie, Francine D. Blau, and Rachel T. A. Croson. 2020. Mentoring Matters for Women in Economics. In *Women in Economics*, ed. Shelly Lundberg, 125–130. London: Centre for Economic Policy.

Guarino, Cassandra M., and Victor M. H. Borden. 2017. Faculty Service Loads and Gender: Are Women Taking Care of the Academic Family. *Research in Higher Education*. 58(April):672–694.

Hengel, Erin. 2020. Publishing While Female. In *Women in Economics*, ed. Shelly Lundberg, 80–90. London: Centre for Economic Policy.

Hopkins, Barbara. 2022. Interview with the author via Zoom. August 3.

Horizon Europe. 2022. Horizon Europe. 2022. *Research and Innovation: Horizon Europe*. research-and-innovation.ec.europa.eu/funding/funding-opportunities/funding-programmes-and-open-calls/horizon-europe_en.

Hospido, Laura, Luc Laeven, and Ana Lamo. 2020. The Gender Promotion Gap: Evidence from Central Banking. In *Women in Economics*, ed. Shelly Lundberg, 109–113. London: Centre for Economic Policy Research.

Hospido, Laura, and Carlos Sanz. 2020. Does Gender Matter to be Accepted into Economics Conferences? In *Women in Economics*, ed. Shelly Lundberg, 98–101. London: Centre for Economic Policy Research.

Khan, Shulamit. 2020. Gender and Promotion in Economics Academia. In *Women in Economics*, ed. Shelly Lundberg, 104–108. London: Centre for Economic Policy.

Kanter, Rosabeth Moss. 1977. *Men and Women of the Corporation*. New York: Basic Books.

Kanter, Rosabeth Moss. 1980. *A Tale of "O": On Being Different in an Organization.* NY: Harper and Row.
Kim, Marlene. 2023a. Gender in Economics Fifty Years Ago and Today: Feminist Economists Speak. *Review of Radical Political Economics* 55(1):8–25.
Kim, Marlene. 2023b. The Problem of Gender in Economics. *Review of Radical Political Economics* 55(4):639–650.
Kim, Marlene. 2024. *Thinking (and Doing) Like an Inclusive Economist.* Mimeo.
Kim, Marlene. 2024. Race and Ethnicity in the Economics Profession: Problems and Remedies. *Forum for Social Economics* 53(2):170–184.
Kleemans, Marieke, and Rebecca Thornton. 2023. Fully Promoted: The Distribution and Determinants of Full Professorship in the Economics Profession. *AEA Papers and Proceedings* 113(May):467–472.
Li, Hsueh-Hsiang. 2018. Do Mentoring, Information, and Nudge Reduce the Gender Gap in Economics Majors. *Economics of Education Review* 64:165–183.
Lundberg, Shelley. Ed. 2020. *Women in Economics.* London: Center for Economic Policy Research.
Lundberg, Shelly. 2020. Women in the Economics Profession: Challenges and Opportunities Along the Pipeline. In *Women in Economics*, ed. Shelly Lundberg, 9–17. London: Centre for Economic Policy Research.
Lundberg, Shelly, and Jenna Stearns. 2019. Women in Economics: Stalled Progress. *Journal of Economic Perspectives* 33(1):3–22.
Nelson, Julie A. 2017. *Gender and Risk-Taking: Economics, Evidence, and Why the Answer Matters.* Routledge.
Nelson, Julie A. 2020. Interview with the Author via Zoom. October 19.
Nunes. Deborah. 2022. Interview with the Author via Zoom. April 19.
Olney, Martha. 2020. Joan Underhill Hannon. *History of Women Faculty in Economics*. August 2020. https://econ.berkeley.edu/abouthistory-women-faculty/joan-underhill-hannon.
O'Meara, KerryAnn, Alexandra Kuvaeva, Gurun Nyunt, Chelsea Waugarman, and Rose Jackson. 2017. Asked More Often: Gender Differences in Faculty Workload in Research Universities and the Work Interactions that Shape Them. *American Educational Research Journal* 54(6):1154–1186.
Porter, Catherine, and Danila Serra. 2020. Female Role Models Inspire Women to Major in Male-Dominated Fields. In *Women in Economics*, ed. Shelly Lundberg, 51–56. London: Centre for Economic Policy Research.
Rodgers, Yana. 2022. Interview with Author via Zoom. May 26.
Ross, Matthew B., Britta M. Glennon, Raviv Murciano-Goroff, Enrico G. Berkes, Bruce A. Weinberg, and Julia I. Lane. 2022. Women are Credited Less in Science than Men. *Nature* 608:135–145.
Sarsons, Heather. 2017. Recognition for Group Work: Gender Differences in Academia. *American Economic Review* 107(5):141–145.

Stevenson, Betsey, and Hanna Zlotnick. 2018. Representations of Men and Women in Introductory Economics Textbooks. *American Economic Association Papers and Proceedings* 108:180–185.

Sugimoto, Cassidy R., and Vincent Lariviere. 2023. *Equity for Women in Science: Dismantling Systemic Barriers to Advancement*. Cambridge, MA: Harvard University Press.

Van der Lee, Romy and Naomi Ellemers. 2019. Gender Contributes to Personal Research Funding Success in The Netherlands. *PNAS* 112(40):12349–12353.

Wu, Alice H. 2018. Gendered Language on the Economics Job Market Rumors Forum. *American Economic Review* 108:175–179.

Exploring the Role of External Characteristics on Gender Equity: A Study of Economics Departments in the United States

Laura Beltran Figueroa

1 Introduction

Gender distribution across faculty has been a long-standing topic of research, and although progress has been made toward gender equality in academia, economics departments continue to be male dominated. According to the 2020 Report on the Status of Women in the Economics Profession (Levenstein 2020), women account for 21% of tenured and tenure-track faculty in economics. Previous empirical studies have identified factors that contribute to these gender disparities in faculty positions, such as gender bias, discrimination, limited access to mentorship and networking opportunities, as well as gendered expectations of work and family responsibilities (Goldin 2015; Gruber et al. 2021; Llorens et al. 2021). The lack of gender diversity in economics deprives the field of diverse perspectives and experiences, which are crucial for high-quality research and teaching (Maruyama et al. 2000; Chang 2002a, 2002b). Therefore, it is imperative to address the issue of gender diversity in

L. B. Figueroa (✉)
Center for Women and Work, Rutgers University, New Brunswick, USA
e-mail: lb1111@smlr.rutgers.edu

© The Author(s), under exclusive license to Springer Nature Switzerland AG 2026

V. Dolar and T. Perry (eds.), *Missing Voices in Economics*,
https://doi.org/10.1007/978-3-031-97180-8_2

economics to advance the field and ensure it reflects diverse viewpoints and experiences.

In this chapter, I extend prior research on gender distribution in economics departments by proposing new variables such as school type and size, religious affiliation, state politics, liberal arts college status, and female department chair presence as external factors potentially affecting faculty gender equity. I utilized web-scraping techniques to compile a database of the leading 240 economics departments in the United States comprising 5,388 professors, as well as detailed data on 1,333 women professors' research interests. I hypothesize that economics departments located in Democratic-leaning states, affiliated with public institutions, and with women chairs will have the most favorable gender distribution among their faculty members. Additionally, I suggest that women professors are more likely to specialize in subfields such as labor, environment, and education, i.e., those perceived to be "soft," whereas male professors tend to focus on macroeconomics and financial economics, subfields associated with higher prestige positions, and occupations outside academia. This specialization trend is significant because historically, journals have favored mainstream economic topics over community-focused areas, impacting tenure prospects (Espinel and Betancourt 2022).

The chapter is divided into four main sections. The first section reviews the prevalent literature on gender distribution among economics departments and explores theoretical frameworks and empirical evidence. I then outline the methodology used to collect and analyze the data for this study. The third section presents the findings, which demonstrate that university location and school type are significant predictors of gender distribution among economics departments. The final section discusses the implications of the study's findings and recommendations for improving gender equity in economics departments.

This chapter contributes to the literature in three main dimensions. Firstly, it expands the current understanding of the external factors related to gender representation in economics departments beyond the traditional variables that prior research has explored. By incorporating school type and size, religious affiliation, state politics, liberal arts college status, and female department chair as potential predictors, this study offers a more nuanced perspective on the contextual factors that shape gender equity in academia. Secondly, this chapter utilizes a novel dataset that provides detailed information on numerous economics departments in the United States, including state and institutional characteristics, and gender distribution among faculty members. I also include data on the research interests and publications from female faculty to determine whether there is an equal distribution in subfields, which may reflect potential issues associated with hiring and tenure prospects. Finally, this study provides guidance for improving gender equity in economics by identifying key external factors, aiding institutions in crafting targeted policies.

2 Literature Review

Over the past few years, there has been a growing body of research highlighting the existence of gender bias and inequity in academia (Llorens et al. 2021; Liu et al. 2021; Carlsson et al. 2021). Despite women earning more PhDs than men, they continue to be underrepresented in tenured academic positions (Conti and Visentin 2015). Lundberg and Stearns reported that as of the mid-2000s, the proportion of women PhD students and assistant professors was just below 35% and 30%, respectively, and these percentages have persisted without significant changes in recent years (Lundberg and Stearns 2019). Alarmingly, women are less represented in economics than in science, technology, engineering, and mathematics (STEM) fields, and there has been little improvement since the 1990s, according to Bayer and Rouse (2016).

This underrepresentation persists across all levels of higher education. Goldin's analysis reveals the stark gender disparity in undergraduate economics education, wherein the number of male majors significantly outnumbers female majors (Goldin 2015). Specifically, the nationwide ratio of male to female economics majors is approximately 2.9:1, with top-ranked universities and liberal arts colleges exhibiting ratios of nearly 2.5:1 and 2.6:1, respectively. Women have consistently made up about one-third of economics bachelor's degree earners for over two decades, with a slight decline since the early 2000s, according to Siegfried (2019). For graduate degrees, the uneven gender distribution is not as pronounced as in the undergraduate level, but still evident. Boustan and Lang argue that over the past 30 years, there has been significant variation in the average percentage of women in graduating classes of economics PhD programs, with figures ranging from as low as 10% to exceeding 50% of the class (Boustan and Langan 2019). However, on average women accounted for 33 percent of the PhD students who graduated (Fraumeni 2011). Despite the progress made in terms of representation in graduate degrees, it appears that women faculty in universities and business schools have not enjoyed the same level of gains, potentially overturning the progress made. Auriol finds that among the 238 universities and business schools included in their sample, women comprise 25% of senior-level positions (full or associate professor) and 37% of junior-level positions in economics (Auriol et al. 2022).

From a subfield specialization point of view, gender gaps are also prevalent. Sierminska and Oaxaca found that over 40% of women who completed their dissertation in the past decade specialized in Labor, Health, or Microeconomics, while the remaining women specialized in 17 other JEL fields. Among men, the top three fields accounting for 40% of specializations were Microeconomics, Macro/Monetary Economics, and Labor (Sierminska and Oaxaca 2022). This specialization pattern in research subfields highlights the presence of gender-specific preferences or barriers that can influence subfield specialization decisions. The implications of such barriers extend beyond individual academic careers, as they can shape research agendas, influence policymaking, and hinder the overall advancement of the economics field.

Some of the factors that have been used to explain the unequal gender distribution in academia have included bias in hiring, promotion, and tenure processes, as well as the "motherhood penalty" that women face when balancing family and career responsibilities (Ginther and Kahn 2004; Kahn et al. 2014; Budig and England 2001). While most of these factors seem to hint at systemic and structural issues within academia, there is also evidence suggesting that cultural and societal factors play a role in perpetuating gender disparities within the field.

In terms of overall gendered employment, regional political leaning is a significant factor. According to a report by the Georgetown Institute for Women, Peace, and Security, the political leaning of a state is a significant factor in influencing the US Women, Peace, and Security Index. The study found that all twelve best-performing states on the index had a Democratic-leaning inclination, and women in these states had better access to employment and education opportunities (Georgetown Institute of Women Peace and Security 2021). Moreover, these states had more robust legal protections against discrimination and access to reproductive healthcare. Red states may have a greater emphasis on traditional gender roles and a lower level of support for policies that promote gender equality in the workplace. On the other hand, blue states may have a more progressive and inclusive culture and may have implemented policies that support women's advancement in the workplace.

Religious affiliation can also impact the faculty hiring process, potentially affecting the representation of women in academic positions. For instance, Johnson et al. contend that religiosity might have a strong effect on intergroup bias and suggest that subliminal priming of religious words can lead to negative attitudes toward value-violating out-groups, such as atheists, Muslims, and gay men (Johnson et al. 2012). These findings highlight religion's influence on attitudes within universities toward underrepresented groups like women and call for increased awareness of biases in faculty hiring.

Evidence suggests that public universities in most countries tend to have a higher proportion of female faculty members than private universities, as the public sector tends to hire more women than men (Cooper et al. 2012). This is attributed to government policies and regulations that prioritize objective criteria and depersonalized hiring processes in public university hiring practices. Additionally, Hoffnar and Green argue that the gender earnings gap is smaller in the public sector than in the private sector, indicating that female faculty members in public universities may have more equitable pay compared to their counterparts in private universities (Hoffnar and Greene 1996). This may be because public universities face less managerial discretion in pay-setting as in hiring, and relatively few faculty positions are collectively bargained in the United States, even at public institutions.

3 Theoretical Framing

The process of recruiting academic faculty members seldom operates independently within the confines of the respective departments. Instead, such appointments are subject to external influences originating from sources within the university and beyond. Prior studies have noted the correlation between state political leaning and women's labor outcomes. May and McGarvey found that the employment gap between men and women is larger in Republican-leaning states than in Democratic-leaning states (May and McGarvey 2017). Accordingly, I can reasonably infer that schools situated in historically Democratic states may exhibit a higher proportion of female professors than schools in Republican-leaning states. There are various reasons for this hypothesis. Firstly, states with Democratic leanings may hold more progressive views on gender equality and thus prioritize efforts toward diversity and inclusivity in academia. Ryan-Hume argues that the interrelation between gender and political preferences became increasingly pronounced in the 1980s, as the Republican Party became more conservative (Ryan-Hume 2021). Additionally, women began to hold more liberal political views during this period; furthermore, gender-equality advocacy groups that arose in the 1960s and 1970s began to institutionalize their activities and capitalize on demographic shifts. Consequently, these groups became more deeply integrated into the internal politics of the Democratic Party.

Similarly, public institutions may have more resources and a stronger commitment to diversity initiatives, which may explain why they tend to have a more favorable gender distribution among their faculty. Gomes and Kuehn conducted a cross-national analysis of 20 countries belonging to the Organization for Economic Cooperation and Development (OECD) and observed that women's representation in the public sector was higher than in the private sector (Gomes and Kuehn 2019). This phenomenon can be attributed to several factors, including (i) lower gender wage gaps in the public sector, which may result in relatively higher wages for women; (ii) greater opportunities for work-life balance in the public sector; and (iii) higher levels of job security in the public sector compared to the private sector. Among private universities, liberal arts colleges may also have a more balanced gender distribution among faculty, as they often prioritize diversity and inclusion as part of their institutional values (Rozier and Scharff 2013).

The influence of religious affiliation on gender representation in economics departments is a potential area of investigation. It is plausible that religious schools may uphold strict societal norms that may hinder the appointment of female professors. Additionally, it is conceivable that women may be disinclined to apply for these positions due to the dearth of female faculty representation. Another explanation could be the presence of a conscious or unconscious bias against women among those responsible for making hiring decisions. Such prejudices may be more widespread in religious institutions that adhere to conventional views on gender roles. For example, Rivera discovered that recruiters often sought candidates who were both competent and shared their cultural backgrounds in terms of leisure activities, experiences, and self-presentation styles (Rivera 2012).

Whether the department had a woman chairman can also impact gender distribution, since the appointment of women to top leadership positions can serve as a powerful symbol and motivator for promoting gender diversity in universities. Research has shown that the appointment of a female governor or senator can lead to a significant increase in the number of women running for office in that state (Harold Windett 2011). Similarly, the appointment of a female university president or chair can send a strong message to faculty, staff, and students about the institution's commitment to diversity and inclusion. This can inspire more women to pursue academic careers and create a more welcoming and supportive environment for women already in academia.

4 Data and Methodology

Using web-scraping techniques, I compiled data on the leading 240 US economics departments according to Michael A. McPherson's (2012) ranking, which was based on the number of publications in the top 50 journals by individuals affiliated with each institution (McPherson 2012). Within each of these economics departments, I collected data on their gender distribution. I restricted my analysis to faculty members holding academic ranks of professor, associate professor, or assistant professor and to those who possess a Ph.D. in economics or a related field. I excluded faculty with adjunct, instructor, retired, or emeritus status. Additionally, I noted any leadership roles held by faculty members within their respective departments. Gender identification relied on a combination of photographic and naming cues, with further verification sought via biographical information, LinkedIn, Google Scholar, or ResearchGate when necessary. Any faculty member for whom gender information could not be obtained was excluded from the analysis.[1]

After compiling the list of women faculty members, I utilized Elsevier's SCOPUS database to identify their current publications and classify them within their specific research field(s), 18 fields of concentration were identified. SCOPUS was chosen due to its extensive citation database of peer-reviewed research literature. To ensure accurate representation, I took great care to match each faculty member to their respective affiliation with the school in question. In cases where discrepancies were found, I cross-referenced SCOPUS publications with those listed on faculty

[1] It is important to acknowledge the existence and experiences of nonbinary individuals within the context of gender analysis. However, for the purposes of this particular analysis, the focus will be limited to the experiences of individuals who identify as either male or female.

members' CVs or school websites. For faculty with only one publication, no further details were obtained beyond the number of documents listed in SCOPUS. In cases where a faculty member was not found in the database, their metrics data was left blank. This data on research fields served as the basis for comparing the distribution of research among women faculty.

The present study incorporated a range of external factors in its analysis, including the state's political leaning, the public or private nature of the school, its size and location, its religious affiliation, whether the department has a woman chair, whether the university identifies as a liberal arts college, and whether the university is a land-grant institution. The state's political leaning was determined based on the outcomes of the 2020 presidential election. The classification of schools as public or private, religious affiliation and departmental and school details were sourced from their respective websites. To ensure methodological consistency, the entire dataset was generated by a single individual.

5 Statistical Analysis and Results

The sample for this study consisted of 240 departments consisting of 5,388 professors, of which 1,343 (24.93%) were women and 4,043 (75.04%) were men. Furthermore, data on research interests was successfully obtained for 99.26% (1333 out of 1343) of the women faculty members included in the sample. An upset plot detailing the characteristics of these institutions is presented in Fig. 1. Specifically, it shows how many schools in the data set have particular combinations of values of the independent variables (Lex et al. 2014). Among the top 240 economics departments, the majority are in democrat states, are public institutions, have no religious affiliation, and are not land-grant institutions.

In Table 1, the means and standard deviations for the percentage of women, total number of women professors, total number of women department chair, total number of professors across economics departments, and university population are presented. The present study discovered an average gender distribution of 26.45% women and 73.55% men across departments. Remarkably, this closely aligns with the findings of Auriol's prior research, which found that women constitute merely 25% of senior-level positions (Auriol et al. 2022). The average department size was 22.45 professors out of which 5.59 were women. Among the surveyed Economics Departments, only 8 departments (3%) were found

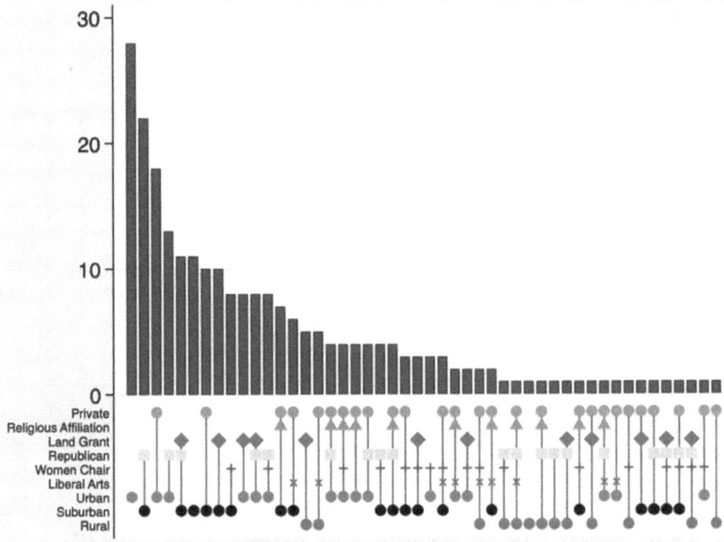

Fig. 1 Upset plot with institutional characteristics of top economics departments

to have a majority of female faculty members. Conversely, two (1%) departments were observed to have no female professors. Additionally, only 47 (19.58%) departments had a women department head.

After conducting an analysis of the fields of concentration among the female professors in the sample, I discovered that most of the professors can be categorized within three specific domains, namely labor economics, development economics, and health economics (Fig. 2). Remarkably, this finding aligns with the research by Sierminska and Oaxaca (Sierminska and Oaxaca 2022), who revealed that a significant proportion of women who completed their dissertations in the past decade specialized in Labor, Health, or Microeconomics.

Upon further disaggregation, several intriguing trends emerged, as illustrated in Fig. 3. Notably, a substantial majority (87.5%) of feminist economists, alongside those researching economics of the household (83.33%) and economics of the family (79.16%), were affiliated with the top 120 economics departments. In contrast, most scholars engaged in law and economics and natural resource economics were found to belong to the bottom 120 departments, at 57.9% and 54.83%, respectively. The

Table 1 Descriptive statistics for the sample of faculty in top economics departments

Variable	*Obs*	*Mean*	*Std. Dev*	*Min*	*Max*
Total Professors Within Department	240	22.45	12.7885	5	70
Women Professors	240	5.59583	3.2714	0	18
Percentage Women Professors	240	0.264497	0.114028	0	0.75
Women Chair	240	0.195833	0.39767	0	1
University Population	240	22,638.75	15,195.71	1300	74,000

remaining fields of research were found to be distributed almost equally between the top 120 and the bottom 120 departments.

5.1 *Political Affiliation and Gender Distribution*

Upon examining the gender distribution across various schools, distinct patterns become apparent. Notably, in the 114 departments where the percentage of female professors exceeds the average—26.45%, 77 departments are situated in states that possess a historical voting record that aligns with the Democratic Party (67.54%), whereas only 37 departments are in states that have recently voted Republican (32.46%). For context, 152 out of the 240 schools that were sampled were in Democratic states (63.33%), while 88 schools were located in Republican states (36.66%). This finding implies that departments with more equitable gender distributions tend to be situated in Democratic states. Overall, this hints at the potential influence of political and cultural factors on the representation of women in academia. Additionally, out of the 47 women department chairs, 31 (69.59%) were in Democrat states, whereas only 16 (34.01%) were in Republican.

5.2 *Institution Type and Gender Distribution*

A detailed analysis revealed that public schools typically have a more equitable faculty gender distribution compared to private schools. Specifically, from the 114 schools that scored above average, 66 (57.89%) schools

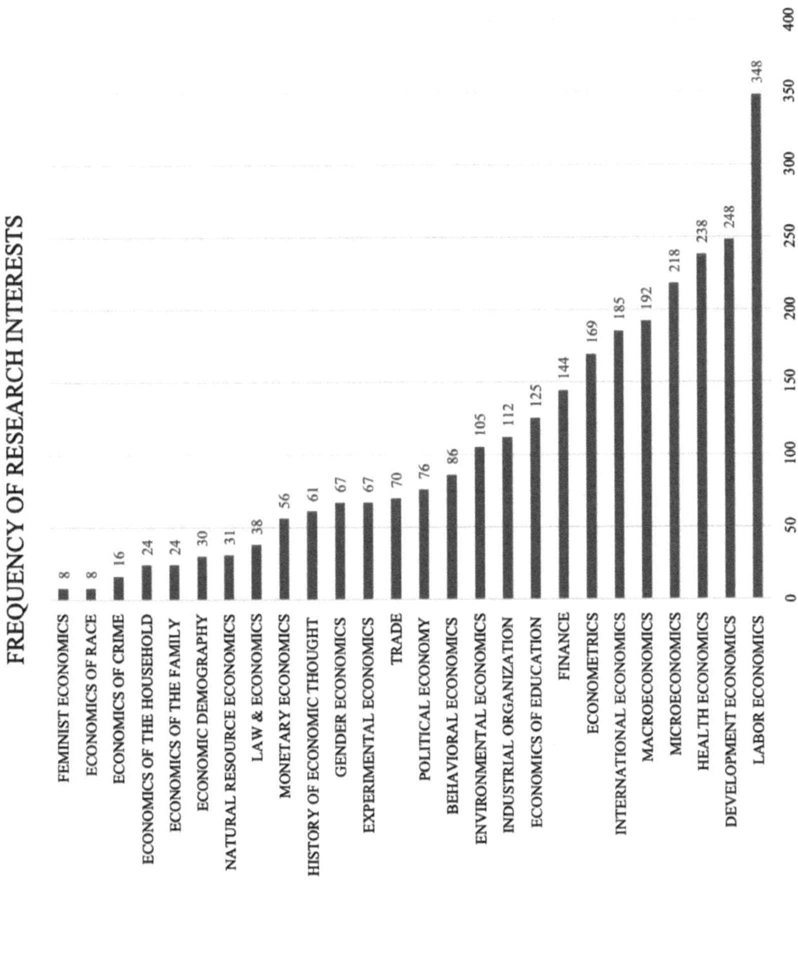

Fig. 2 Field categorization among women professors

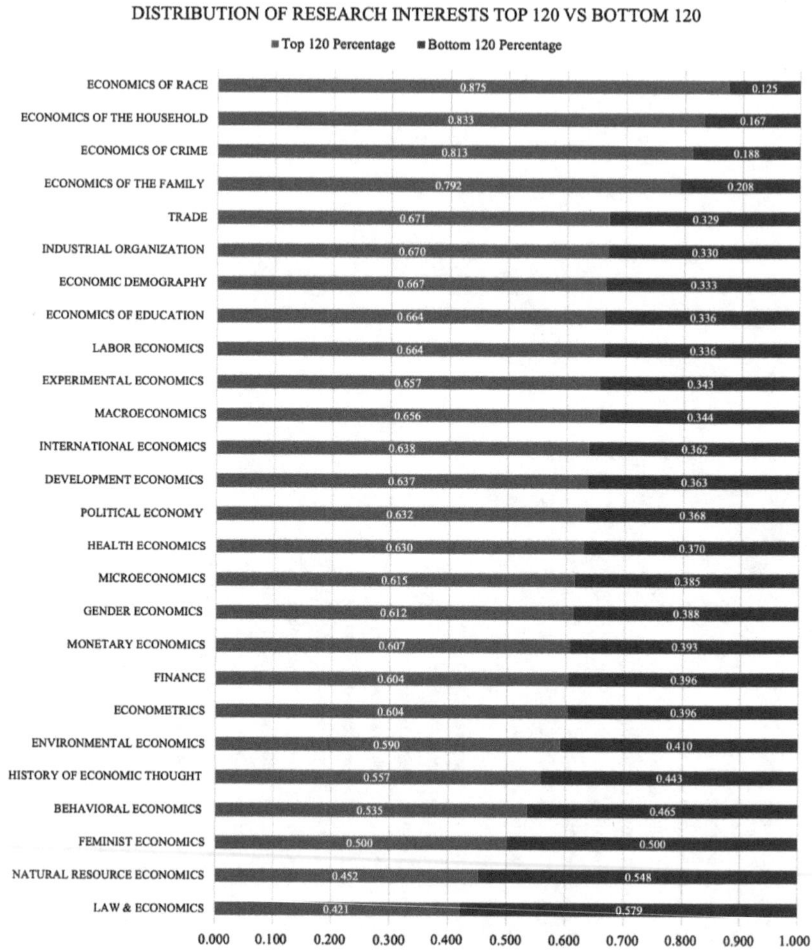

Fig. 3 Distribution of research interests among women

were public and 48 (42.11%) were private. For context, 90 out of the 240 schools that were sampled were private (37.5%), while 150 schools were public (62.25%). This evidence suggests that public institutions are more effective at attracting and retaining female faculty than private ones. Nonetheless, this trend was not uniform across all schools, as certain private institutions in select regions boasted a higher proportion of female professors than public institutions. Additionally, out of the 47 women department chairs, 31 (69.59%) were in Democrat states, whereas only 16 (34.01%) were in Republican states.

When examining the intersection of institutional characteristics and state political affiliation, it becomes evident that among the 66 public schools that perform better than average, the majority (56.06%) are situated in states with a Democratic political affiliation. However, there was no significant difference in the distribution of political affiliations among public schools that performed below average. Among private schools that perform above average in terms of gender distribution, 83.33% are in states with a Democratic political affiliation.

5.3 *Religious Affiliation and Gender Distribution*

The present study is characterized by a limited sample size, encompassing only 31 academic departments affiliated with religious institutions. Among these departments 14 departments scored below the average gender distribution. The distribution of departments in the sample was heterogeneous, with 11 departments located in states characterized as Republican and 20 departments located in Democrat states.

6 OLS Regressions with the Variables of Interest

To delve further into the determinants affecting the gender distribution among economics faculty, Ordinary Least Squares (OLS) regression analyses were conducted. The dependent variable in these analyses was the percentage of female faculty members in economics departments. Several independent variables were considered, including political affiliation of the state, type of institution (public vs. private), religious affiliation, department size, student population, whether the department head is a woman, and whether the institution identifies as a liberal arts college. In the baseline model, the dependent variable is the percentage of female faculty members in economics departments and the independent variables include political affiliation of the state (Democratic or Republican), type of institution (public or private), and department size as measured by the total number of professors in the department. This was designed to serve as a reference point before adding more variables into the mix.

Results from the baseline model indicated that department size was statistically significant at the 1% level, suggesting that the size of the department plays a substantial role in the gender distribution among faculty members. Specifically, larger departments tended to have a lower percentage of female faculty members compared to smaller departments. Additionally, state political affiliation emerged as a significant variable, at the 1% level, suggesting that economics departments located in states with Democratic leanings are somewhat more likely to have higher percentages of female faculty than those in states leaning Republican. More so, institution type—private vs. public—was not significant in the baseline model, suggesting that the public or private nature of an institution does not have a statistically significant relationship with on the percentage of female faculty within economics departments at the 10% significance level or better.

In light of these findings, I introduced additional variables into subsequent models to test for potential nuances. When including a variable for whether the department head is a woman, I found it to be significant at the 1% level. More specifically, having a woman chair in the department increases the gender distribution of women by 7%. This adds another layer of complexity, suggesting that having a woman in a leadership role within the department can positively influence the gender distribution of faculty members. This finding may hint at a more supportive culture or specific initiatives led by female department heads that help improve gender representation. Additionally, in the second regression (M1), the type of institution became significant at the 10% level, suggesting that when the department head's gender is considered, the nature of the institution (public vs. private) begins to play a more noticeable role in determining the gender distribution of faculty members. Specifically, private institutions showed a slightly higher likelihood of having more female faculty members compared to public institutions, albeit the effect being modest.

When including a variable for whether the institution considered itself a liberal arts college (M2), the variable was found to be statistically significant at the 1% level, suggesting that the academic orientation of the institution does, in fact, play a role in the gender distribution of economics faculty. In this case, liberal arts colleges appear to have a higher percentage of female faculty in economics departments compared to other types of institutions. In the last iteration (M3), I controlled for ranking, student population, and whether the department was in an urban area, with none of these variables showing statistical significance.

Table 2 presents the output for these models, capturing the influences of these additional variables on the gender distribution in economics

Table 2 Regressions depicting the relationship between gender distribution among economics faculty and external factors

	Baseline	*Model 1*	*Model 2*	*Model 3*
Republican	−0.0409***	−0.0372**	−0.0335**	−0.0322**
Private	0.0245	0.0272*	0.0093	0.0074
Total Professors	−0.0025***	−0.0022***	−0.0018 ***	−0.0009
Woman Chair		0.0725***	0.0708***	0.0675***
Liberal College			0.0680***	0.0588**
Ranking				0.0002
Student Population				0.0000
Urban				−0.0055
Intercept	0.3254***	0.3029***	0.2937***	0.2515***
R-squared	0.1051	0.1680	0.1924	0.2034
Sample Size	240	240	240	240

*$p < 0.1$, **$p < 0.05$, ***$p < 0.01$

faculty. The coefficients for female department chair, liberal arts college status, and state political affiliation remain highly significant at the 1% and 5% confidence levels, confirming the robustness of these variables as predictors.

7 Discussion

This study investigated the gender distribution and research interests of faculty members in top economics departments in the United States. I found an average gender distribution of 26.45% women and 73.55% men across the departments in my sample, which closely aligns with prior research. Additionally, the study found that female professors tended to specialize in labor economics, development economics, and health economics, which is consistent with prior research. However, upon further inspection, a substantial majority of feminist economists, as well as those researching economics of the household and economics of the family, were affiliated with top-ranked departments, whereas scholars engaged in law and economics and natural resource economics were found to belong to the bottom-ranked departments. One possible explanation is that scholars who specialize in law and economics or natural resource economics may have different career trajectories or academic backgrounds that lead them to be affiliated with lower-ranked departments. Another possible explanation is that top departments are more likely to support women professor's research in less orthodox fields.

Political affiliation and institution type were found to be correlated with gender distribution. For instance, departments with more equitable gender distributions tend to be situated in Democratic states, and public schools generally exhibited a more favorable gender distribution among their faculty. Additionally, the majority of public schools that perform better than average are situated in states with a Democratic political affiliation. Two possible mechanisms that may explain this pattern are a higher level of support for diversity and inclusion in Democratic states and public schools, and a stronger emphasis on gender equity and representation in their hiring and promotion practices. It is also possible that Democratic states and public schools attract a more diverse pool of applicants, leading to a more equitable gender distribution among faculty members.

Meanwhile, the influence of religious affiliation on gender representation in economics departments is less clear and may require further investigation. Due to the limited sample, it is impossible to conclude whether religion plays a significant role in shaping gender representation in economics departments or not. Having a woman department chair also seemed to have a positive association with women's representation, with departments led by female chairs having a higher percentage of female faculty members on average. This finding underscores the importance of having more women in leadership positions to promote gender diversity and equity in academia.

8 Conclusion

There are broader societal, political, and cultural factors that influence the career paths of women in academia. It is impossible to analyze the experiences of women in academia without considering these external factors. For instance, cultural stereotypes and biases against women can impact their ability to advance in their academic careers. Additionally, gender inequality in society can limit women's access to educational opportunities and resources, which can affect their academic achievements and career prospects. Political affiliations of a state can also play a role in shaping the academic environment for women. For instance, departments located in very Republican states may have a different political culture and agenda than those in Democratic or more liberal states, which can influence policies and attitudes toward diversity and inclusion.

It is important for academic institutions to be aware of these external factors and to actively work toward creating a supportive and inclusive environment for all members of their community, regardless of their background or beliefs. For example, given that Republican states are known to have less equitable gender distributions in their economics departments, institutions in those states could take proactive measures to increase diversity and inclusivity, such as offering more resources and support for women in economics, implementing bias training for faculty and staff, and actively recruiting and promoting women faculty members. In terms of hiring decisions, departments can take steps to ensure that their hiring practices are fair and equitable, such as using blind review processes or establishing diversity targets. They can also prioritize diversity and inclusion in their job postings and outreach efforts to attract a more diverse pool of applicants. Additionally, providing mentorship and professional development opportunities for women and other underrepresented groups can help to support their career advancement and retention in academia. The concentration of women in certain economics subfields such as Health and Labor should be addressed by encouraging and promoting diversity in all subfields and disciplines. For example, to attract a more diverse range of scholars, public and lower-ranked institutions could consider expanding their offerings to include emerging fields and interdisciplinary studies or offer dual or joint appointments whenever financial constraints prevent the creation of new positions. Academic institutions can work to increase access to resources and opportunities for women in underrepresented fields, as well as address cultural and societal biases that may discourage women from pursuing careers in certain areas. Lastly, it is also important to involve women in academia in the policymaking process to ensure that their perspectives and experiences are considered.

To enhance our understanding of gender-based wage disparities in elite academic institutions, future research should seek to quantify the wage differentials between men and women in these schools. Furthermore, investigating the relationship between funding for Diversity, Equity, and Inclusion initiatives in public and private academic institutions would provide valuable insights into how these efforts are being supported across the higher education landscape. Ultimately, it is imperative that we continue to recognize and address the systemic barriers that women face in academia. By acknowledging and addressing these external factors, academic institutions can create more equitable and supportive environments that foster the success of all members of their community. This not only benefits individual women in academia but also contributes to a more diverse and inclusive academic culture that benefits the entire field.

References

Auriol, Emmanuelle, Guido Friebel, Alisa Weinberger, and Sascha Wilhelm. 2022. Underrepresentation of Women in the Economics Profession More Pronounced in the United States Compared to Heterogeneous Europe. *Proceedings of the National Academy of Sciences* 119(16):e2118853119.

Bayer, Amanda, and Cecilia Elena Rouse. 2016. Diversity in the Economics Profession: A New Attack on an Old Problem. *Journal of Economic Perspectives* 30(4):221–242.

Boustan, Leah, and Andrew Langan. 2019. Variation in Women's Success Across PhD Programs in Economics. *Journal of Economic Perspectives* 33(1):23–42.

Budig, Michelle J., and Paula England. 2001. The Wage Penalty for Motherhood. *American Sociological Review* 66(2):204–225.

Carlsson, Magnus, Henning Finseraas, Arnfinn H. Midtbøen, and Guðbjörg Linda. Rafnsdóttir. 2021. Gender Bias in Academic Recruitment? Evidence from a Survey Experiment in the Nordic Region. *European Sociological Review* 37(3):399–410.

Chang, Mitchell J. 2002a. Preservation or Transformation: Where's the Real Educational Discourse on Diversity? *The Review of Higher Education* 25(2):125–140.

Chang, Mitchell J. 2002b. The Impact of an Undergraduate Diversity Course Requirement on Students' Racial Views and Attitudes. *The Journal of General Education* 51:21–42.

Conti, Annamaria, and Fabiana Visentin. 2015. A Revealed Preference Analysis of PhD Students' Choices Over Employment Outcomes. *Research Policy* 44(10):1931–1947.

Cooper, David, Mary Gable, and Algernon Austin. 2012. *The Public-Sector Jobs Crisis: Women and African Americans Hit Hardest by Job Losses in State and Local Governments*.

Espinel, Camila Orozco, and Rebeca Gomez Betancourt. 2022. A History of the Institutionalization of Feminist Economics Through Its Tensions and Founders. *History of Political Economy* 54(S1):159–192.

Fraumeni, Barbara M. 2011. Report of the Committee on the Status of Women in the Economics Profession 2010. *American Economic Review* 101(3):731–736.

Georgetown Institute of Women Peace and Security. 2021. U.S. Women, Peace and Security Index. Georgetown Institute of Women Peace and Security. March 11. https://giwps.georgetown.edu/usa-index/.

Ginther, Donna K., and Shulamit Kahn. 2004. Women in Economics: Moving Up or Falling off the Academic Career Ladder? *Journal of Economic Perspectives* 18(3):193–214.

Goldin, Claudia. 2015. *Gender and the Undergraduate Economics Major: Notes on the Undergraduate Economics Major at a Highly Selective Liberal Arts College.* Manuscript, April 12.

Gomes, Pedro, and Zoë Kuehn. 2019. You're the One that I Want! Public Employment and Women's Labor Market Outcomes.

Gruber, June, Jane Mendle, Kristen A. Lindquist, Toni Schmader, Lee Anna Clark, Eliza Bliss-Moreau, Modupe Akinola, et al. 2021. The Future of Women in Psychological Science. *Perspectives on Psychological Science* 16(3):483–516.

Harold Windett, Jason. 2011. State Effects and the Emergence and Success of Female Gubernatorial Candidates. *State Politics & Policy Quarterly* 11(4):460–482.

Hoffnar, Emily, and Michael Greene. 1996. Gender Discrimination in the Public and Private Sectors: A Sample Selectivity Approach. *The Journal of Socio-Economics* 25(1):105–114.

Johnson, Megan K., Wade C. Rowatt, and Jordan P. LaBouff. 2012. Religiosity and Prejudice Revisited: In-Group Favoritism, Out-Group Derogation, or Both? *Psychology of Religion and Spirituality* 4(2):154.

Kahn, Joan R., Javier García-Manglano, and Suzanne M. Bianchi. 2014. The Motherhood Penalty at Midlife: Long-Term Effects of Children on Women's Careers. *Journal of Marriage and Family* 76(1):56–72.

Levenstein, Margaret. 2020. Report: Committee on the Status of Women in the Economics Profession (CSWEP). In *AEA Papers and Proceedings*, vol. 110, 726–736. American Economic Association.

Lex, Alexander, Nils Gehlenborg, Hendrik Strobelt, Romain Vuillemot, and Hanspeter Pfister. 2014. UpSet: Visualization of Intersecting Sets. *IEEE Transactions on Visualization and Computer Graphics* 20(12):1983–1992.

Liu, Xiaohong, Wei He, Li Zhao, and Jon-Chao Hong. 2021. Gender Differences in Self-Regulated Online Learning During the COVID-19 Lockdown. *Frontiers in Psychology* 12:752131.

Llorens, Anaïs, Athina Tzovara, Ludovic Bellier, Ilina Bhaya-Grossman, Aurélie Bidet-Caulet, William K. Chang, Zachariah R. Cross, et al. 2021. Gender Bias in Academia: A Lifetime Problem that Needs Solutions. *Neuron* 109(13):2047–2074.

Lundberg, Shelly, and Jenna Stearns. 2019. Women in Economics: Stalled Progress. *Journal of Economic Perspectives* 33(1):3–22.

May, Ann Mari, and Mary G. McGarvey. 2017. Gender, Occupational Segregation, and the Cultural Divide: Are Red States Different than Blue States? *Review of Regional Studies* 47(2):175–199.

Maruyama, Geoffrey, Jose F. Moreno, Roxane Harvey Gudeman, and Patricia Marin. 2000. *Does Diversity Make a Difference? Three Research Studies on Diversity in College Classrooms.*

McPherson, Michael A. 2012. Ranking US Economics Programs by Faculty and Graduate Publications: An Update Using 1994–2009 Data. *Southern Economic Journal* 79(1):71–89.

Rivera, Lauren A. 2012. Hiring as Cultural Matching: The Case of Elite Professional Service Firms. *American Sociological Review* 77(6):999–1022.

Rozier, Michael, and Darcell Scharff. 2013. On Academics: The Value of Liberal Arts and Practice in an Undergraduate Public Health Curriculum. *Public Health Reports* 128(5):416–421.

Ryan-Hume, Joe J. 2021. The National Organization For Women And The Democratic Party In Reagan's America. *The Historical Journal* 64(2):454–476.

Sierminska, Eva, and Ronald L. Oaxaca. 2022. Gender Differences in Economics PhD Field Specializations with Correlated Choices. *Labour Economics* 79:102289.

Siegfried, John J. 2019. Trends in Undergraduate Economics Degrees, 2001–2018. *The Journal of Economic Education* 50(3):333–336.

Is Economics What Women Economists Do? Gender Differences in Fields of Research Among Top Economists

Giulia Zacchia and Izaskun Zuazu

1 Introduction

Almost 30 years ago, Backhouse et al. (1997), providing excellent research on "what economists do," made a plea for more quantitative analysis of economists' publications. Recently, there has been an increase in quantitative studies of research production in economics based on bibliometric and scientometric methods (Baccini et al. 2022; Rousseau and Rousseau 2021). This literature has produced an extensive body of work on trends in publications (Ambrosino et al. 2018; Marcuzzo and Zacchia 2015; Duarte and Giraud 2016) and the development of different networks of economists (D'Ippoliti et al. 2023; Baccini et al

G. Zacchia (✉)
Sapienza University of Rome, Rome, Italy
e-mail: giulia.zacchia@uniroma1.it

Minerva, Laboratory on Diversity and Gender Inequality, Sapienza University, Rome, Italy

I. Zuazu
Institute for Socio-Economics (IfSO), University of Duisburg-Essen, Duisburg, Germany
e-mail: izaskun.zuazu-bermejo@uni-due.de

© The Author(s), under exclusive license to Springer Nature Switzerland AG 2026

V. Dolar and T. Perry (eds.), *Missing Voices in Economics*,
https://doi.org/10.1007/978-3-031-97180-8_3

2023). However, relatively less attention has been devoted to identifying the gender dynamics of these processes. The studies on women in the economics profession mainly focused on gender gaps and gender discrimination in institutions, or rather, in human resources organizations (Acker 1990; Kahn 1995; Bayer and Rouse 2016; Lundberg and Stearns 2019).

As Acker (1990) argues, organizations are gendered processes where "advantage and disadvantage, exploitation and control, action and emotion, meaning and identity, are patterned through and in terms of a distinction between male and female, masculine and feminine" (Acker 1990, p. 146). The main aim of the organizational approaches to the question of women in the economics profession is to identify the gendered patterns in universities and research institutions, looking at internal processes, department organization, research activities, and criteria for evaluation and career paths (Acker 2008; Johansson and Śliwa 2014). In that sense, the concept of equality is central in terms of both equal opportunity issues and performance improvement of institutions. Therefore, a crucial aspect in this body of research is thus understanding how universities and research institutions can avoid discrimination in hiring decision-making and in the promotion of career development and how they can provide a research environment that can benefit from the creativity and productivity of diverse research groups (Zacchia 2021; Lundberg 2020; Lundberg and Stearns 2019; Hospido and Sanz 2021; Allgood et al. 2019; Vettese 2019).

Another approach within the literature on the role of gender in the economics profession is devoted to identifying and uncovering the contribution of women to the economic discipline, increasing our knowledge about women and academic production, and providing information about trends in the number and type of publications by women in economics and also laying out the evidence of the "old boy network" in publishing (May 2022, p. 122). For example, Groenewegen and King (1994) analyzed women authors in top economic journals from 1900 to 1939. A broader survey of women researchers, including less-known titles, is in Madden et al. (2004), which provides a quantitative analysis of almost 1,160 women authors of economics journals published between 1900 and 1940. Other researchers study gender differences in economic foci, methodologies, research approaches, and interests. For example, Davis (1997), Davis et al. (2011), Hedengren et al. (2010) and, for the Czech Republic, Stastny (2010) find that women typically reach a much stronger consensus on issues of equity and fairness both in the economics profession and in policy recommendations, calling for greater governmental intervention than their male colleagues. Albelda (1997) defines how men economists are much less interested in topics such as women's labor force participation, the impact of fiscal and monetary policies on women and the family structure, wage discrimination, and the economic status of minority women. Finally, May et al. (2014) report important and significant gender differences among economists in research about minimum wages, health insurance, and equal opportunities in the labor market. However, looking at the main research foci of PhDs in economics from 1991 to 2017 in almost all major PhD-granting departments in the United States, Lundberg and Stearns (2019) find the absence of differences in the distribution of men and women across fields is identified by Journal of Economics Literature (JEL) codes. Instead, Chari and Goldsmith-Pinkham (2017) and Hospido and Sanz (2021) analyzing papers selected for conference programs show that women are particularly scarce in macro and finance, and more abundant in applied microeconomic fields. Moreover, if intergenerational gender differences are considered, Dolado et al. (2012), studying the scientific production of tenured economists in top international departments in 2005, find that the tendency of women to specialize in fields more female dominated (with a high share of women already in the field) is weaker for younger female researchers who spread more evenly across fields.

This chapter contributes to the analysis of trends in gender differences in academic production by field of research among world-wide top economists. Using bibliometric tools, we provide a systematic analysis of the level of gender segregation by field of research among those economists who are considered top in economic science. To do so, we construct a unique database, with information collected from Research Papers in Economics (RePEc), which identifies the top 10% of economists with their most used JEL code over 1983–2017. We combine broad and narrow classifications of the field of research to provide more nuanced trends of field specialization by gender. We compute the level of gender segregation by field of research and consider the patterns of field of research by women and men. Our results show that gender segregation by field of research has decreased and stalled. This is mainly due to the shift of women toward male-dominated fields, such as macroeconomics and monetary economics, and the abandonment of female-dominated fields, such as labor and demographic economics. The study of the gender distribution across research fields within economics is just a first step in the direction of conceiving economic research as a social activity imbued with gendered dynamics which we hope will become a thriving area of research in the coming years.

2 Data Sources and Research Design

The first step of this analysis is the identification of the sample of women and men economists to study, to have the possibility to compare similar profiles that diverge just for the sex. For that reason, we concentrate on male authors present in the ranking of the top 10% of authors (with references to their publications in all year; it is composed of 2,595 authors[1]), and female economists listed in the ranking of the top 10% of female economists (966 authors) in RePEc. RePEc, to compensate for the under-representation of women among authors listed in the datasets, computes a "ranking of female economists"[2] that is performed solely among women, and that gives a wider overview of the presence and contributions of women economists to the profession. RePEc can be currently considered one of the largest bibliometric databases in the field of economics and related fields. A considerable amount of data has been collected regarding publications, authors (in terms of sex,[3] current affiliation, and in a few cases educational backgrounds[4]), citations, and even social activities of economists such as their visibility on social media, in particular on X, formerly known as Twitter. RePEc is based on the "active participation principle," where authors, institutions, and publishers have to register and provide information to the network. Currently, it contains almost 2.8

[1] The list of top 10% authors in RePEc, retrieved in August 2019, is made up of 2,808 top economists of whom 213 are women. In my analysis, I consider just the men since 213 women are also present in the list of top 10% Female Economists.

[2] More info here https://ideas.repec.org/top/top.women.html.

[3] Since 2006, RePEc also provided data about "Female representation in Economics," mainly statistics are drawn on economists registered in the RePEc Author Service. The identification of the sex of an author is inferred from her/his first and middle names: gender attribution contemplates that if there is more than 90% confidence that the gender is correct using a name data bank, it is attributed. Ambiguous and unrecognized names are then manually entered into "exception tables" for case-by-case attributions. In the end, only almost 0.4%.

[4] RePEc Genealogy is now implementing information that tries to document, within the field of economics, who was a student of whom, when, and where. More info is available at: https://genealogy.repec.org/

million works authored by more than 55,000 authors from 101 countries. We focus on top economists to uncover gender differences in the pressure to publish on a specific field(s) of research among those who are considered now "excellent" (according to different criteria[5]).

We next proceed to analyze the gender differences in the main research interests over time of top economists. To do so, we follow the methodology reported by Dolado et al. (2012), which uses JEL codes to identify research fields. JEL codes are alphanumerical codes made up of three levels used by authors or editors to classify scholarly literature in the field of economics. The first level of a JEL code is a letter and classifies papers according to 19 codes plus one residual category. The second level (128 classes) consists of a single letter followed by a single digit. At the third level, the code consists of a single letter followed by two digits.[6] We compute for each author her main JEL code (according to all the three levels above described), based on the most frequent JEL code used in articles published in seven five-year sub-periods (1983–1987; 1988–1992; 1993–1997; 1998–2002; 2003–2007; 2008–2012; 2013–2017).[7] We calculate trends by looking at the first level of JEL codes and different aggregations of fields of study. With the available data, we proxy the dichotomy between gender economics and feminist economics (the former grounded on Gary Becker's theory of economic human capital and the New Home Economics' perspectives, and the latter instead defined as a rejection of neoclassical framework due to its biases in the foci and methods used in the discipline, see Nelson (1995)), as clearly defined in Becchio (2020). We investigate how much those specific third-level JEL codes are used to describe (B54 for feminist economics and J16 for gender economics—economics of gender; non-labor discrimination) top women and men economists' publications, since 2006, when the specific JEL code B54 was created to identify better this dichotomy between

[5] The ranking of the top 10% of authors in RePEc is the result of 36 different rankings based on the number of works, citation counts, journal page counts, popularity on RePEc services (i.e., abstract views or downloads), and measures of centrality in networks of authors (closeness and betweenness).

[6] For a complete review of the history of the JEL code system, see Cherrier (2017).

[7] Björk and Solomon (2013) report that economics journals typically have average review times (submission to publication) close to two years, so a five-year period seems appropriate to allow us to detect changes in trends. We couldn't analyze the publications before 1983 due to the low availability of data recorded in RePEc.

gender and feminist economics, clarifying the heterodox perspective of the latter.

3 Distribution of Women and Men Across Fields in Economics

3.1 Broad Classification

We first provide the distribution of women and men's top economists by field of research over the period 1983–2017. We use a classification of fields that collapses the JEL codes into seven broad categories to ease the interpretation of results.[8] Figure 1 depicts the percentage of women's top economists in each field out of all women's top economists, as well as the percentages for men. On average, the main field of research of women and men top economists tends to concentrate on macro/finance (34.1% and 31.7%, respectively, for men and women) and microeconomics (19.1% and 15.8%, respectively, for men and women), where there is a relative higher relevance for men top economists than that for women top economists, and labor/public (24.4% and 14.5% for women and men, respectively), with a higher representation of women in labor/public and the highest gender gap. This descriptive analysis confirms what Lundberg and Stearns (2019) find for the United States, but now considering economists around the world who are considered the top 10% of economists.

Figure 2 provides the evolution of the gender distribution of the field of research during the seven 5-year periods considered in the database. The distribution across the seven fields between men and women is similar, as well and there are some similarities in the directions of trends: both women and men increased their publications about microeconomics and decreased those about macro/finance, environmental, and history/development (even if the reduction is higher for women) from the 1980s to nowadays. Instead, gender differences are evident in labor/public since women decreased their interest in this field while men increased their attention to the field.

[8] "Micro" is JEL code D; "Macro/Finance" is codes E, F, and G; "Labor/Public" is H, I, and J; "IO" is L; "Environmental" is Q; "History/Development" is N and O; and "Other" contains the remaining JEL codes A, B, C, K, M, P, R, Y, and Z.

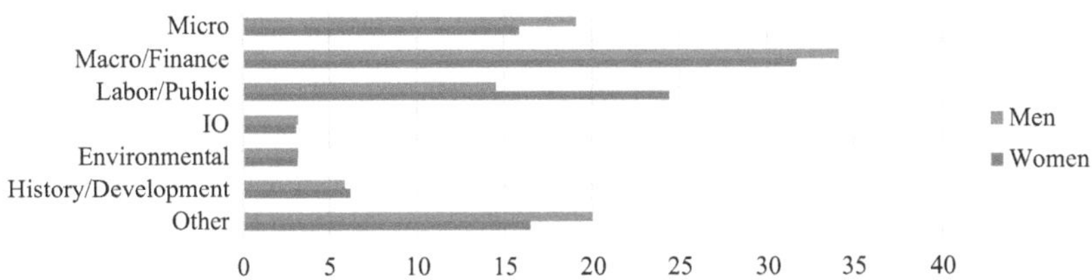

Fig. 1 Main field of women and men top economists 1983–2017 (share). *Data source*: own elaboration based on the database constructed from RePEc (1983–2017 averages)

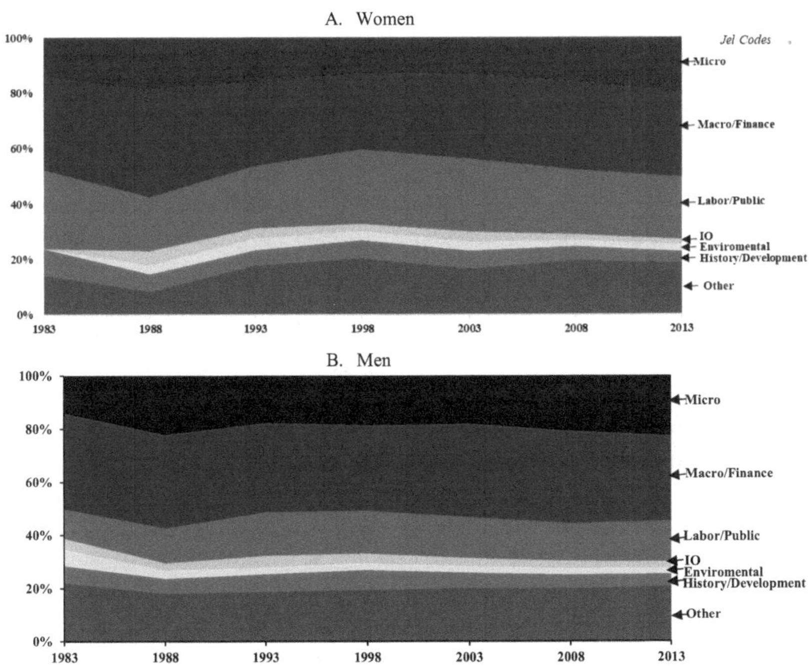

Fig. 2 Main field of women and men top economists by year (share). *Data source*: own elaboration based on the database constructed from RePEc. Note: Data collapsed into five-year bins for smoothness, i.e., the 2013 bin contains data from 2013 to 2017

3.2 Narrow Classification, Selected Fields

We next look at the more disaggregated classification of fields of research using the 19 first-level JEL codes.[9] We zoom in on the main research fields of both women and men top economists, namely microeconomics, mathematical and quantitative methods, macroeconomics and monetary economics (male-dominated) labor and demographic economics, and health, education, and welfare (female-dominated), as well as gender-neutral fields, such as financial economics. Recall that male or female domination refers to the fact that a specific share is more relevant in relative terms respectively for women and men economists. Gender domination can be identified as the gap between the male share and female share of a certain field.

Figure 3 describes the share of the above-mentioned fields of research for academic production by gender. The relevance of microeconomics for men remained the same from the 1980s, while women have slightly converged toward this field, especially in the last three periods (2003–2017). The importance of macroeconomics and monetary economics for top economists converged by gender in 1993–1997 and has been stagnant ever since.

The evolution of the share of fields traditionally female or male dominated provides further insights. Even though the differences are somehow reducing over time, there are persisting gender gaps in certain fields of research. For instance, labor and demographic economics, a commonly female-dominated field, has reduced its gender disparity, mainly due to the abandonment of women in such fields. Women remained more interested and even increased their production in health, education, and welfare, and this field has also increased for men's top economists.

At the other end, in male-dominated fields, we find the fields of mathematical and quantitative methods and financial economics. In the former, men's share has slightly increased and women followed this trend, thus reducing the gender disparity over time. Financial economics posits an interesting case, as it was a female-dominated field at the beginning of

[9] We do not consider the miscellaneous JEL code (Y) because it is a residual category created to include unclassifiable objects in the classification system, mainly for editorial convenience. It includes tables and charts, introductory material, or book reviews that do not give any information about the research field preferences.

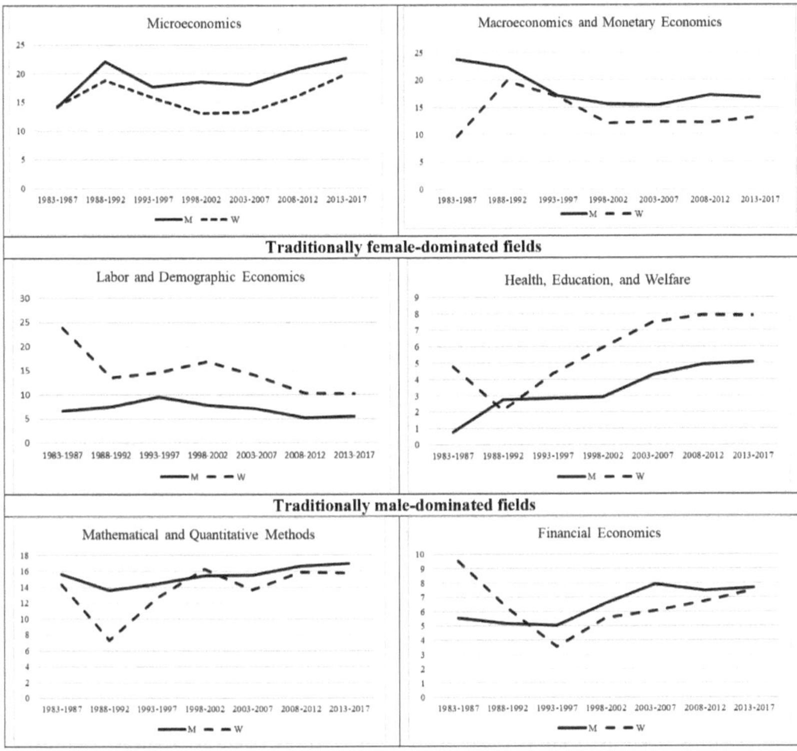

Fig. 3 Women and men top economists in selected fields by year (share). *Data source*: own elaboration based on the database constructed from RePEc

the period at scrutiny (1983–1992), and then transformed into male-dominated field in the three subsequent periods (1993–2007), to finally be a gender-neutral field in the last two periods (2008–2017).

3.3 Gender Segregation by Field of Research

We turn our analysis to the context of gender segregation. So far, this chapter has analyzed the relevance of different fields of research, using two classifications—one broad and one narrow—for the academic production of women and men top 10% of economists. To measure the extent to which women concentrate in certain fields and men in others, we compute the Duncan and Duncan (1955) index of dissimilarity, commonly used in economics and sociology to measure segregation. The formula of the index of dissimilarity goes as follows:

$$S = \frac{1}{2}\sum_{i=1}^{n} |m_i - w_i|$$

where w_i (m_i) is the proportion of women (men) who wrote in the JEL code i. This index computes the proportion of women (men) who must swap fields to have the same distribution across fields that of men. It describes the extent to which women and men are unevenly distributed over research fields in economics (JEL codes), so it measures the distance (in percentage) from an equal distribution of women and men across JEL codes. Higher values of the index of dissimilarity mean higher gender segregation, whereas lower values refer to lower gender segregation by field of research. Figure 4 provides the evolution of the index of dissimilarity that measures gender segregation by field of research, during the seven periods considered in this chapter (1983–2017). The average gender segregation by field of research among top economists is 21.5% over this period. Nevertheless, gender segregation dropped drastically between 1983 and 1997 (37% in 19,983–1987 to 10.1% in 1993–1997), and then was stagnant over the rest of the period at scrutiny, with values around 12.3%. Putting together the trend in gender segregation with the evidence previously provided, we can consider that this reduction in segregation was because women top economists shifted toward male-dominated fields, such as microeconomics, macroeconomics, and monetary economics, while at the same time, abandoning traditionally female-dominated fields, such as labor and demographic economics. However, it should be highlighted one exception to this is the persisting and increasing relevance of health, education, and welfare among women top economists, an already female-dominated field, which came along also with a rise of that field for men top economists.

3.4 Gender Economics and Feminist Economics

We complement our empirical analysis of the field of research of women and men's top economists with a specific analysis of the subfields of gender economics and feminist economics. As suggested by Backhouse

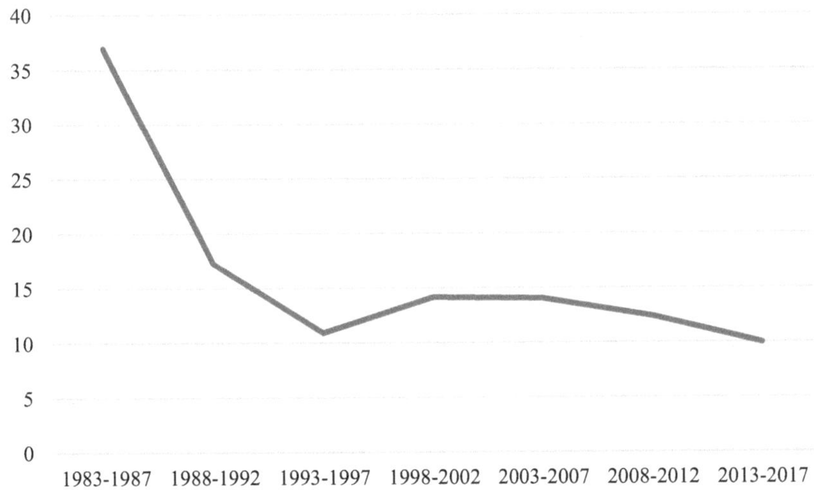

Fig. 4 Evolution of gender segregation by field of research among top economists. *Data source*: own elaboration based on the database constructed from RePEc

et al. (1997), more quantitative research on economics' scientific production should be conducted to understand what economics is about, and what economists do. Gender approaches to the differences in economic outcomes between women and men, and by the same token, to gender disparities in academic production, are embedded in gender economics and feminist economics. We thus allow for an introspection on the main methodological approaches adopted from a gender perspective in this subsection, by considering how gender and feminist economics, as fields of research, are conducted by top economists.

Since 2006, the JEL code classification has evidence of the dichotomy between gender economics (JEL code J16) and feminist economics (JEL code B54). While gender economics comes from a neoclassical tradition, grounded on the New Home Economics' school of thought, feminist economics is placed under the umbrella of heterodox economics. Feminist economics is rooted in the rejection of the normativity of neoclassical economics and moves beyond the *Home Oeconomicus* framework to bring the study of human life and its interaction with the environment to the center of economics (Nelson 1993, p. 34). Feminist economics acknowledges the non-market activities and the relevance of paid and unpaid work for the functioning of the economy (Berik and Rodgers 2009), and highlights the benefits of both quantitative and qualitative methods of analysis.[10]

Figure 5 provides the gender economics and feminist economics fields that share women and men's top economists; only a marginal share of top economists has one of these fields as the main field of research. Gender economics is the main field of research of 1.2% of women's top economists in 2013–2017, which has increased from the previous period (0.9%), while for men this field represents 0.3% (0.2% in 2008–2012). When considering the JEL code of feminist economics, the numbers are even lower. There are no men top economists whose main field of research is feminist economics, and this is also true for women top economists in the period from 2013 to 2017. However, we have to stress that here we are analyzing women and men top economists, which are the most visible authors according to standardized bibliometrics, a classification that, by definition, tends to penalize diversity and pluralism (Zacchia 2021; D'Ippoliti 2020; Roncaglia 2019).

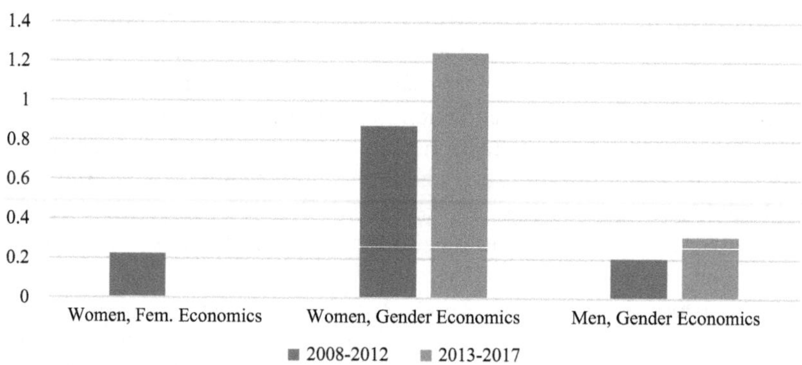

Fig. 5 Gender economics and feminist economics ad fields of research (%). *Data source*: own elaboration based on the database constructed from RePEc

[10] For a complete analysis of the differences between feminist and gender economics, also from a historical perspective, see Becchio (2020).

4 Conclusions

This chapter contributes to the analysis of gender diversity in the economics profession by providing a systematic empirical analysis of the gender distribution of top economists across research fields. To do so, we constructed a unique database with information on the academic production of top female and top male economists from 1983 to 2017, distributed over seven five-year periods, using RePEc as the main data source. The results of our analysis can be summarized in six points: (i) Gender segregation by field of research decreased drastically from 37 to 10% between 1983 and 1997, and remained stagnant for the rest of the considered period. This reduction is mainly due to the shift of top female economists into male-dominated fields of research, although some exceptions such as health, education, and welfare and financial economics should be taken into account. (ii) There is a stable male dominance in microeconomics, macroeconomics, and monetary economics. These two fields together account for an average of 37% of the academic output of top male economists over the whole period considered (1983–2917), compared to 30% for women. However, there is an increasing trend of women top economists whose main field is one of these two fields. (iii) There is a narrowing of the gender gap in the share of labor economics and demography, which is one of the reasons for the narrowing of gender segregation by field among top economists. Female top economists have reduced their share in labor and demographic economics from 23% (1983–1987) to 10% (2013–2017). (iv) There is an increasing and persistent gender gap in health, education and welfare, which is a female-dominated field. Although both female and male top economists have increased their representation in this field, the gap has persisted. (v) There has been a catch-up effect in traditionally male-dominated fields, such as mathematical and quantitative methods and financial economics, thus closing the gender gap in the relevance of these fields for top economists. (vi) Gender economics and feminist economics, two fields that could provide gender-sensitive quantitative analyses of economists' publications, remain marginal for both genders in the last two periods for which data are available. In the last period 2013–2017, no top economist has feminist economics as his or her main field of research.

It is important to remember that we have analyzed a small sample of economists who are among the most cited, more productive in terms of publications, and more connected in peer networks, as they are present in the ranking of the top 10% of authors or, for women, in the list of the top 10% of female economists produced by RePEc. Our analysis here confirms previous findings on gender differences in fields of specialization at other stages of the academic career and at different hierarchical levels (Fortin et al. 2014; Sierminska and Oaxaca 2014). Many interesting questions remain. Is there also a convergence in the quality of publications by men and women? Is the choice of research fields determined by institutional features such as different national research evaluation systems? Is the definition of excellence in economics so embedded in gender bias that only women who more closely resemble the male profile are allowed to be included in the ranking of top economists? This last question is of particular interest because, in contrast to the call for "responsible" metrics for research assessment, a bibliometric approach to defining the quality of research outputs and researchers is becoming increasingly prevalent in economics. Given the increasing popularity of bibliometric indices in higher education, it is important to open a debate on how best to take diversity into account, using a range of indicators that reflect and support pluralism in research and researchers' careers, trying to anticipate the systemic gender biases in the adoption of any policy for the distribution of funds to research institutions, as well as for the evaluation of individual researchers. In this sense, in order to maintain diversity in economics, it would be useful to monitor future trends in research foci from a gender perspective.

References

Acker, J. 1990. Hierarchies, Jobs, Bodies: A Theory of Gendered Organizations. *Gender & Society* 4(2):139–158.

Acker, J. 2008. Helpful Men and Feminist Support: More than Double Strangeness. *Gender, Work & Organization.* 15(3):288–293.

Albelda, R. 1997. *Economics and Feminism: Disturbances in the Field.* New York: Twayne Publishers.

Allgood, S., L. Badgett, A. Bayer, M. Bertrand, S. E. Black, N. Bloom, L. D. Cook. 2019. AEA Professional Climate Survey: Final Report. American Economic Association. https://www.aeaweb.org/resources/member-docs/final-climate-survey-results-sept-2019.

Ambrosino, A., M. Cedrini, J. B. Davis, S. Fiori, M. Guerzoni, and M. Nuccio. 2018. What Topic Modeling could Reveal About the Evolution of Economics. *Journal of Economic Methodology* 25(4):329–348. https://doi.org/10.1080/1350178X.2018.1529215.

Baccini, A., F. Baccini, L. Barabesi, M. Cioni, E. Petrovich, and D. Pignalosa. 2023. Fine-Grained Classification of Journal Articles Based on Multiple Layers of Information Through Similarity Network Fusion: The Case of the Cambridge Journal of Economics. *Scientometrics* 129(1):373–400.

Baccini, F., L. Barabesi, A. Baccini, M. Khelfaoui, and Y. Gingras. 2022. Similarity network fusion for scholarly journals. *Journal of Informetrics* 16(1):101226.

Backhouse, R., R. Middleton, and K. Tribe. 1997. Economics Is What Economists Do, But What Do the Numbers Tell Us? Paper for Annual History of Economic Thought Conference. University of Bristol. September 3–5, 1997, Available at SSRN: https://ssrn.com/abstract=2942733 or https://doi.org/10.2139/ssrn.2942733

Bayer, Amanda, and Cecilia Elena Rouse. 2016. Diversity in the Economics Profession: A New Attack on an Old Problem. *Journal of Economic Perspectives* 30(4):221–242.

Becchio, G. 2020. *A History of Feminist and Gender Economics*. Abingdon: Routledge.

Berik, G., and Y. van der Meulen Rodgers. 2009. Engendering development strategies and macroeconomic policies. In *Social Justice and Gender Equality. Rethinking Development Strategies and Macroeconomic Policies*, vol. 4, ed. G. Berik, Y. van der Meulen Rodgers, and A. Zammit. New York: Routledge.

Björk, B. C., and D. Solomon. 2013. The Publishing Delay in Scholarly Peer-Reviewed Journals. *Journal of Informetrics* 7(4):914–923. https://doi.org/10.1016/j.joi.2013.09.001.

Chari, A., P. Goldsmith-Pinkham. 2017. *Gender Representation in Economics Across Topics and Time: Evidence from the NBER Summer Institute*. Available at SSRN: https://ssrn.com/abstract=3053492 or https://doi.org/10.2139/ssrn.3053492

Cherrier, B. 2017. Classifying Economics: A History of the JEL Codes. *Journal of Economic Literature* 55(2):545–579.

Davis, W. L. 1997. Economists' Perceptions of Their Research: Survey of the Profession. *The American Journal of Economics and Sociology* 56(2):159–172.

Davis, W. L., B. Figgins, D. Hedengren, and D. B. Klein. 2011. Economics Professors' Favorite Economic Thinkers, Journals, and Blogs (along with Party and Policy Views). *Econ Journal Watch* 8(2):126–146.

Dimand, R. W., G. Black, and E. L. Forget. 2011. Women's Participation in the ASSA Meetings. *Economia History, Methodology, Philosophy* 1(1):33–49.

Dimand, R. W., M. A. Dimand, and E. L. Forget. 2000. *A Biographical Dictionary of Women Economists*. Aldershot, UK and Brookfield, USA: Edward Elgar.

Dolado, J. J., F. Felgueroso, and M. Almunia. 2012. Are Men and Women Economists Evenly Distributed Across Research Fields? *Some New Empirical Evidence, SERIEs* 3:367–393. https://doi.org/10.1007/s13209-011-0065-4.

Duarte, P. G., and Y. Giraud. 2016. The Place of the History of Economic Thought in Mainstream Economics, 1991–2011, Viewed Through a Bibliographic Survey. *Journal of the History of Economic Thought* 38(4):431–462.

D'Ippoliti, C. 2020. *Democratizing the Economics Debate: Pluralism and Research Evaluation*. Routledge.

D'Ippoliti, C., L. Gobbi, C. A. Mongeau Ospina, and G. Zacchia. 2023. Social Determinants of Citations: An Empirical Analysis of UK Economists. *Kyklos* 76(4):827–858.

Duncan, O. D., and B. Duncan. 1955. A Methodological Analysis of Segregation Indexes. *American Sociological Review* 20(2):210–217. https://doi.org/10.2307/2088328.

Forget, E. 1995. America Women Economists, 1900–1940: Doctoral Dissertation and Research Specialization. In *Women of Value*, ed. M. A. Dimand, R. Dimand, and E. Forget, 25–38. Edward Elgar.

Fortin, Nicole, Thomas Lemieux, and Marit Rehavi. 2021. Gender Differences in Fields of Specialization and Placement Outcomes Among PHDs in Economics. *AEA Papers and Proceedings*. Vol. 111. 2014 Broadway, Suite 305, Nashville, TN 37203: American Economic Association.

Groenewegen, P., and S. King. 1994. *Women as Producers of Economic Articles: A Statistical Assessment of the Nature and the Extent of Female Participation in Five British and North American Journals 1900–39*, 201. School of Economics WP: University of Sydney.

Hedengren, D., D. B. Klein, and C. Milton. 2010. Economist Petitions: Ideology Revealed. *Econ Journal Watch* 7(3):288–319.

Hospido, L., and C. Sanz. 2021. Gender Gaps in the Evaluation of Research: Evidence from Submissions to Economics Conferences. *Oxford Bulletin of Economics and Statistics* 83: 590–618. https://doi.org/10.1111/obes.12409.

Johansson, M., and M. Śliwa. 2014. Gender, Foreignness, and Academia: An Intersectional Analysis of the Experiences of Foreign Women Academics in UK Business Schools. *Gender, Work & Organization* 21(1):18–36.

Kahn, Shulamit. 1995. Women in the Economics Profession. *Journal of Economic Perspectives* 9(4):193–205.

Kelly, M. A., and S. Bruestle. 2011. Trend of Subjects Published in Economics Journals 1969–2007. *Economic Inquiry* 49(3):658–673.

Kosnik, L. R. 2015. What have Economists been Doing for the Last 50 Years? A Text Analysis of Published Academic Research from 1960–2010. *Open-Assessment E-Journal* 9: 1–38.

Lundberg, S. 2020. *Women in Economics*. London: CEPR press.
Lundberg, S., and J. Stearns. 2019. Women in Economics: Stalled Progress. *Journal of Economic Perspectives* 33(1):3–22.
Madden, K., P. Michele, and J. Seiz. 2004. *A Bibliography of Female Economic Thought up to 1940* (1st ed.). Routledge. https://doi.org/10.4324/9780203482063
Marcuzzo, M. C., and G. Zacchia. 2015. Is History of Economics What Historians of Economic Thought Do? A Quantitative Investigation. *History of Economics Ideas* 24(3):29–46.
May, A. 2022. *Gender and the Dismal Science*. New York: Columbia University Press.
May, A., M. G. McGarvey, and R. Whaples. 2014. Are Disagreements Among Male and Female Economists Marginal at Best? A Survey of AEA Members and Their Views on Economics and Economic Policy. *Contemporary Economic Policy* 32(1):111–132.
Nelson, J. A. 1993. The Study of Choice or the Study of Provisioning? Gender and the Definition of Economics. In *Beyond Economic Men Feminist Theory and Economics*, ed. M. A. Ferber and J. A. Nelson. Chicago: The University of Chicago Press.
Nelson, Julie A. 1995. Feminism and Economics. *Journal of Economic Perspectives* 9(2):131–148.
Rath, K., and K. Wohlrabe. 2016. Trends in Economics Publications Represented by JEL Categories Between 2007 and 2013. *Applied Economics Letters* 23(9):660–663.
Roncaglia, A. 2019. *The Age of Fragmentation A History of Contemporary Economic Thought*. Cambridge: Cambridge University Press.
Rousseau, Sandra, and Ronald Rousseau. 2021. Bibliometric techniques and their use in business and economics research. *Journal of Economic Surveys* 35(5):1428–1451.
Sierminska, Eva, and Ronald L. Oaxaca. 2021. Field Specializations Among Beginning Economists: Are There Gender Differences? *AEA Papers and Proceedings*. Vol. 111. 2014 Broadway, Suite 305, Nashville, TN 37203: American Economic Association.
Stastny, D. 2010. Czech Economists on Economic Policy: A Survey. *Econ Journal Watch* 7(3):275–287.
Vettese, T. 2019. *Sexism in the Academy, N+ 1 Magazine, 34.*
Zacchia, G. 2021. What Does It Take to Be Top Women Economists? An Analysis Using Rankings in RePEc. *Review of Political Economy* 33(2):170–193. https://doi.org/10.1080/09538259.2020.1848624.

Institutional Discrimination: An Analysis of Women in Economics in Italian Universities

Giulia Zacchia and Marcella Corsi

1 Introduction

When it comes to women in economics, there are usually three spheres of analysis:

- the absence of women and the concept of gender in economic analysis and models (Ferber and Nelson 1993, 2003);
- the neglected contribution of women economists to the evolution of economic thought (Kuiper 2022; Chassonnery-Zaïgouche et al. 2022);
- the low presence of women in the economic discipline, particularly in top positions in academia (Lundberg and Stearns 2019; Ginther and Kahn 2021).

G. Zacchia (✉) · M. Corsi
Sapienza University of Rome, Rome, Italy
e-mail: giulia.zacchia@uniroma1.it

Minerva, Laboratory on Diversity and Gender Inequality, Sapienza University, Rome, Italy

M. Corsi
e-mail: marcella.corsi@uniroma1.it

© The Author(s), under exclusive license to Springer Nature Switzerland AG 2026

V. Dolar and T. Perry (eds.), *Missing Voices in Economics*,
https://doi.org/10.1007/978-3-031-97180-8_4

In this chapter, we focus on this last point in order to examine the working conditions of women economists in academia and whether and how they have been discriminated against in their career paths. In our analysis, we seek to define how institutional practices can systematically penalise minorities (Colander and Woos 1997; Zacchia 2021; May 2022), for example reproposing the doctrine of the separate spheres (Becchio 2024) in the academic work through a gendered division of labour between research—well evaluated in the academic career progression—and teaching and bureaucratic practices, that just like the unpaid care work is not considered as 'productive'.

We focus on Italy since, in the global context, the 'Italian case' from 2010 has been used several times as a field experiment to analyse gender differences in competitive environments, given the reform of the university system (Law 240, 2010) that changed the rules for entering the academic profession that imposed strict bibliometric criteria for the evaluation of researchers (Abramo and D'Angelo 2020; Corsi et al. 2019a, b; De Paola et al. 2018; Bagues et al. 2017; Baccini et al. 2019).

Unlike the analyses conducted up to now, we focused on a qualitative analysis, providing a study of the Italian context regarding self-perceived gender differences in academia in the field of economics. We define how women in economics in Italian universities perceive their working environment once bibliometrics become a cornerstone for the recruitment and upgrading of researchers in universities. To do so, we analyse the data collected through a qualitative analysis on the condition of women in the academic profession in economics distributed among the members of the Italian Economic Society (SIE), looking at gender differences in family status, educational background, scientific production, care responsibilities, division of labour within the workplace and the self-perception of discrimination suffered.

2 Women in Economics in Italy

The hierarchical structure in Italian universities in the economic sector is strongly influenced by gender: for men, a classic pyramid structure is observed, with the majority being full professors, followed by associate professors and then researchers. Among women, on the other hand, most are associate professors, followed by researchers and full professors. This figure leads to a reflection on the gender gaps in career paths: while for women persistence in the lower ranks seems to be more frequent and career advancement slower and more difficult, for men the role transition seems to be faster and more linear, so much so that most Italian academic economists have already reached the top of their careers.

It is well known that the scarce presence of women among economists, particularly in full professorship, is not limited to the Italian context. This has given rise to various associations in the western world (and not only: in 2003, the *Chinese Women Economists Network* was born in Shanghai) with the aim of monitoring and promoting the status of women in the economics profession; in particular, we recall, in the early 1970s, the initiative of the *American Economic Association* (AEA) to set up a *Committee on the Status of Women in the Economics Profession (CSWEP)*, which initiated a large number of studies, particularly in the United States[4]. In the United Kingdom, the *Committee for Women in Economics (CWE)* under the *Royal Economic Society* has performed a similar function since 1996, as has the *Committee for Women Economists* in Australia (2002). At the European level, *Women in Economics (WinE)* at the *European Economic Association* promotes women's networks in economics research and data collection since 2005, as has the *Committee on the Situation of Women in Economics* (COSME) in Spain (since 2006).

In Italy, thanks to the gender budgeting exercises of universities and the activities of the gender commission of the Italian Economics Society, gender gaps in the 'numbers' of academic economists are increasingly visible at the national level. However, there is a lack of permanent monitoring of the conditions and self-reported job satisfaction of women in economics that follows the comprehensive analysis on the status of women in economics in Italian universities in 1999 (Carabelli et al. 1999). A systematic survey on the state of women in economics would make it possible to identify the impact of institutional reforms in terms of worsening or improving their working conditions and to define how best to act to eliminate institutional discrimination in the profession. With this chapter, we try to fill this gap by conducting a survey among the members of the Italian Economics Society to analyse whether being a woman is still a factor of discrimination in Italy and what 'survival' strategies have been adopted by Italian women academic economists in recent years, also highlighting generational differences.

3 Women in Economics and Discrimination: Gender Analysis of the Economic Profession in Italy

To provide a snapshot of Italian women economists, including self-perceptions of their work environment and discrimination suffered, a questionnaire was sent via e-mail to the members of the Italian Economic Society between August and September 2013. The Italian Economic Society[1] was founded in 1950 to promote and stimulate economic research in Italy. Its members are mainly professors and researchers in the various fields of economics. The survey was conducted in 2013, the year following the implementation of the last university reform that changed the rules for hiring and upgrading individual researchers in Italian universities and introduced bibliometric standards for the national evaluation of researchers.

The response rate to the questionnaire was 20.8%, with a response of 185 members (of which 62 are women) out of 891 total members. In almost all cases (there were only three non-academics), responses were received from teaching staff in Italian universities. The response rate of women was significantly higher (29.2%), representing 33.5% of all female members of the Italian Economic Society.

3.1 Age and Family Status

From an age point of view, the age group most represented is between 41 and 45 years of age, while the presence of younger people (under 35 years of age) is lower (they are just 4.3% of responders). Among women economists, on the contrary, the largest representation is for the 61–65 age group (29%). Connected to the age distribution of the sample, at an aggregate level the highest percentage of responses was given by full professors (42.7%) followed by associate professors (24.3%) and researchers 21.6%. However, breaking down the data by gender one finds a greater presence of female researchers than male researchers in

[1] To know more please visit https://www.siecon.org/en. However, the Italian Economic Society well represents the universe of economists in Italy, suffice it to say that in the year under review (2013), the total number of academic economists employed in Italian universities was 1413 and the active members of the Italian Economic Society amounted to 892.

the analysis conducted. We can speculate that younger women are more motivated to be included in surveys that monitor their own activities.

Cross-referencing the data by age group with academic role, the greatest discrepancies are found for female economists aged 41–45 years among whom the researcher role is more common (46%) than their male colleagues of the same age (27%). We then checked the average age by teaching group: for researchers, there is no gender difference as the average age is 41 years for both men and women; for associate professors, the average age is slightly higher for women, 50 years compared to 48 for men, while for full professors, there is no big difference (58 years on average age for women full professors and 59 for men).

Always looking at personal characteristics, substantial gender differences in family status are found: 62% of female economists are in couple (married or cohabiting with a partner) compared to 78.9% of men, a gap persistent for all age groups and particularly true for women between 61 and 65. Moreover, 39% of female economists have no children compared to 23% of their colleagues. The greatest differences are recorded for women over 65, among whom 40% have no children compared with 10% of their male colleagues of the same age. For all age groups, the percentage of women without children is higher than for their male colleagues, decreasing only for the 51–55 age group. Although we do not have a direct question on the choice of parenthood and how it was influenced by academic activity, for women more than for men having children is a less frequent option even among the youngest. However, other studies in other contexts confirm our intuition. Zheng et al. (2022) find that in North American academia women are less likely than men to have children. However, mothers who are academics have fewer children than their male colleagues and are significantly more likely than fathers to report higher levels of negative impact on careers due to children (Bonache et al. 2020; Misra et al. 2011). Analysing the academic context in Canada and New Zealand, Baker (2012) concludes that academia is a profession where men have higher rates of marriage and fertility than women.

In economics and business in the German-speaking academia (Austria, Germany and the German-speaking part of Switzerland) Joecks et al. (2014) find that only the most productive female researchers can afford to have children. Similarly, for Spanish early-career academics, Bonache et al. (2020) find evidence that research excellence and parenthood are perceived as mutually exclusive.

3.2 Educational Background

Looking at the educational backgrounds of the sample analysed, 75.8% of women have a PhD, slightly lower is the percentage of men (71.5%). This figure is, however, conditioned by the gender gaps in age in our sample, since all the youngers have obtained at least a PhD, and we have already shown that among women the percentage of youngers is higher than among men. Approximately 45% of Italian economists obtain their PhD abroad, with no gender differences; furthermore, about one in ten economists who have obtained a PhD in Italy have subsequently obtained his/her PhD abroad. The percentage of those with a double degree is higher for men than for women.

On average, the age of doctoral attainment is 31 for both men and women. There are therefore no gender differences at the beginning of the academic career: the profiles in terms of educational background and age are homogeneous. The first divergences occur in the choice of research areas for the PhD. For both sexes, the largest percentage of the respondents had followed a generic doctorate in economics; going into more details, however, it can be seen that women economists concentrated their studies in three areas:

- economics of development, growth and social capital,
- international economics and
- microeconomics.

In contrast, their male colleagues were mainly engaged in PhD in political economy, industrial economics and history of economic thought (see Fig. 1). This is in line with other studies that find that the distribution of men and women varies across field of specialisation (Barbezat 2010; Chari and Goldsmith-Pinkham 2017; Beneito et al. 2018; Lundberg and Stearns 2019; Sistelo and Teixeira 2022).

We then analysed the PhD dissertation asking for the key words that describe the doctoral theses, and thus assigning a JEL Code[2] to enable a comparison; for both sexes, the majority of PhD theses focused on microeconomic topics; women developed, in a higher percentage,

[2] The JEL classification is a standardised classification system developed by the Journal of Economic Literature to provide a categorisation system for research articles pertaining to economics and finance subjects.

Fig. 1 PhD research area (%). *Source:* survey distributed to members of the Italian Economic Society in 2013–185 respondents

topics pertaining to labour economics, public economics and international economics in their doctoral theses, while men focused more on economic development, growth theory and innovation, macroeconomics and monetary economics (see Fig. 2).

We therefore calculated a segregation index between the different research fields chosen for the PhD thesis, using the Duncan segregation index (1955). The Duncan segregation index is mainly used as a measure of horizontal gender segregation in the labour market. An index value of 1 indicates complete segregation on the labour market, i.e. a greater presence of one gender than the other in each economic sector. In our case, we calculated the index by looking at different research topics to define whether men and women have similar or completely different research interests (in the latter case, the Duncan segregation index would be equal to 1).

The Duncan segregation index calculated to define gender segregation in research topics for PhD theses is 0.32. However, it is interesting to compare the index values by age group. Contrary to analyses conducted in other countries (Hale 2005; Dolado et al. 2012) that report a contraction of gender segregation in the choice of research topics for the younger generations, in our case the segregation index is higher (0.57) for those under 40 years of age, highlighting a greater divergence of topics chosen for the PhD thesis between the sexes.

What is striking is that it is precisely for this age group that there is a greater interest among women for so-called feminised research fields, since 53% of women economists oriented their PhD theses in health, education and welfare and labour economics and demography. By contrast, the segregation index is lowest for the 41–50 age group, (0.3). We then asked whether the research topic chosen for the PhD thesis was continued throughout the professional career: in 57% of the observed cases, for which data is available, the PhD research topic is then developed over the years as the main topic of research declared by the respondents. 61% of the women keep their research interest constant over time compared to 55% of their male colleagues. However, correcting the data for age, taking into account only those over 40 years of age, the gap narrows and only 43% of women declared that they maintained in the years the same research interests as their PhD against the 44% of men.

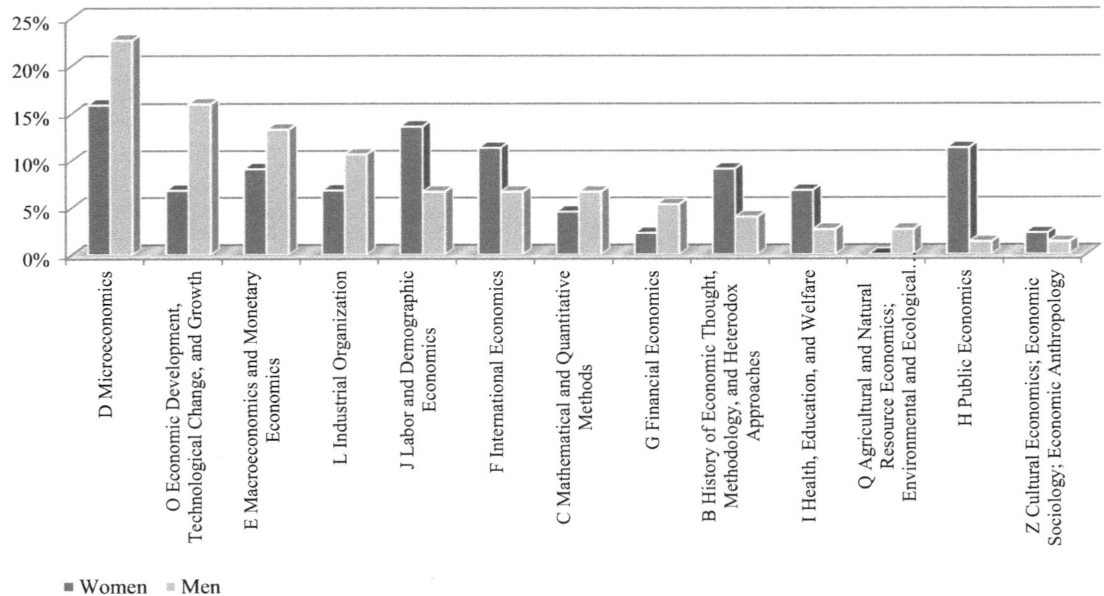

Fig. 2 Distribution of research topics (JEL Code) chosen for the PhD thesis (%). *Source*: survey distributed to members of the Italian Economic Society in 2013–185 respondents

3.3 Academic Production

On average, irrespective of age and gender, economists interviewed declared to have produced 3 publications per year in the last 5 years, of which at least two in peer-reviewed journals (see table 1).

Women, on average, publish less than men: 2 publications per year and 1.5 in peer-reviewed journals. Considering also age, it can be seen that among women the median number of publications is higher for the age groups at the extremes, or better for the youngest (under 35 years), and for those between 61 and 65 years. Considering also the academic status, the greatest difference is for researchers, among whom there is a median number of 3.6 publications per year for men, 2 in peer-reviewed journals, while for women the number of publications is reduced to 2 and 1.5 in peer-reviewed journals.

Table 1 Average number of publications per year over the last 5 years

Age group		*Average number of publications per year over the last 5 years*		*Average number of publications per year in peer-reviewed journals in the last 5 years*	
		Women	*Men*	*Women*	*Men*
< 35	Mean	2.7	3.0	1.4	3.0
	Median	3.0	3.0	1.1	3.0
36–40	Mean	2.4	3.9	1.7	2.2
	Median	2.0	4.5	2.0	2,2
41–45	Mean	3.7	4.2	2.0	2.7
	Median	2.2	3.2	1.9	2.4
46–50	Mean	2.1	3.6	2.1	2.4
	Median	1.9	3.0	1.9	3.0
51–55	Mean	3.6	3.2	0.8	1.8
	Median	1.3	4.0	0.5	2.0
56–60	Mean	2.2	3.3	1.7	3.0
	Median	1.8	3.0	1.0	3.0
61–65	Mean	3.3	3.2	2.1	1.5
	Median	3.0	3.0	2.0	1.0
> 65	Mean	3.5	3.4	2.8	1.8
	Median	2.5	2.0	2.0	1.0

Source: survey distributed to members of the Italian Economic Society in 2013 - 185 respondents

We then tried to define how and what Italian economists publish. On average, women make more use of co-authorship: 34% of women economists have published with at least 2 co-authors against 23% for men.

The use of co-authorship is more evident for women researchers, highlighting a trend towards networking among younger women. However, we must remember that much of the literature on the subject has shown that co-authored publications are not equally valued in promotion decisions, with the implication that co-authored publications carry less weight for women by providing them with fewer opportunities for access to academia or career advancement than their male counterparts (Sarsons et al. 2021; Hussey et al. 2022; Ductor et al. 2023; D'Ippoliti et al. 2023). We also asked them to indicate the gender of the co-authors with whom they mostly publish: the most significant finding is that men publish in 41% of cases with an author of the same gender, while among women only 3% have a woman as a regular co-author. The use of mixed co-authorship, regardless of gender, is more frequent among women (71%) than men (50%). While for women economists there is a progressive increase in the use of co-authors of the same sex as their academic status progresses (11% of female researchers choose to permanently publish with other women, 14% of female associate professors, and 15% of female full professors), the opposite phenomenon is observed for men: as their academic status progresses, the use of male co-authors decreases (46% of researchers, 42% of associate professors and 30% of full professors). This is in line with the study by Ductor et al. (2023), which found that women have fewer collaborators, and they use to collaborate more often with the same co-authors.

We also analysed the relationship with editors by checking the rejection rate of publications submitted for refereeing and the average time between submission and the publication of the article.

Contrary to expectation, women economists report a higher rate of acceptance of their publications, as many as 18% have never had a publication rejected by editors, while for men the percentage is slightly lower at 15%.

Among women (34%), the largest percentage declares a rejection rate between 1 and 25%, while among men, the largest group (35%) is of those who declare a rejection rate between 26 and 50%. For both sexes, the figure is strongly influenced by the academic role held, with the rejection rate decreasing with increasing academic status.

Slightly different between the sexes is the length of time to refereeing of publications: on average, women publish after 15 months from submission to refereeing of the publication, while for men the time span is 13 months. For full professors there are no gender differences, the average number of months between submission to the journal and publication being 13 months. In contrast, for both associate professors and researchers, the refereeing times are on average much longer for women than for their colleagues, as verified in the international context by Hengel (2022).

3.4 Care Responsibilities and Time Devoted to Research

The literature has often attributed women's lower productivity to their more intense domestic responsibilities (Johnson and Stafford 1974; Vohlídalová 2020; Günçavdi et al. 2017; Suitor et al. 2001). However, in empirical analyses carried out for economics, the gender gap in publications remains significant even among those without children (Ginther and Kahn 2004; Ceci et al. 2014; Lundberg and Stearns 2019) suggesting that other obstacles should be considered such as the gender discrepancy in the use of working time, which is strongly conditioned by social norms, since women use to spend more time on teaching, service, and other non-research academic activities (Xie and Shauman 2003; Misra et al. 2011).

We then formulated a generic question on the burden of domestic work among Italian economists. In this case the gender gaps are more pronounced: if the total work within households is taken as 100, women economists declare, in most cases, a care and domestic burden of between 51 and 75%, while men a care and domestic burden of between 25 and 50% (see Fig. 3). The extremes are also striking: no women declared that they had no family commitments at all, compared to 5% of the men interviewed, while on the contrary, among those who cannot count on the help of anyone in the family, the percentage of women is significantly higher: 11% compared to 2% of men.

From a generational point of view, gender differences remain strong for all age groups: not even among the youngest there is a more equal distribution, since among those under 40 years of age 82 per cent of women carry out more than 50 per cent of domestic and care work compared to only 6 per cent of their male colleagues. Analysing the data further, if we look at the teaching ranks, as many as 40% of women full professors

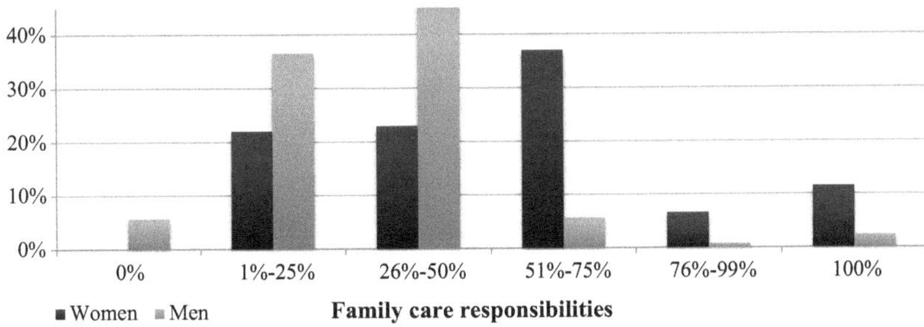

Fig. 3 Distribution by domestic and care workload within the household. *Source*: survey distributed to members of the Italian Economic Society in 2013–185 respondents

support more than 50% of housework, while among male full professors the percentage drops to just 6%; the gap widens for researchers, among whom 72% of women support more than 50% of housework against just 9% of men. The figure suggests policy recommendations: gender policies aimed at promoting the role of women at the top of academic careers cannot disregard a consideration of the different distribution of domestic and care work in their households. Consequently, services (e.g. child-care services within universities, etc.) and ad hoc policies are needed to rebalance and redistribute care activities within households.

Looking instead at the distribution of working time between research and non-research activities such as teaching or bureaucratic tasks, it is interesting to note that women declare to devote more than half of their working time to research activities (see Fig. 4) more time than men do. For all teaching groups, women declare that they devote between 50 and 75% of their working time to research. The same can be said of men, except for full professors who, on the contrary, state that they devote only 26% to 50% of their working time to research activities.

Once the domestic workloads and the division of working time between research and non-research activities were defined, we tried to see how these factors impact the productivity of economists.

For women, the different domestic workload does not seem to affect the number of publications (the median number of publications is 2 for all women regardless their care and domestic burden), whereas for men, the median number of publications decreases as the care and domestic workload within their households increases. Among those who declared

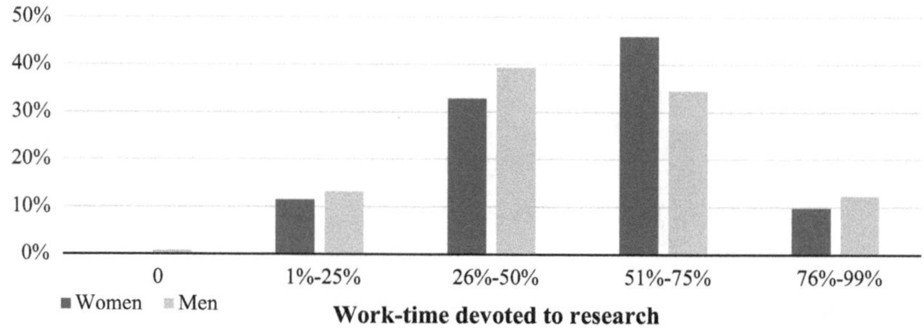

Fig. 4 Distribution by work time spent on research. *Source*: survey distributed to members of the Italian Economic Society in 2013–185 respondents

less than 50% of domestic work, there are 3.5 publications per year, 3 for those who declared more than 50%, and among those who declared 100%, the median number of publications drops to 2. On the contrary, women economists are strongly influenced by the percentage of time devoted to research, as opposed to time devoted to teaching or more 'bureaucratic' work: as this percentage increases, the median number of publications rises substantially, as shown in Table 2. Among female economists who manage to carve out a substantial part of their work for research, the median number of publications is significantly higher than that of their colleagues. Consequently, the assessment practices for entering and upgrading in academia should also take the teaching load into account in the evaluation of individuals and not only scientific production.

3.5 Research interests

We also asked respondents to describe their fields of specialisation, or better their main research interests. In aggregate terms, Italian economists are most concerned with economic development, growth theory and technological innovation, while only 0.6% of respondents state economic history as their main research topic. Once again, we propose a gender approach to verify the presence of a thematic segregation by gender. The three subject areas most frequently covered by women are microeconomics (14%), labour economics and demography (13%) and growth theory and technological innovation (10%). While among men, the main

Table 2 Number of publications per year in the last 5 years in relation to time spent on research

Percentage of time spent on research		*Average number of publications per year in the last 5 years*		*Average number of publications per year in peer-reviewed journals in the last 5 years*	
		Women	*Men*	*Women*	*Men*
1–25%	Mean	1.2	2.7	0.9	1.6
	Median	1	2.5	1	1
26–50%	Mean	2.2	4	1.4	2.1
	Median	2	4	1,03	2
51–75%	Mean	3.7	3.5	2.1	2.4
	Median	2.5	3	2	2.5
76–99%	Mean	4.7	3.8	2.3	2.6
	Median	5	3.5	2	2.5

Source: survey distributed to members of the Italian Economic Society in 2013—185 respondents

areas of specialisation are growth theory and technological innovation (14%), macroeconomics and monetary economics (13%) and industrial organisation (12%).

The thematic segregation index was also calculated in this case: the Duncan segregation index is 0.25, so there are fewer gender differences than in the previously analysed PhD theses. We can speculate that when women enter the university system, there is a tendency towards homogenisation of the research topics developed.

Analysing the topics by academic status, there is greater homologation in the research topics chosen among full professors (0.26), followed by researchers (0.35) and finally associate professors, for whom the topic segregation index is the highest, at 0.48. We then checked how the age factor affects the choice of research topics: the most evident divergence between the sexes is recorded for the 46–50 age group, while the greatest homogeneity in the choice of research topics is recorded for the 51–55 age group. Among the youngest (30–40 years), the thematic segregation index stands at 0.43 (see Fig. 5). It is interesting to note that, when considering the age groups at the extremes, the respondents aged 36–40 and those aged 61–65, the main research topic chosen varies considerably for women: among the youngest the most developed topic is labour

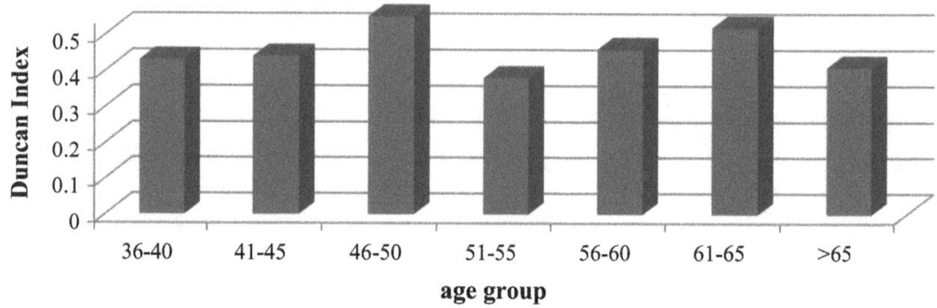

Fig. 5 Thematic segregation index by age group. *Source*: survey distributed to members of the Italian Economic Society in 2013–185 respondents

economics, while for the other group analysed it is history of economic thought. In contrast, for men, the most frequently chosen research topic is, for both groups analysed, growth theory and technological innovation, regardless of age.

3.6 *Discrimination*

The last section of the questionnaire offers a subjective analysis of the career paths of Italian academic economists, identifying average time to gain a tenure position and perceptions of having suffered discrimination during their career.

With regard to the number of years that have elapsed since the last upgrade, the differences are evident. From a gender perspective, on average women need more years to full professorship: the transition from associate to full professorship is on average 9 years for women compared to 6 years for men.

We then proposed a generic question, namely 'Do you think you have ever been discriminated against in your work?'. It was precisely on the definition of discrimination that an initial remark was made, considering the term too 'strong', and preferring to speak of *penalisation, a* term considered more correct.

The figure, however, is alarming: 42% of the women interviewed stated that they have been discriminated against compared to 15% of the men. For both sexes, full professors aged between 61 and 65 years stated in the highest percentage that they had suffered discrimination during their career.

Let us now go into the details of the main causes: as many as 73% of women economists claim discrimination on the grounds of sex. In this regard, we quote in full the comment of one respondent: "I *don't think that there was conscious discrimination, but at the same time I think that, all things being equal, if I had been a man, I would have moved up the career ladder a bit faster*". This is a clear perception of institutional discrimination. The remaining 27% of the women, who stated that they had suffered unequal treatment, identified age, research topic and non-being a member of strong networks as the causes of discrimination. Among those who identified the research topic as discriminatory, the main topics addressed in the course of the research activity are environmental evaluation and the history of economic thought.

Among men, on the other hand, 44% of those who stated that they felt discriminated against reported their chosen research topic as the reason, 31% not being part of strong networks, and, in a lower percentage, because of expressed political views and age.

4 Concluding Remarks

The taxonomy of the economics profession in Italy, carried out thanks to the analysis of a questionnaires circulated among members of the Italian Economics Society, reveals important hints for emancipation policies and gender equality in academic career paths. Specifically, it was shown that female productivity is associated with the percentage of working time devoted exclusively to research. Therefore, within departments, more attention is needed to the division of working time between research, teaching and more bureaucratic tasks in order to make women's contribution to the profession more visible and to foster greater equity in career paths. This is particularly relevant in the light of the actual assessment practices that place scientific productivity in terms of number and quality of publications as the cornerstone of careers' advancements.

Another element that emerged concerns conformism in research topics. In fact, we found a greater tendency towards homologation among full professors: women economists at the top of their academic careers tend to deal with a greater percentage of the same topics chosen by male colleagues. On the contrary, when analysing the beginning of the academic career and specifically PhD theses, the gender divergences are more marked. We can speculate that women to break the glass ceiling adopt a strategy of conformism in their choice of research areas on which to publish.

Finally, it is important to emphasise that 42% of the women economists interviewed believe that they have been discriminated against during their working lives (among men, the percentage drops to 15%), due, in 73% of cases, not to their main research topics or other reasons, but merely to the fact of being a 'woman'.

To highlight the contribution of women to the profession and above all to combat institutional discrimination, it is necessary in Italy, as is already the case in other countries, to develop a systematic activity to monitor the status of women in the economics profession.

Lastly, given that the mechanisms of access and upgrading in the academic careers for economists are based on research evaluation practices in Italy nowadays, in order to unhinge mechanisms of institutional discrimination, even unconscious ones, it is necessary that gender impacts would be considered right from the phase of defining criteria. Just as an example, the steps towards a responsible and inclusive evaluation of research should include an assessment that is not limited to the evaluation of scientific publications alone but that evaluates candidates' complete CVs (possibly a narrative CV) including teaching experience and the overall correspondence with the needs of the recruiting institution(s). Furthermore, it is necessary not to equate the quality of an article with the relevance of the journal in which it is published or with the number of citations received. And finally, it is important to ensure that diversity in terms of gender, academic rank, research subfield, orientation and school of thought (where applicable) is guaranteed in the evaluation committees to guarantee not only diversity but also pluralism in economics.

References

Abramo, G., and C. A. D'Angelo. 2020. Were the Italian Policy Reforms to Contrast Favoritism and Foster Effectiveness in Faculty Recruitment Successful? *Science and Public Policy* 47(5):604–615.

Baccini, A., G. De Nicolao, and E. Petrovich. 2019. Citation Gaming Induced by Bibliometric Evaluation: A Country-Level Comparative Analysis. *PLoS ONE* 14(9):e0221212.

Baker, M. 2012. Fertility, Childrearing & the Academic Gender Gap. *Women's Health and Urban Life* 11(2):9–25.

Bagues, M., M. Sylos-Labini, and N. Zinovyeva. 2017. Does the Gender Composition of Scientific Committees Matter? *American Economic Review* 107(4):1207–1238.

Barbezat, D. A. 2010. Gender Differences in Research Patterns Among PhD Economists. *The Journal of Economic Education* 37(3):359–375.

Becchio, G. 2024. *The Doctrine of the Separate Spheres in Political Economy and Economics*. London: Palgrave.

Beneito, P., J. E. Boscá, J. Ferri, M. García. 2018. Women across Subfields in Economics: Relative Performance and Beliefs. FEDEA Working Paper Series, no. 2018-06.

Bonache, H., V. Carballo, A. Chas, and N. Delgado. 2020. Go the Extra Mile: A Gender Approach Towards Parenthood in Early-Career Academics. *Journal of Gender Studies* 31(1):125–135.

Carabelli, A., D. Parisi, and A. Rosselli, eds. 1999. *Che "genere" di economista?* Bologna: Il Mulino.

Ceci, S. J., D. K. Ginther, S. Kahn, and W. M. Williams. 2014. Women in Academic Science: A Changing Landscape. *Psychological Science in the Public Interest* 15(3):75–141.

Chari, A., and P. Goldsmith-Pinkham. 2017. Gender Representation in Economics Across Topics and Time: Evidence from the NBER Summer Institute. National Bureau of Economic Research Working Paper Series, nr. 23953.

Chassonnery-Zaïgouche, C., E. L. Forget, and J. D. Singleton. 2022. Women and Economics: New Historical Perspectives. *History of Political Economy* 54(S1):1–15.

Colander, D., and J. W. Woos. 1997. Institutional Demand-Side Discrimination Against Women and the Human Capital Model. *Feminist Economics* 3(1):53–64.

Corsi, M., C. D'Ippoliti, and G. Zacchia. 2019a. Diversity of Backgrounds and Ideas: The Case of Research Evaluation in Economics. *Research Policy* 48(9):1038.

Corsi, M., C. D'Ippoliti, and G. Zacchia. 2019b. On the Evolution of the Glass Ceiling in Italian Academia: The Case of Economics. *Science in Context* 32(4):411–430.

De Paola, M., M. Ponzo, and V. Scoppa. 2018. Are Men Given Priority for Top Jobs? Investigating the Glass Ceiling in Italian Academia. *Journal of Human Capital* 12(3):475–503.

D'Ippoliti, C., L. Gobbi, C. A. Mongeau Ospina, and G. Zacchia. 2023. Social Determinants of Citations: An Empirical Analysis of UK Economists. *Kyklos* 76(4):827–858.

Dolado, J., F. Felgueroso, and M. Almunia. 2012. Are Men and Women-Economists Evenly Distributed Across Research Fields? Some New Empirical Evidence. *Journal of the Spanish Economic Association* 3(3):367–393.

Ductor, L., S. Goyal, and A. Prummer. 2023. Gender and Collaboration. Department of Economic Theory and Economic History of the University of Granada, Papers 23/01.

Duncan, O. D., and B. Duncan. 1995. A Methodological Analysis of Segregation Index. *American Sociological Review* 20(2):210–217.

Ferber, M. A., and J. A. Nelson. 1993. *Beyond Economic Man: Feminist Theory and Economics*. Chicago: University of Chicago.

Ferber, M. A., and J. A. Nelson. 2003. *Feminist Economics Today: Beyond Economic Man*. Chicago: University of Chicago.

Ginther, D. K., and S. Kahn. 2021. Women in Academic Economics: Have We Made Progress? *AEA Papers and Proceedings* 111: 138–142.

Ginther, D. K., and S. Kahn. 2004. Women in Economics: Moving Up or Falling Off the Academic Career Ladder? *Journal of Economic Perspectives* 18(3):193–214.

Günçavdi, G., S. Göktürk, and O. Bozoglu. 2017. An Insight into the Challenges Faced by Academic Women with Pre-school Age Children in Academic Life. *Universal Journal of Educational Research* 5(6):953–959.

Hale, G. 2005. *How Do Women-Economists Choose their Field? Evidence of Path-dependence*. Yale: Yale University mimeo.

Hengel, E. 2022. Publishing While Female: Are Women Held to Higher Standards? Evidence from Peer Review. *The Economic Journal* 132(648):2951–2991.

Heather, S., K. Gërxhani, E. Reuben, and A. Schram. 2021. Gender Differences in Recognition for Group Work. *Journal of Political Economy* 129(1):101–147.

Hussey, A., S. Murray, and W. Stock. 2022. Gender, Coauthorship, and Academic Outcomes in Economics. *Economic Inquiry* 60(2):465–484.

Joecks, J., K. Pull, and U. Backes-Gellner. 2014. Childbearing and (Female) Research Productivity: A Personnel Economics Perspective on the Leaky Pipeline. *Journal of Business Economics* 84: 517–530.

Johnson, G. E., and F. P. Stafford. 1974. The Earnings and Promotion of Women Faculty. *American Economic Review* 64(6):888–889.

Kuiper, E. 2022. *A Herstory of Economics*. Hoboken: Wiley.

Lundberg, S., and J. Stearns. 2019. Women in Economics: Stalled Progress. *Journal of Economic Perspectives* 33(1):3–22.

May, A. M. 2022. *Gender and the Dismal Science*. New York: Columbia University Press.

Misra, J., J. H. Lundquist, E. Holmes, and S. Agiomavritis. 2011. The Ivory Ceiling of Service Work. *Academe* 97(1):22–26.

Sistelo, M., and P. N. Teixeira. 2022. Women PhDs in Economics in Portugal (1980–1999). A Late Emergence and a Distinctive Profile Femmes docteures en économie au Portugal (1980–1999): émergence tardive et caractère distinctif. *Oeconomia* 12(3):663–686.

Suitor, J. J., D. Mecom, and I. S. Feld. 2001. Gender, Household Labor, and Scholarly Productivity Among University Professors. *Gender Issues* 19(4):50–67.

Vohlídalová, M. 2020. Early-Career Women Academics: Between Neoliberalism and Gender Conservatism. *Sociological Research Online* 26(1):27–43.

Xiang, Z., Y. Haimiao, and N. Chaoqun. 2022. Meta-Research: How Parenthood Contributes to Gender Gaps in Academia. *eLife* 11:e78909. https://www.ncbi.nlm.nih.gov/pmc/articles/PMC9299837/pdf/elife-78909.pdf

Xie, Y., and K. A. Shauman. 2003. *Women in Science: Career Processes and Outcomes*. Cambridge: Harvard University Press.

Zacchia, G. 2021. What Does It Take to Be Top Women Economists? An Analysis Using Rankings in RePEc. *Review of Political Economy* 33(2):170–193.

Zheng, X., H. Yuan, and C. Ni. 2022. How Parenthood Contributes to Gender Gaps in Academia. *eLife*. 1110.7554/eLife.78909.

Gender Diversity in Economics in South Asian Academic Spaces

Asma Hyder

1 Introduction

Over the past century, there has been a movement to integrate women into various fields, particularly those traditionally considered male-dominated domains, such as economics, finance, public policy, and STEM. Despite the progress, female labor force participation is still low globally, and their representation in the global south is a judgment call for the intelligentsia and policy-makers, mainly in higher education institutions. While numerous studies have explored the role and work of women in economics, there is a conspicuous gap in research within the specific context of South Asia. By shedding light on this overlooked area, this chapter not only contributes valuable insights but also sparks crucial discussions. It attempts to serve as a promoter for considering the importance of such conversations within the broader context of the global south.

Economics, encompassing the study of human behaviors in consumption and investment, plays a pivotal role in shaping societies through

---

A. Hyder (✉)
School of Economics and Social Sciences, Institute of Business Administration, Karachi, Pakistan
e-mail: ahyder@iba.edu.pk

© The Author(s), under exclusive license to Springer Nature Switzerland AG 2026

V. Dolar and T. Perry (eds.), *Missing Voices in Economics*,
https://doi.org/10.1007/978-3-031-97180-8_5

public policy. The limited representation of women in this subject raises concerns about the potential for an unjust society. Apart from this, the literature indicates that gender diversity brings innovative thinking and diverse problem-solving approaches (Gupta and Patel 2021), and gender-balanced teams produce a comprehensive and broader range of perspectives (Jones and Williams 2023). Several recent studies highlight the persistent gender gap in leadership positions and decision-making in academic and professional settings (Smith et al. 2021; Brown and Johnson 2022). In developing countries, especially in the context of South Asia, the issue is exacerbated due to deeply entrenched misogynistic cultural norms. This disparity can be illustrated by the fact that the *Reserve Bank of India* and *The Bangladesh Bank* have only one woman on their boards, and the board of the *State Bank of Pakistan* consists solely of male members. This situation is a blatant indication of the exclusion of women from high-level policy-making roles, reflecting a concerning state of affairs. Therefore, it is important to study the behavior toward economics at different levels. The chapter examines the status of women economists in academia and their interests within the subfields of economics discipline. The RePEc metadata has been utilized for this analysis. The later part of the chapter presents the outcomes of structured and semi-structured interviews with female heads of the top ten percent of economics departments in three countries.

A lot has been done to encourage women and to make them visible, for instance, strengthening policies and laws against gender harassment at workplaces, encouraging women in academia through advocacy, provision of flexible working hours, etc. However, their visibility in the subject is still a question mark. Elinor Ostrom, Esther Duflo, and Claudia Goldin are the only three women who got the Nobel Prize among the total of 93 Nobel laureates in economics. This drastic imbalance starts from the lower level and continues toward the higher end of the labor market. This phenomenon may be attributed to multiple things including broken pipelines, lack of networks, preferences, culture, and more than that. Thus, the visibility of women economists at leading roles is not only a stock variable rather it should be acknowledged as a process of societal advancement. The discussion on later requires the study of the journey and experiences of women economists. For this, the interviews of the leading economists and authors were conducted in these countries to examine the factors restraining women from being in careers related to economics and policy circles.

2 The South Asian Context

There are distinctions and commonalities in the status of women across three countries, namely India, Pakistan, and Bangladesh. Their position in society is intertwined with various forms of societal exclusion. The diversity in women's circumstances can be attributed to socioeconomic inequality, geographical regions, and the rural–urban divide, which are shaped by uneven socioeconomic progress. Despite these differences, a prevailing traditional and patriarchal culture is shared among them. Nonetheless, regardless of these variations, women consistently encounter systemic subordination compared to men, as patriarchy exerts its pervasive influence across different social classes, geographical regions, and the rural–urban continuum.

Tharakan and Tharakan (1975) presented an interesting argument, suggesting that understanding the role of women in society necessitates an examination of their involvement in the production process and their control over resources required in the production process. Thus, the framework that has been followed in this exploration considers the women in the production process (as faculty members and researchers) and the authority to use resources (women economists in leading positions). While it is difficult to dismiss the notion of certain preferences, which, I assume, should be normally distributed across all genders, I further tried to explore the phenomena of taste and certain preferences, through a survey among university students of the economics department to get ideas from the new generation or emerging economists; the outcomes of this analysis are presented in the later part of this chapter.

3 Data

For the analysis in this chapter, I exploited one secondary and two primary data sets. First of all, the analysis in the initial section includes a description of the top 25% of economics departments headed by women and top authors and their subfields of specialization. I extracted the metadata from RePEc (Research Papers in Economics), which is an initiative that seeks to enhance the dissemination of research in economics and related areas. This data is available on http://repec.org. The further insights on women economists I obtained data from New Economic Papers (NEP), an announcement service which filters information on new additions to RePEc into edited reports. The goal is to provide subscribers with up-to-date information about the research literature. For this analysis, we considered 'the field of specialization' only if the author appeared at least five or more times in NEP reports. For instance, if an author appears five or more times in NEP-DEV or NEP-AGR is counted as a development economist or agricultural economist and vice versa.

Secondly, I have conducted twelve leading semi-structured interviews with a few women economists. The selection criteria include: (1) the institution/department should be among the top 10% of departments according to RePEC ranking, and (2) the interviewee is heading the institution. The interviews were conducted through a Zoom meeting. The duration of each interview was approximately one hour. The third section of this chapter provides insights from the experiences of these women economists.

Finally, a survey was conducted in universities in Karachi, a metropolitan city in Pakistan, targeting undergraduate economics major students. While acknowledging that the sample may not be fully representative, it provides a preliminary insight into the preferences of the younger generation of economists. The semi-structured interviews and Google survey from ECON major students were utilized throughout the discussion in the chapter. These two small primary data sets, but very useful, helped to understand the reasons for the low representation of women economists in the region and also their challenges in the context of academia.

4 Stylized Facts from the Top 25% of Economics Departments

The RePEc data provides sufficient information on rankings; hence I initially focused on the presence of female economists in the top 25% of economics departments in three countries. In Pakistan, the average proportion of female economists in the top 25% of departments is 34%, with a maximum proportion of 70%. In leading economics departments in India, the female proportion is 29%, with a maximum proportion of 89%. Similarly, the average female proportion in Bangladesh's leading departments is 37%, with a highest proportion of 56%. While these statistics are neither very encouraging nor very discouraging, it is important to note that only three departments in Pakistan, five departments in India, and two departments in Bangladesh have equal or more than 50% female faculty. Thus, the distribution of faculty is still far from normal. Additionally, it's crucial to recognize that these numbers represent only a small fraction of the overall number of departments.

The statistics presented above are just a preliminary picture of facts that have been used from statistics available on RePEc website. Considering that ample evidence is available from the rest of the world that there is a significant gender difference in recognition (Wu 2019; Card et al. 2019; Hengel 2022), I pursued a more in-depth analysis by focusing on female economists heading in the top 25% of economics departments in three countries. In Pakistan, only five out of twenty-one departments (24%) are led by female economists, in India, it's ten out of sixty-two (16%), and in Bangladesh, only three out of fifteen departments (20%) are led by women. These two indicators, departments led by women and departments with at least fifty percent female economists, are not only scarce but also concentrated in major cities like Lahore, Karachi, New Delhi, and Dhaka. This observation opened other venues of thinking especially, the correlation between larger cities and women in the economics discipline. This evidence strongly suggests that traditional culture acts as a barrier to women's upward career mobility. In major cities women are more normalized, and acceptability is higher in policy and in leadership positions.

The exploration of the culture and dynamics of big cities is necessary and is discussed in the later part of this chapter. Here I would like to give the reference of our recent experience during COVID-19 lockdowns uncovers the realities regarding the division of work within households which are linked to norms and culture in this part of the world, where women are supposed to do all household chores and men can easily isolate themselves for scholarly work that can be produced from home. During this period, female authorship significantly decreased globally, with high inequalities less in favor of underdeveloped countries (Gabster et al. 2020). In the larger cities, the stereotypical thinking regarding women's responsibilities within households is evolving due to increased women's participation in the labor market and levels of education. These statistical facts raised critical questions for further investigation. The representation of female faculty members at least in leading economics departments is decent in three countries, but the absence of women in leadership positions raises concerns. It remains uncertain whether this gap signifies a leak in the pipeline, indicating barriers preventing women's progression, or if women themselves are hesitant to assume the responsibilities of top positions. Also, we don't know the difference in the degree of influence of culture in larger and smaller cities, as the leadership positions, if held by women, are mostly in larger cities.

5 A Closer Look at Top Authors

There is a prevailing perception that women economists tend to concentrate in specific sub-themes of economics, such as health, education, development, or labor economics, with fewer women authors observed in sub-themes like monetary policy and macroeconomics. To investigate this perception, the data from New Economic Papers (NEP) of top authors was collected, revealing significant findings. The statistics indicate that very few women economists are placed in the top 10% of authors in Bangladesh and Pakistan, and those who do lack a distinct field of specialization (five or more papers in a specific sub-discipline). Furthermore, it is noteworthy that among those with specialization, the representation of women in sub-disciplines like macroeconomics, monetary policy, finance, econometrics, and stock market analysis is almost non-existent. Similar evidence has been documented in various studies worldwide, including Beneito (2018), Chari and Goldsmith-Pinkham (2017), and Dolado et al. (2012) which are few among many others. However, no study is available focusing on the global south, especially South Asia, and the numbers we found here in this region the representation is far below than those reported in papers in the west.[1] This led to an interesting question, whether the glass walls exist in this horizontal distribution or it's a matter of taste and preferences? In this highly skewed distribution, the idea of self-selection cannot be ruled out.

On the flip side, in the context of India, a noteworthy trend emerges where not only many women are placed among top economists but also many of them are in macroeconomics, international trade, monetary policy, and banking and are mostly in think tanks like National Council of Applied Economic Research, Indian Statistical Institute, and Indira

[1] An analysis done by Women in Economics Initiative shows that Oceania, as in 2022, has the highest share of women among top authors with 15%. Africa has the second highest share of women with 13%, followed by Europe with 11%, Latin America with 8%, North America with 8%, and Asia with 6%. (See The Women in Economics Index 2023, https://www.women-in-economics.com for more details).

Gandhi Institute of Development Research. Once more, it's essential to highlight that these institutes, universities, or think tanks with heightened women authorship are predominantly situated in major cities.

6 Women Economists Leading Premier Economics Departments

The top 25% of economics departments/ institutions were identified in each country through IDEAS/RePEc database ranking.[2] Examining the heads of departments in these premier institutions, we found that in Pakistan only 5 out of 22, in India 10 out of 63, and in Bangladesh, 3 out of 15 are led by women. I conducted semi-structured interviews[3] with these women economist leaders in top institutions, uncovering several noteworthy points for consideration as elaborated below.

Many women don't reach top positions in their professional journeys due to missed or compromised opportunities along the way. The substantial dropout of women at each step starting from undergraduate to graduate levels, entering the labor market and finally attaining leadership positions, represents not just a simple loss but a loss of talent and diversity. Mobility emerges as a major obstacle in the labor market journey, especially in South Asian region, where relocation for a woman with or without a family poses significant challenges for her career and family life. There are varied reasons for that, for instance, joint family systems and families are large with high dependency on women for routine livelihood, patriarchy, limited freedom women have in this region, and safety and religions are just a few among others.

While I tried not to emphasize breaks in women's career due to family issues as this barrier is not limited to economics, however, this is one of the significant reasons that came as a result of interviews. In academic spaces, other than career breaks, usually women face a lack of sponsorships for being part of academic committees, academic boards, and other such voluntary positions, which can significantly enhance their careers. Men

[2] ht@@tps://ideas.repec.org/top/top.econdept.html

[3] I am thankful to Dr. Ratna Sahay, Dr. Nisha Pandey, Dr. Sumita Sarkar from India, Dr Alia H. Khan, Dr. Hadia Majid, Dr. Noureen A. Khan, Dr. Alia Ahmed, Dr Sundus Saleemi, Maryam Zia Baloch from Pakistan and Dr. Hasneen Jahan from Bangladesh for their participating in discussion and sharing their experiences and thoughts. I also extend my gratitude to all students those who participated in our survey.

often are hesitant while nominating women for such positions, fearing that their nomination will be challenged as women wouldn't be able to perform their responsibilities in these additional positions due to their household responsibilities. For example, during a conversation, a woman economist said that the only solution for women is to work hard and to prove themselves, eliminating any excuse for others not to nominate them. Typically, women encounter a double burden, balancing responsibilities at home and in the labor market, expected to excel in both domains. They are required to be perfect in all places. Such expectations raise concerns about the overall well-being of women. Thus, as a result of the lack of sponsorships, due to the perception and experiences, women find it difficult to sit late in the office due to family responsibilities, patriarchal culture, women usually have limited network, and last but not least lack of socializing is another reason for not being part of voluntary positions—which requires additional working hours and efforts.

The interviewees shared their experiences overcoming societal and familial obstacles to pursue their career paths. They highlighted the specific difficulties encountered by women in conservative societies, prevalent in most of South Asia, where traditional norms can limit educational and career options. Throughout their journeys, spanning from entering the labor market to reaching leadership positions, women have to face discrimination, lack of support, and harassment in professional settings. Additionally, women in the education system and even otherwise often defer promotions due to family constraints, opting to wait until their children are settled. Many women refrain from advocating for better positions or salaries, choosing to remain at home due to family obligations. This complex interplay of societal expectations and family responsibilities underscores the intricate challenges that women in these contexts navigate in their professional lives.

Few interviewees emphasized the role of families, parents, in-laws, and husbands in enabling their careers. Gender biases at workplaces, including unequal treatment, lack of promotions, and societal expectations regarding women's roles, are embedded in societal mindsets. They stressed that women often face difficulties managing work and family responsibilities, with societal pressure to prioritize motherhood. The conversation also highlighted the significance of social and family harmony in supporting women's career growth. Mariyam Zia Baloch, born and raised in Pakistan, now at IMF Washington DC said that we don't see women on policy-making tables, banks, and governments, that's why young girls don't aspire to be economists. Society has restricted the career roles that a woman can take up. Career-oriented women are either doctors or teachers; besides this, everything else is taboo. Thus, stereotype threats refrain women from being in economics and policy-making.

In the private sector, educated and highly ambitious women frequently encounter obstacles after marriage, such as maternity leaves and motherhood leaves, impeding their career advancement. This hinders their progress in the professional sphere. However, in the government sector, factors like marital status and pregnancy do affect career advancement but to a lesser degree. In India, there is a growing inclination toward placing women in administrative roles, driven by the perception that they exhibit greater dedication, punctuality, and productivity than their male counterparts. Despite possessing commendable education and experience, women are often disregarded due to constraints on their mobility. Mobility is a challenging experience for women globally and poses a particularly significant barrier in the context of South Asia.

Furthermore, the prevailing patriarchal norms in the region emphasize the necessity for gender equality initiatives and inclusion in development agendas. Women in patriarchal societies encounter challenges marked by limited opportunities and persistent discrimination. Despite some achievements, there are significant prevalent gender disparities in academia and policy-making positions, underscoring the need for both societal and systemic change to promote gender equality and inclusion. One of the key findings gleaned from interviews with accomplished women economists in prominent institutions was the significance of networks and connections. Typically, men tend to possess robust professional networks. In contrast to their male counterparts, women in South Asia face restricted opportunities for regular social interactions with friends and colleagues, resulting in a limited professional network. The importance of such networks becomes evident in processes like nominations, transitions between workplaces, and securing prestigious voluntary positions. The networks and connections are also reflected in recognition both within their own organizations and at larger forums. Women are not taken seriously during the conversation. Wu (2020) reported a similar argument in her paper that women are less recognized, and the discussion becomes less academic or professional while discussing the work done by women. She found that the shift in conversation becomes more often about their personal information and conduct rather on their professional and intellectual contribution.

The interviews with leading women economists from India, Pakistan, and Bangladesh shed light on the challenges faced by women in leadership roles, particularly within governmental and organizational settings. An illustrative example is the sole female representative among the team members working on high-level decision-making and policies related to China Pakistan Economic Corridor (CPEC), one of the mega projects in Pakistan. During the conversation, she emphasized that whenever she tried to bring a different perspective in policy dialogue related to CPEC, but never heard seriously.

Intersectionality compounds these challenges, as discrimination based on class, ethnicity, and caste further constrains opportunities for women in policy and administrative positions. The World Inequality Database 2023 reports that levels of inequality vary widely across South and Southeast Asia. The class and ethnic divides are sharp and clear in these three countries, and thus cannot be ignored. To address the intersectionality, there is a need to be unglued from a patriarchal mindset, merit-based promotions, and objective assessment of candidates. The labor market in this region predominantly consists of informal employment. However, in the formal labor market policies are hardly implemented and thus lead to exploitation, low wages, and limited bargaining opportunities. The impact of these practices in the overall labor market is many times higher for women.

Sponsorship plays a crucial role in career advancement, but the opportunities for women remain limited to get sponsorships from their male peers. Specifically, women are seldom sponsored for high positions because of unavailability in late evening meetings and limited networks. The lack of inclusion of women in policy-making processes leads to policies that do not adequately address women's needs and lose a great opportunity for a better society through inclusivity. Efforts should be made to create more opportunities for women based on their capabilities, recognizing the academic achievements of female economists, rather than solely relying on sponsorship. The other way to address this issue can be by defining a mechanism for high-level voluntary positions.

7 The New Generation of Female Economists and Rethinking Economic Theory

The expert opinions revealed a transformation in education, where traditional career paths such as economics, engineering, or sociology are being challenged by emerging fields like innovation, technology, and creative disciplines, i.e., art, design, and media. Social media and technology are creating awareness about these evolving career possibilities, expanding horizons beyond conventional subjects. However, there seems to be a lack of awareness among students regarding niche areas within the economics discipline. Many students opt for core subjects like microeconomics and macroeconomics, not out of genuine interest, but rather by chance, as they choose these subjects due to insufficient awareness and guidance. Consequently, there's a reluctance to deeply engage with these subjects, resulting in a lack of enthusiasm for learning. There is only a minority, around 20 to 30 percent, are genuinely passionate about their subjects, particularly in econometrics, and aspire to become researchers. Despite this, the education system predominantly emphasizes on job prospects rather than nurturing expertise or passion for a subject. Furthermore, there's a societal trend where students, particularly girls, tend to gravitate toward traditional or creative disciplines. During interviews with women economists, a consensus emerged on the need to shift this trend. They emphasized the importance of encouraging students to explore and choose courses based on their passion and interest rather than conforming to societal expectations or limited awareness.

Among female economics majors, 15% expressed a complete disinterest in economics, while 18% of male counterparts shared a similar sentiment. Only 21% of female respondents and 38% of male respondents indicated an intention to specialize in macroeconomics or monetary policy for their advanced studies. Though acknowledging the limitations of concluding a small sample, it is tentatively suggested that the emerging cohort of female economics majors may not be considerably ambitious to pursue economics as a lifelong career. This survey led to the inference that these female graduates in economics need counselling, interaction with role models to follow, and the need for women to be in the economics profession. This assertion aligns with the findings of a larger survey articulated by Avilovo and Goldin (2020), which posits that such behavior may be attributed to the phenomenon of 'stereotype' threat. In the context of patriarchal societies, where such threats are likely to be more pronounced, women, when convinced that they are expected to perform poorly in a given subject, tend to shy away from it. Consequently, female economics majors, influenced by the stereotype notion that women may not excel in the discipline, may divert to other fields with more favorable gender perceptions.

An interviewee from Bangladesh, the head of an economics department observed that, regardless of gender, a significant number of undergraduate students tend to dislike studying core economics courses. One plausible explanation for this phenomenon is the use of complex economics jargons, which make it challenging for students to connect economic theories with quite unrealistic assumptions with real-world scenarios and integrate them into everyday conversation. This raises questions about the effectiveness of teaching pedagogies within the field of economics, suggesting a potential need for rethinking the discipline. During the conversation, some participants further asserted that women often lean toward subjects that allow them to explore and understand societal issues, placing a greater emphasis on those marginalized by competition and economic forces. The fundamental principles of economics, rooted in the maximization of material phenomena, may contribute to its perceived lack of empathy. Women driven by their preferences and inclinations may find it challenging to strongly identify with the core principles of the subject. On a similar note, Dr. Sundus Saleemi expressed an interesting perspective on conventional economic theories, pointing out that these theories commence with a rational agent primarily focused on optimizing the utility function related to consumption and leisure. Within this framework, leisure is defined as time away from the labor market. Notably, the inadequacy and absence of care and domestic work in the models reveal an implicit bias. The definitions of work and leisure in early texts of economics correspond more closely to a rational economic man than a genderless economic agent and hence are unconvincing and inadequate for analyses of the behavior of all agents in an economy. This conversation provided a plausible explanation on diminishing the appeal and acceptance of the subject, particularly among female undergraduate students. This discourse underscores the necessity for contemplating an alignment of the subject matter with diverse preferences and inclinations, thereby advocating for a rethinking of the methodologies employed in the presentation and delivery of economics education.

In the case of India, we have identified a few positive developments. Unstructured interviews have revealed that organizations particularly in the private sector and high-ranking administrative positions like head of departments and deans are now deliberately given to women due to their level of commitment. One interviewee emphasized that women are being chosen for these roles because of their punctuality, conscientiousness in meeting deadlines, and their avoidance of extended breaks such as smoking or socializing with friends during office hours. This contrasts with their male counterparts. It is noteworthy, however, that the observation of a deliberate effort to increase the representation of women in management roles is not a prevalent theme in discussions with experts in Pakistan and Bangladesh.

8 Women in the Frontlines: Catalysts of Resilience

Women empowerment requires interventions through public policy on certain laws, i.e., labor market policies in favor of women, deliberate and well-designed awareness campaigns to increase awareness and empower women, and interventions in schools and colleges to encourage women to participate in all academic disciplines or join those labor market sectors which are dominated by men, etc. However, during the survey, we encountered women who struggled and fought with the system and societal patriarchy. It is important to highlight their perspective, which was very common but important because it highlights the double burden women have to carry while being in ambitious careers.

The interviews with women in leadership positions reveal that a few passionately advocate for women at the forefront, akin to warriors overcoming all barriers and exemplifying resilience. Along with many challenges in transitioning between states and managing familial responsibilities, women need to remain confident and knowledgeable, and perhaps work harder than their male counterparts, albeit without expecting special concessions. Few participants in the study refrain from blaming society, government, or family, insisting that a woman's decisions, actions, and strength are paramount. Their argument centers on empowering women to make their own choices, work diligently, and challenge traditional norms, showcasing their own experiences as a testament to what women can achieve with determination without external support. Some interviewees also challenge the term 'woman economist' and they said that they want to be called simply economists. However, with this argument, they agree that such thinking places a double burden on women: first to compete in their discipline and second to navigate all cultural, societal, and familial barriers with resilience. With this approach, the well-being of women cannot be ignored.

9 Conclusion

Developing nations, particularly those in South Asia, need to take various affirmative measures at the institutional level to facilitate women in labor force in general, and economics in particular. These initiatives could emulate the formation of 'The Committee on the Status of Women in the Economic Profession'. Their primary objectives should include strengthening the network, providing mentorship, and supporting women in career advancement within the professions related to economics through sponsorships and other strategic measures. To address the underrepresentation of women in senior positions across all sectors, particularly in policy-making, there is a crucial need for mechanisms that monitor and track women's participation.

To bring a change it is important to nurture the current and future generations of undergraduates especially those who opt for economics majors in a way to increase their interest in the discipline. This can be achieved by providing them with accurate and detailed information about the various career paths within the field of economics. Additionally, the implementation of mentoring programs, coupled with the introduction of female economics major students to accomplished role models, can substantially enhance their professional growth. The establishment of supportive networks among students not only facilitates the exchange of experiential knowledge but also cultivates a sense of community. Ultimately, this approach addresses the prevailing issue of inadequate networking opportunities faced by women economists.

To mend the leaky pipelines, it is advisable to establish guidelines promoting women during crucial stages such as PhD admissions, faculty hiring, the formation of gender-balanced committees, participation in seminars, and ensuring an equitable promotion process throughout their careers. Additionally, a notable observation is the scarcity of publicly accessible statistics on women staff in universities in South Asian countries. It is imperative for South Asian and other developing nations to compile gender-segregated statistics of academic and policy spaces, entry and exit points in the profession, among other factors, to enhance our understanding of these phenomena. Undoubtedly, further research is warranted to comprehensively explore the role of women in economics, particularly within the global south and the specific context of South Asia.

Finally, it is crucial to reassess the language and content of basic economic theory textbooks and curricula. This need for rethinking has been underscored not only by a few interviewees but is also a recognized concern in economic literature. Scholars such as Siminski and Yetsenga (2020), Kabeer (1991), and Akerlof and Kranton (2000) have made arguments addressing this issue. Despite advancements in empirical models and research papers taking a more modern approach, undergraduate students are still exposed to traditional models that were originally developed by and for men, neglecting the consideration of social identities related to gender and their contribution to society.

References

Brown, C., and M. Johnson. 2022. Breaking the Glass Ceiling: Women in Economics Leadership Positions. *Economics Diversity and Inclusion* 15(4):57–69.

Card, D., S. Della Vigna, P. Funk, and N. Iriberri. 2019. Are Referees and Editors in Economics Gender Neutral? Working Paper No. 25967. National Bureau of Economic Research. http://www.nber.org/papers/w25967.

Chari, A., and P. Goldsmith-Pinkham. 2017. Gender Representation in Economics Across Topics and Time: Evidence from the NBER Summer Institute, NBER Working Papers 23953.

Dolado, J. J., F. Felgueroso, and M. Almunia. 2012. Are Men and Women-economists Evenly Distributed Across Research Fields? *Some New Empirical Evidence. Series* 3(3):367–393.

Gabster, B. P., K. Daalen, R. Dhatt, and M. Barry. 2020. Challenges for the Female Academic During the COVID-19 Pandemic. *The Lancet* 295:10242.

Akerlof, George A., and Rachel E. Kranton. 2000. Economics and Identity. *The Quarterly Journal of Economics* 115(3):715–753.

Gupta, R., and S. Patel. 2021. The Impact of Gender Diversity on Research Quality in Economics. *Journal of Economic Research* 36(1):45–58.

Hengel, E. 2022. Publishing While Female. Are Women Held to Higher Standards? Evidence from peer Review. Cambridge Working Papers in Economics 1753, Faculty of Economics, University of Cambridge.

Jones, P., and D. Williams. 2023. Diverse Research Teams and their Impact on Economic Analyses. *Diversity in Economics Journal* 10(2):78–92.

Kabeer, N. 1991. Gender, Production and Well-being: Rethinking the Household Economy, IDS Discussion Paper 288, Institute of Development Studies, University of Sussex, England, 191.

P. Beneito, J. E. Boscá, J. Ferri, and M. García. 2018. Women Across Subfields in Economics: Relative performance and Beliefs. Working Papers 2018-06, FEDEA.

Smith, A., and L. Johnson. 2021. Gender Disparities in Economics: A Comprehensive Study. *Journal of Gender Economics* 28(2):215–223.

Siminski, Peter, and Rhiannon Yetsenga. 2020. Rethinking, Specialization, and the Sexual Division of labor in the 21st Century. IZA Discussion Papers 12977, Institute of Labor Economics (IZA).

Tharakan, S. M., and M. Tharakan. 1975. Status of Women in India: A Historical Perspective. *Social Scientist* 4(4/5):115–123. https://doi.org/10.2307/3516124.

Women in Economics. 2020. What Can UWE do for Economics? In *A VoxEU Book*, Authored by Avilovo, T., and Goldin, C. ed by Shelly Lundberg. Centre for Economic Policy and research Press.

Wu, A. H. 2020. Gender Bias Among Professionals: An Identity-Based Interpretation. *The Review of Economics and Statistics* 102(5):867–880.

Diversity, Equity, and Inclusion in the Undergraduate Economics Curriculum: A Patch for the Leaky Pipeline of Women in Economics?

Ariane Agunsoye and Jacqueline Strenio

1 Introduction

In recent years, two discussions have come to the forefront of undergraduate economics education: the continued underrepresentation of women in the discipline and an increasing focus on diversity, equity, and inclusion (DEI) initiatives (often referred to as EDI when employing the term equality rather than equity), a buzzword that has come to dominate university discourse and policy in the UK, but is now banned in the US. But what does that mean in practice? In this chapter, we analyze the role EDI may play in addressing the lack of women in economics.

While the history behind the EDI movement in higher education was radical, the current focus lies often on finding quick solutions within the

A. Agunsoye
Goldsmiths, University of London, London, UK
e-mail: a.agunsoye@gold.ac.uk

J. Strenio (✉)
Norwich University, Norwich, VT, USA
e-mail: jstrenio@norwich.edu

© The Author(s), under exclusive license to Springer Nature Switzerland AG 2026

V. Dolar and T. Perry (eds.), *Missing Voices in Economics*,
https://doi.org/10.1007/978-3-031-97180-8_6

existing system. In line with a neoliberal university, metrics and measurements are developed and taken as key guides for improving EDI within the university, with "success" coming in the form of awards certifying their treatment of women, people from minority racial or ethnic groups, and people identifying as LGBTQ + . Yet, the underlying systemic issues which have contributed to the creation of an unequal system are often not questioned. Moreover, despite the increased attention on EDI at the university level, such focus has not translated into the economics classroom.

Failing to bring issues related to EDI and gender specifically into the classroom is a contributing factor to the lack of diversity in the economics discipline overall. Women continue to be underrepresented in reading lists and textbooks (Guizzo 2024; Kuiper 2022; Small 2023; Stevenson and Zlotnik 2018), and topics taught in economics ignore gendered dimensions (Berik and Rodgers 2023; Strenio and Rodgers 2023). These oversights reinforce the leaky pipeline, especially for women students who fail to see their own experiences and identities represented throughout the curriculum (Agunsoye et al. 2022a). Indeed, most undergraduate economics programs that do incorporate gender discuss these topics in elective classes that focus solely on women in the economy rather than systematically incorporating gender throughout the curriculum. The result? Women are more likely to report feeling different than the typical economics major, namely men students (Bayer et al. 2020).

This chapter will explore what diversity, equity, and inclusion can look like in the classroom and what it means for women in economics. We will discuss how feminist economics and gender-aware pedagogical tools can contribute to increasing inclusivity in economics. While being critical of current approaches to EDI, the widespread discussion of these could be exploited to diversify the curriculum and pedagogy.

2 Systemic Inequalities Within Economics

EDI initiatives have been upsurging in the past two decades with universities competing to become EDI champions, although this has changed in the US as of January 2025 with President Trump's Executive Order 14173, "Ending Illegal Discrimination and Restoring Merit-Based Opportunity" and Executive Order 14151, "Ending Radical and Wasteful Government DEI Programs and Preferencing." There is little evidence, however, that existing EDI measures tackle the persistent discriminatory practices inherent in economics.

Women are largely underrepresented. Only 19% of economists worldwide are women (Boring and Zignago 2018), with even fewer in senior positions. In the UK, while 33% of lecturers (assistant professors) and 27% of senior lecturers or readers (associate professors) are women, only 15% of full professors are women. This trend, referred to as the "leaky pipeline," is even worse in the case of women with a racial or ethnic minority background. Between 2012 and 2018, there was not a single Black female economist working as a professor in the UK (Bateman et al. 2021; Gamage et al. 2020). Women economists are similarly underrepresented in the US. Only 22% and 6.6% of economics faculty in the US are female or come from a minority racial or ethnic background, respectively, and they are often in lower-ranked or part-time positions (Berland et al. 2022; CSMGEP 2019). Underrepresentation starts in undergraduate programs. The average undergraduate economics department in the US lacks racial and gender inclusion relative to other fields (Bayer and Wilcox 2019). For example, male students are 2.5 times more likely to choose economics compared to female students and only 2% of economics bachelor's degrees are awarded to Black women (Avilova and Goldin 2018; Cook and Opuku-Agyeman 2019). A similar picture can be found in the UK where only 27% of undergraduate economics students are women. While a third of economics students that identify as Black or Asian are female, they often do not stay within academia (Bateman et al. 2021).

The leaky pipeline is, in part, caused by discriminatory practices inherent in the discipline. In 2018, Alice Wu brought attention to the misogyny in economics by analyzing posts on one of the major anonymous online economics discussion platforms, the Economics Jobs Market Rumors (EJMR) website. She found that words about physical appearance and being single or married, for example, most likely predicted that a post was about a woman, while posts about men were predicted by words related to academic or professional qualifications (Wu 2018). A more recent study has unveiled that the most sexist and racist comments posted on EJMR originated from leading universities, the same universities which dominate economic theory and policymaking (Rugaber 2023). Differential treatment by gender is also reflected during research presentations. Research shows that women receive more probing questions than men and that such questions are often patronizing or attempting to undermine their knowledge (Dupas et al. 2021). These discriminatory practices are intensified for those with a minority racial or ethnic background. For instance, 62% of African American female economists who responded to the American Economic Association's climate survey reported some form of gender and/or racial discrimination (Allgood et al. 2019).

Gendered and racialized discriminatory practices also infiltrate the institutions of knowledge dissemination essential for promotion. While women make up one-third of academics, only 11% of papers published in the top five economic journals include a female author, just 8% of papers had a majority of female authors, and only 4% were written solely by women. Not only are women held to higher publishing standards, they also experience lengthier review processes and are less likely to be recommended as reviewers due to editors preferring to assign papers to reviewers with the same characteristics as them (Hengel 2022; Card et al. 2020). This homophily can also be found within citations where men are more likely to cite other men (Fox et al. 2017; Helmer et al. 2017), negatively impacting women's promotion possibilities and reinforcing a dominance of theories and methodologies which downplay and/or deepen power imbalances based on gender and race. Even when women are similarly, or more, qualified than men, they are not promoted equally (which is exacerbated for women belonging to a minority racial or ethnic background (Cook and Opoku-Agyeman 2019). Characteristics seen as acceptable for men are viewed less favorably for women, for instance, co-authorship is more detrimental for women than for men when applying for promotions, because of the implicit assumption that women contribute less within co-authored papers (Sarsons et al. 2021).

Finally, women in academia face an imbalanced workload. Women are still predominantly responsible for caring duties when having children and conducting the day-to-day domestic tasks, reducing the time they can devote to the labor market (Ghodsee 2019). Having two children, for instance, culminates in lowering the research output of female academics by 2.5 years (Santos and Dang van Phu 2019). The impact of unpaid care on female academics has been highlighted by the pandemic, during which men's submission of papers upsurged while women's submissions declined (Gabster et al. 2020). At the same time, women are often assigned more service work than men within their departments, taking time away from their academic and teaching work, and are frequently assigned to administrative tasks which are less beneficial for promotion (Ashencaen Crabtree & Shiel 2019; Sümer & Elsen-Ziya 2022).

The lack of diverse identities and perspectives in economics resulting from these discriminatory practices is highly problematic, not only from a moral perspective, but also from an economic perspective, as it limits the breadth of economic theory and research topics. As economic theory influences policy, this can result in the marginalization of essential issues for developing an equitable society such as social mobility, labor market inequalities, and the role of unpaid care. If policies are set without taking into consideration women's perspectives and lived experiences, valuable opportunities for income and growth are missed. A prime example is the current pension system in the UK which was developed based on assumptions of a male, well-earning work trajectory, ignoring caring duties (Grady 2015). As a consequence, women are not only forced out of the labor market and earn less when becoming mothers but are also not able to contribute sufficiently to pensions throughout their lifetime (Agunsoye and James 2022), increasing their likelihood of relying on the state during retirement. Ignoring unpaid care is not surprising given that the demographic background of an academic influences research topics and that economics is dominated by white, often privileged, men in the Global North (May et al. 2018).

3 The Rise of EDI/DEI Measures

Although the terms diversity (who is studying), equity (resources for studying), and inclusion (culture of studying), combined as "DEI" or "EDI," have become a buzzword in higher education, EDI initiatives have a more radical history in higher education in the US, stemming from the Civil Rights Movement of the 1950s and 1960s. At the time, these movements were specifically focused on colleges becoming more racially inclusive, including complying with the integration requirement under Title VI of the Civil Rights Act of 1964—a goal that was pushed to the forefront of many higher education institutions in the aftermath of the assassination of Reverend Martin Luther King Jr. in 1968 (Charles 2023). The core goal of diversifying institutions of higher education and making college campuses more inclusive continued into the early 2020s in the US, even though the focus expanded beyond racially diversifying predominantly white institutions to examining and supporting EDI efforts across many social identities of students, faculty, and staff, including gender, sexual orientation, (dis)ability, and religion. Besides diversifying the student population through admissions, initiatives were broadened to include retention, support of marginalized populations, and often involved and complemented work on other important institutional goals such as accessibility, belonging, and justice (Stephen et al. 2023). While indicators of EDI success varied by university, key goals were to narrow graduation gaps and increase the diversity of the student population. Other common EDI practices at the faculty and staff level included requiring job candidates to submit diversity statements and mandating diversity training.

By 2024, this manifestation of EDI had become mainstream at colleges and universities around the world, albeit with different interpretations. While both the UK and the US focused on *diversity*, which means embracing differences, and on *inclusion*, which means having a campus culture that is welcoming where all students and staff feel they belong and that their opinions are valued, a key difference can be detected in the third term (Stephen et al. 2023). Up until January 2025, US universities had tended to use *equity* while in the UK, the focus lies on *equality* in their EDI frameworks. Equality refers to giving everyone access to the same resources whereas equity acknowledges that the starting point might not be the same for each student and therefore ensures that the material is adjusted to the individual needs (University of Oxford 2023). UK universities in particular focus on attainment and retention gaps as research has found that students coming from minority ethnic backgrounds are less likely to achieve an honors degree and are more likely to discontinue studying (Advani et al. 2020). At the same time, UK universities have increasingly moved toward decolonizing and diversifying strategies. A recent survey of UK business schools found that 67% of surveyed schools have implemented decolonizing and diversifying initiatives which include student ambassadors, guest speakers, policy guidelines, and even named race champions (Everett and Linton 2023). Although often viewed as synonymous to EDI, these initiatives do not fundamentally change the institutional structure and curriculum content, a key task when taking decolonization and diversification seriously.

Despite these differences, the codification of EDI into a more formal, mainstream initiative became widespread in both countries in the past few decades. Up until January 2025, it was rare to find a university in the US or UK without an EDI strategy or assigned staff responsible for their implementation and success, including senior administrators. EDI initiatives were (and continue to be in the UK) increasingly operationalized and professionalized through development of key performance indicators (KPIs) and EDI offices, dedicated staff and regulators intervening. In the UK, measurements are sought to evaluate the success of EDI activities and to integrate them into the wider KPIs of universities with questions being asked at learning and teaching conferences such as: “If decolonization and diversification interventions are part of a business school’s strategy, how are we measuring the success of these interventions?” A particular emphasis is put on costs, seeking to ensure the profitability of new initiatives. At the same time, those working on EDI moved from generic staff roles to more senior administrative positions, including Chief Diversity Officers, Vice Presidents of DEI, or other highly visible cabinet-level roles (Charles 2023). Now, however, these positions and roles are increasingly being dismantled among institutions of higher education in the US (Dutton 2025). In contrast, the Office for Students, the regulatory body for UK universities, has defined an action plan with success measurement indicators to achieve its five goals: “elimination of discrimination, equality of opportunity, and the fostering of good relations between different people in respect of universities, colleges and students” (OfS 2018). One of its measures includes fining universities if attainment and retention gaps fall below a certain threshold, seeking to push forward EDI initiatives.

While the reach of, and demand for, EDI initiatives had generally been expanding over the past two decades, they had also become increasingly politicized in the US. The US Supreme Court banned race-conscious admissions in 2023 with their ruling on affirmative action, and as of April 4, 2025, 129 bills with anti-DEI legislation have been introduced across 29 states and the US Congress, 19 of which have become law (The Chronicle of Higher Education 2025). This new wave of anti-DEI legislation includes proscriptions that have banned or restricted DEI offices and staff, mandatory DEI training, diversity statements, and identity-based preferences for hiring and admissions. Such anti-DEI policy culminated in President Trump’s 2025 pair of executive orders, Executive Order 14173, “Ending Illegal Discrimination and Restoring Merit-Based Opportunity” which attempts to categorize any “diversity, equity, and inclusion (DEI)” efforts as illegal, requiring federal agencies and contractors, and encouraging private entities, to end such “discrimination” (Exec. Order No. 14173 2025) and Executive Order 14151, “Ending Radical and Wasteful Government DEI Programs and Preferencing” which attempts to end federal DEI programs and offices, including ending celebrations of demographic groups, such as Black History Month (Exec. Order No. 14151 2025).

Despite the vague language in the executive orders, political pressure and the threat of withholding federal funding have resulted in many colleges and universities removing DEI language, ending programs, and closing offices. Other higher education organizations have pushed back, filing a lawsuit against the two executive orders. While the legal and political landscape regarding DEI in the US remains in flux, such policies only emphasize the urgency of programs adopting gender-aware and decolonized curriculum and pedagogies to continue to create inclusive spaces regardless of whether DEI remains banned or comes back into the mainstream as in the UK.

4 EDI as Panacea to Reduce Economics' Inequalities?

While EDI offices and measures are now commonplace (although this is rapidly changing in the US (Dutton 2025)), they continue to be narrowly defined. Success is often determined solely by indicators of the demographic composition of the student body and graduating classes, retention numbers, the utilization of services, or campus climate surveys. A former EDI officer Ariana González Stokas reflects on her experience within diversity work in higher education, arguing that it is purposefully structured to be superficial and decorative (2023):

> It became quickly apparent that one could work on diversity so long as one did not too dramatically unsettle the institution's traditions and seek to reassemble them, or to open up the arteries of inequity and dig around to find what needed to be abolished. I have come to realize that despite the best efforts of highly competent people, diversity efforts often function as a decorative shield.

Reminiscent of a key issue within economics with its focus on changing individual behavior rather than tackling structural constraints, she goes on to hint at the inability of EDI officers, policies, and strategies to address the systemic issues:

> Remedies, if ever enacted, were individually focused. There was rarely a mention of a problematic system or culture or set of practices...Some people were interested in talking about white privilege in the abstract, but not so much in investigating how the systems they relied on day after day were privileging whiteness, wealth, ability, or masculinity.

This superficial approach often results in employing figureheads and requiring substantial documentation and evaluation without real change. Too often EDI measures are planned top-down without active involvement by students, for instance mainly focusing on subconscious bias trainings and behavior within classrooms. From discussions on current EDI approaches within universities in Italy, South Africa, the UK, and the US in a recent workshop we organized, it became clear that EDI work involves a lot of unpaid work within departments. As this work is often not recognized within promotion processes, it can reinforce gendered inequalities within academia (Sümer and Elsen-Ziya 2022).

Current measures also do not tackle the underlying causes of attainment and retention gaps but rather treat their symptoms, often ignoring the impact of curriculum, assessment methods, and an underrepresentation of women faculty on student outcomes. Even when implementing measures to increase diversity within economics, such interventions tend to incorporate dominant economic methodologies such as randomized controlled trials and monetary incentives. One such example is incentivizing schools to conduct interventions to increase female economics graduates. Interventions include providing more course information, mentoring programs, career counseling, and improving instructional content, for instance, by making first-year content more relevant through integration of community-based projects and "evidence-based material" (Avilova and Goldin 2018, p. 8). Yet, the focus on mentoring and career counseling initiatives lies on adapting individual behavior to the existing system without challenging its discriminatory practices.

Perhaps even worse, these measures do not fundamentally change the underlying assumptions of economics which are rooted in the utility-maximizing agent and efficient market dynamics. For instance, while "the CORE project attempts to reinvent economic education by linking economic concepts to current events and research" (Al-Bahrani 2022, p.261), it does not fundamentally question the concept of utility and the separation into internal and external elements (Mearman et al. 2018). Economic concepts are presented as "neutral," yet they ignore gendered and racialized dimensions within society. A national survey of economics instructors in the US found that 91% of principles-level classes did not include a single lesson or activity related to diversity, inclusion, or gender issues (Asarta et al. 2021) and such references were similarly nonexistent in intermediate theory, statistics, econometrics, and other upper-division field courses in the economics curriculum in the US (Harter and Asarta 2022). Similarly, recent surveys in the UK found that 99% of surveyed economics courses did not make reference to racism and colonialism (Choat et al. 2023; Kvangraven and Kesar 2023). Integrating a view of the world that does not represent a multiplicity of identities and ideas results in women and students from minority racial and ethnic backgrounds disproportionately choosing not to study economics, or not to pursue further economic studies. Economics feels too detached from real-world problems: ("I'm not convinced I'm doing anything that matters outside the tower of academia" [Colander 2005, p. 179]). This is a contributing factor to the leaky pipeline as interviews with students have shown that this can lead to them not choosing and not continuing with economics (Agunsoye et al. 2022a).

For EDI to be truly successful, it must be synthesized within all levels of the university and the economics discipline, reflecting the day-to-day experiences of students in the classroom in terms of who is represented as economists. Interviews with high school students in the UK have revealed that economics is perceived as being dominated by white, privileged men (Agunsoye et al. 2022a). Not seeing female economics professors and famous female economists discussed in class results in female students having less interest in studying economics (Porter and Serra 2020) and can culminate in attracting students who are biased against women (Paredes et al. 2023) and/or incorporate racial bias (Ajzenman et al. 2023). These biases are only intensified when studying economics. Male faculty, for instance, often reinforce gendered inequalities by elevating the voices of male students and marginalizing female voices, resulting in female students indicating that they do not feel heard in the economics classroom (Agunsoye et al. 2022a).

The content of textbooks also reflects the lack of gender diversity in the discipline. For example, Stevenson and Zlotnik (2018) find that men account for more than 90% of leaders, policymakers, and economists mentioned in introductory economics textbooks. Moreover, women are less likely to be mentioned in fictional examples and when they do appear, they are more likely to be involved in food, fashion, or household tasks. Even in textbooks dedicated to pluralistic perspectives, highlighted "great" economists are disproportionately white and male (Strenio 2023). The lack of representation in textbooks, case studies, and examples is problematic because it reinforces the "othering" of nonwhite, nonmale voices. Yet, current EDI measures do not tackle the lack of diversity within pedagogy and curriculum, preventing the improvement of attainment and retention gaps within universities.

5 EDI Measures in the Economics Classroom: The Way Forward

If one takes seriously the mission to make universities more inclusive, it is not enough to recruit and retain underrepresented students. Rather, it is essential that students are able to see themselves reflected in faculty. Teaching staff should be representative of all groups in society inclusive of women and different ethnicities. A diversity of faculty identities also allows for more breadth of research and teaching topics and often results in different policy prescriptions which are even more important given the recent policy changes in the US. Male economists are more likely to prefer market solutions to government intervention, are more skeptical of environmental protection, and are less keen on redistribution. In contrast, female economists are more likely to acknowledge labor market inequalities and give more importance to social policy (Bayer and Rouse 2016; May et al. 2018). EDI initiatives need to acknowledge the importance of gender diversity in economics staff and gender-aware research, including pedagogical research. In addition to staff being representative of all groups in society, the curriculum needs to reflect a realistic picture of society, with a diversity of content and pedagogies so that all students feel welcome. This entails: (1) including theoretical viewpoints with a gendered lens and scholars who reflect the diversity of society, and (2) rethinking methodological approaches to knowledge creation within the classroom. Developing a holistic approach to introducing EDI measures in economics is key to advancing a truly inclusive environment within the university.

5.1 Gender-Aware Curriculum

Even though there has been a rise in offering feminist economics and gender studies modules, gendered content in economics programs is often only represented in upper-division, elective classes on gender and the economy or in specific assignments within other elective classes. And even within those elective classes, gender is largely addressed solely in specific sections rather than systematically integrated throughout the semester and text (Berik & Rodgers 2023; Strenio and Rodgers 2023). Much of the standard curriculum in introductory-level classes discusses "core" economics concepts as if they are gender neutral and focuses exclusively on visible economic activities, such as production by waged labor in a capitalist firm. This standard approach ignores a range of everyday economic activities, including unpaid work, care work, sharing, and gifting. Yet, while narrowly defining economics as the study of scarcity has become ubiquitous across textbooks, departments, and countries, there is a growing appetite to redefine what economics is, and what economists study.

A more gender-aware economics must make "gendered content and processes central to the study of the economy" (Strenio and Rodgers 2023, p. 41), integrating gender from the beginning in the introductory classroom and carrying through the entirety of the curriculum. Such gender mainstreaming should start with a more expansive definition of the discipline itself. Feminist economists have long embraced defining economics as the study of social provisioning, which incorporates both paid and unpaid, market and nonmarket economic activity, and emphasizes measuring economic success using indicators of human well-being, such as acknowledging the "heterogeneity of humans needs" rather than just "aggregate or average distributions of income and wealth" (Power 2004, p. 5). This approach allows for the centering of ethical questions and concerns (Nelson 2018). Defining economics as the study of social provisioning is well aligned with the core goals of EDI as the central tenets of the approach also include analyzing differences based on gender, race/ethnicity, and other social identities, explicitly incorporating discussions of power hierarchies and processes as well as considering ethical values (Power 2004). A social provisioning approach reinforces true EDI work in the economics classroom and beyond, by encouraging a focus not only on evaluating and assessing the demographic composition of majors, graduating classes, and overall student bodies, but also on the structural power hierarchies within universities and societies with the ultimate goal of altering the processes to make economics more inclusive.

Within a truly inclusive EDI framework, inequality should also be included as an alternative starting point for economics. Inequality is particularly relevant to the EDI mission as it speaks to the lived experiences of historically underrepresented students and faculty in the discipline. Recognizing inequality rather than scarcity as a point of origin allows for

> establishing important distinctions between the measure and sources of disparities across individuals, households, ethnic, racial, and gender groups, regions, and nations...[where] discrimination becomes a major topic rather than a subject buried in the module of a principles course that provides the student's first exposure to labor economics. (Darity 2022, p. 6)

Introductory classes should introduce students to the history of the field, with the ability to explore competing perspectives on what economics is and what role social provisioning and inequality play within it. In addition to discussing the social and historical construct of knowledge in introductory classes, requiring classes in the history of economic thought is a key way in which economic programs can better prepare students to understand economic theory within its socially and historically constructed context. However, adding economic history and history of economic thought courses is not sufficient if such courses do not include female scholars and scholars from the Global South nor acknowledge the dominant role colonialism and slavery have played in the economic success of Global North countries. As Small (2023) uncovers and cautions, such history of economic thought courses have typically focused narrowly on contributions by predominantly white men from the Global North. However, resources exist to help design history of economic thought courses more inclusively (see, for example: Guizzo (2024), Kuiper (2022), and Small (2023)).

Gendered and racialized perspectives should be part of the core modules and included across the entirety of the economics curriculum. While some resources exist that describe ways in which instructors of development economics (Berik and Rodgers 2023) and labor economics (Strenio and Rodgers 2023) might do this, much of that work remains with the individual instructor and can therefore reinforce disparities in unpaid, unrecognized work for instructors who are interested in radically reimagining their courses. EDI initiatives, at both the university and professional organization level, that provide incentives (monetary or course releases) to allow instructors to do this, then can be imperative in patching the leaky pipeline for women in economics by both allowing women faculty the time and space to restructure their courses and reward them in terms of retention and promotion measures, and simultaneously, making economics more inclusive for students of all identities and backgrounds. That change must also come from textbook authors and publishers as well. Bayer and Wilcox (2019) recommend that they "design and revise their materials with a central question in mind: Are issues of race, gender, and class integrated into the material in a way that will allow a broader swath of students to see economics as relevant to people like them? (p. 311)."

Indeed, key recommendations from Bayer et al. (2020) on creating a more inclusive economics classroom for underrepresented minority students entail both broadening the principles-level courses and incorporating more examples and content that are relevant to students of all backgrounds and reflect the multiplicity of identities within society. To ensure students see economists that look like them, Strenio (2023) has proposed a "Great Economist" assignment in which students pick an economist from a pre-set, curated list representing a wide range of social identities and lived experiences. Students then present a biography and research summary of their great economist to the class. A wider approach could be to introduce different schools of thought including female scholars and scholars from the Global South in the beginning of the degree and carry them throughout the program when discussing diverse economic topics.

5.2 *Gender-Aware Pedagogical Tools*

In addition to more inclusive course content, feminist economists have highlighted the need for changes in teaching and assessment methods. Shackelford (1992) identifies three essential features of feminist pedagogy for economics which fit well within the EDI goal of inclusivity, but go further in acknowledging that those that have historically had their voices, ideas, and experiences suppressed by patriarchy must be elevated. In the following, we outline how these features could be integrated within an EDI framework along with insights from the critical pedagogies of Freire (1970), Freire and Macedo (2014), and hooks (1994).

First, feminist pedagogy must have as a goal "empowering or giving voice and influence to those disempowered by patriarchal structures" (Shackelford 1992, p. 571) while critical pedagogy insists that "everyone's presence is acknowledged" (hooks 1994, p.8). This fits well within an EDI framework for economics by emphasizing the importance of acknowledging, validating, and connecting students' lived experiences to the study of economics. In the previous section, we discussed ways of purposefully including diverse voices in the curriculum as one way of doing this. Pedagogically, this means that all students must have an opportunity to feel heard and be acknowledged in the classroom, through the provision of opportunities to interact not only with the content and the instructor, but also with other students. This can be achieved by employing non-formal teaching methods such as integrating extensive group discussions in the lectures to empower students to develop their own ideas, letting students explore a topic which is relevant to their everyday life in small research projects, and giving the possibility to students to choose one or two topics of the lectures. Second, feminist pedagogy requires a "focus on practice, with an emphasis on process over product or content" (Shackelford 1992, p. 571) which Freire calls "problem-posing" education (Freire & Macedo 2014, p. 79). To ensure a focus on process within an EDI framework, space should be given to all students to express themselves and excel. That means teaching and assessment methods should be diversified including not only essays and exams but podcasts, blogs, presentations, posters, and group learning (Agunsoye et al. 2022b).

An example of how these two goals can be tackled is found in one of our courses where students are exposed to this type of "problem-posing" education and expected to investigate a current economic issue. Students are asked to identify a relevant topic based on a recent newspaper article, analyze it with the help of an economic theoretical viewpoint and empirical data, and develop policy recommendations. The key results are then summarized in a case study report and presented in front of a panel consisting of experts from diverse industries including government services, financial consultancies, and non-governmental organizations. By giving students the ability to choose the topic for their research projects, they make the projects more relevant to their lives and explore an issue of importance to them. This has often led students to recognize limitations of existing dominant economic theories and explore alternative theoretical viewpoints. Moreover, they work together throughout the whole module and learn how to engage in teams.

Finally, Shackelford (1992) emphasizes the importance of incorporating other ways of knowing, especially in economics, a discipline rife with "'objective,' 'hierarchical,' or 'authority-laden' models" (p. 571).

Economics is often described as the "most scientific of the social sciences" (Colander 2005, p. 185) based on the use of an "objective", mathematical deductive approach (Coyle 2012). This mathematization has created barriers for female students in studying economics if they have internalized the stereotypical norms of being less financially and/or mathematically inclined (Avilova and Goldin 2018; Eswaran 2014). Mathematization can also result in missing essential key insights due to misrepresenting the economy. Pluralism in theoretical and pedagogical approaches thus needs to go hand in hand with pluralism in methodological approaches.

We need to move beyond only teaching quantitative approaches to economics. Students should also learn to use qualitative and mixed methods in research projects. This can be combined with EDI goals such as belonging and inclusiveness by letting students choose the methodology for a research project and conduct primary data collection after learning how different methodologies can be employed in economics. By integrating qualitative research or mixed methods into economic analysis, a non-formalistic, methodological framework can be employed where intra-group relationships, power imbalances, and everyday life and its meanings and values can be explored, representing a realistic view of the world. The necessity of pluralism in methods has also recently been acknowledged by the OECD in the frame of exploring change processes in the public sector encouraging practitioners "to synthesize different approaches" and thus "aligns itself with recent developments towards methodological pluralism and problem-based approaches" (OECD 2017, p. 136). Yet, while diverse methodological approaches have been thriving in other, related disciplines such as economic geography and among practitioners (see for instance Money Advice Service), economists have been reluctant to adopt a pluralist methodological approach, and the discipline remains disproportionately focused on causal analysis and quantitative methods.

Interdisciplinarity is another essential pedagogical tool for a more gender-aware economics, allowing the discipline to overcome its insular culture "divorced from related subjects such as politics, psychology and sociology" (Prowse 1993 in [Coyle 2012, p. 188]). Integrating insights from different disciplines is particularly important for EDI initiatives. Despite having included topics which have originally been discussed in sociology or psychology such as social mobility, economists rarely cross-reference (Fourcade, Ollie and Algan 2015) and economic concepts dominate discussions. The widespread adoption of universal principles and individual rationality creates an economic framework that is detached from its social and political surroundings. Through this, cultural and social norms are downplayed and differences based on gender, race, and ethnicity ignored.

Moving outside of economics and integrating valuable knowledge from other disciplines enables students to explore real-world issues while recognizing underlying power relationships and the impact of social and cultural norms on economic behavior. Interdisciplinary insights should be included in modules when discussing a topic, revealing perspectives from other disciplines such as anthropology, sociology, and psychology and their interconnection with economics. An example is introducing students to political economic thought, decolonial viewpoints, and feminist theories while critically evaluating current structures of capitalism and the impact of institutions on economic outcomes. At the same time, students should be able to choose optional modules from other disciplines throughout their degree. By creating a truly interdisciplinary degree, diversity and inclusive knowledge comes alive which can both serve as a patch for the leaky pipeline in economics and support broader EDI goals.

6 Conclusion

While EDI has raised awareness of unequal student access and outcomes, it remains focused on its symptoms and not underlying causes. One of the oversights in EDI work in higher education is that it has largely concentrated on measurement metrics aimed at the institutional or individual school or college level, where "success" is narrowly defined as reductions in retention and graduation gaps between students of different racial, ethnic, and gender identities. When looking at economics, gender diversity represents an important step for making economics a more inclusive field of knowledge, yet current EDI measures do not focus on the content of the economics curriculum, pedagogy, or faculty composition. Even worse, such EDI measures have been abolished in the US. As a result, economics remains riddled with a lack of representation of women and theoretical viewpoints devoid of gendered, racialized, and ethnic dimensions.

Being dominated by a small part of the wider society and by narrowly defined theoretical viewpoints has led to prioritizing certain cultures and backgrounds more than others, preventing the improvement of attainment and retention gaps within universities, one of the core goals of

EDI measures. Developing a holistic approach to increasing diversity, equity, and inclusion in economics through curricular and pedagogical change can serve as an important patch for the leaky pipeline of women in economics and prove successful in countries in which EDI is a buzzword, as well as in countries in which it is now a banned word. However, increasing gender diversity needs to entail change across multiple dimensions and levels: the classroom—including individual instructors and the content and pedagogies they use; departments—including the chairs and tenure and promotion committees; and university-wide administrators—including EDI offices and staff. Research on inclusive pedagogies and content should also be equally recognized, supported, and rewarded in faculty retention and promotion decisions.

References

Advani, A., S. Sen, S., and R. Warwick. 2020. *Ethnic Diversity in UK Economics*. ESRC Research Centre on Micro-Social Change. Retrieved from https://www.iser.essex.ac.uk/wpcontent/uploads/files/misoc/reports/explainers/ethnic-diversity-UK-economics.pdf.

Agunsoye, A., L. Ambler, J. Earle, M. Groenewald, D. Guizzo, B. Roberts-Dear, and N. Scott. 2022a. Undiverse and Uninclusive. In *Reclaiming Economics for Future Generations*, ed. J. Earle, L. Amber, and N. Scott, 23–54. Manchester: Manchester University Press.

Agunsoye, A., L. Amber, J. Earle, M. Groenewald, D. Guizzo, K. Ramburuth-Hurt, and N. Scott. 2022b. Reforming Academia. In *Reclaiming Economics for Future Generations*, ed. J. Earle, L. Amber, and N. Scott, 203–241. Manchester: Manchester University Press.

Agunsoye, A., and H. James. 2022. I Had to Take Control: Gendered Finance Rationality in the UK. *Review of International Political Economy* 30(4):1486–1509.

Ajzenman, N., B. Ferman, and P. C. Sant'Anna. 2023. Discrimination in the Formation of Academic Networks: A Field Experiment on EconTwitter. IZA DP No. 15878. Bonn: Institute for Labor Economics.

Al-Bahrani, A. 2022. Classroom Management and Student Interaction Interventions: Fostering Diversity, Inclusion, and Belonging in the Undergraduate Economics Classroom. *The Journal of Economic Education* 53(3):259–272.

Allgood, S., L. Badgett, A. Bayer, M. Bertrand, S. E. Black, N. Bloom, and L. D. Cook. 2019. *AEA Professional Climate Survey: Final Report*. American Economic Association. Retrieved from https://www.aeaweb.org/resources/member-docs/final-climate-survey-results-sept-2019.

Asarta, C. J., R. G. Chambers, and C. Harter. 2021. Teaching Methods in Undergraduate Introductory Economics Courses: Results from a Sixth National Quinquennial Survey. *The American Economist* 66(1):18–28.

Ashencaen Crabtree, S., and C. Shiel. 2019. Playing Mother: Channeled Careers and the Construction of Gender in Academia. *Sage Open* 9(3).

Avilova, T., and C. Goldin. 2018. What can UWE do for Economics? *NBER Working Paper* 24189. Retrieved from https://www.nber.org/system/files/working_papers/w24189/w24189.pdf.

Bateman, V., D. K. Gamage, E. Hengel, and X. Liu. 2021. *The Gender Imbalance in UK Economics*. London: Royal Economic Society.

Bayer, A., and C. E. Rouse. 2016. Diversity in the Economics Profession: A New Attack on an Old Problem. *Journal of Economic Perspectives* 30(4):221–242.

Bayer, A., and D. W. Wilcox. 2019. The Unequal Distribution of Economics Education: A Report on the Race, Ethnicity, and Gender of Economics Majors at U.S. Colleges and Universities. *The Journal of Economic Education* 50(3):299–320.

Bayer, A., S. P. Bhanot, E. T. Bronchetti, and S. A. O'Connell. 2020. Diagnosing the Learning Environment for Diverse Students in Introductory Economics: An Analysis of Relevance, Belonging, and Growth Mindsets. *AEA Papers and Proceedings* 110:294–98.

Berik, G., and Y. Rodgers. 2023. Teaching Development Economics From a Gender Perspective. *The Journal of Economic Education* 54(1):60–75.

Berland, O., O. Harman, and N. Moreau-Kastler. 2022. Female Representation in Economics. Retrieved from https://ideas.repec.org/top/female.html#cohort.

Boring, A., and S. Zignago. 2018. Economics: Where are the Women? *Banque de France Eco Notepad*, July 3 Retrieved from. https://blocnotesdeleco.banquefrance.fr/en/blogentry/economics-where-are-women.

Card, D., S. Della Vigna, P. Funk, and N. Iriberri. 2020. Are Referees and Editors in Economics Gender Neutral? *Quarterly Journal of Economics* 135(1):269–327.

Charles, J. B. 2023. The Evolution of DEI. *The Chronicle of Higher Education*, June 23 Retrieved from https://www-chronicle-com.library.norwich.edu/article/the-evolution-of-dei.

The Chronicle of Higher Education. 2025. DEI Legislation Tracker. *The Chronicle of Higher Education*, April 4 Retrieved from https://www-chronicle-com/article/here-are-the-states-where-lawmakers-are-seeking-to-ban-colleges-dei-efforts.

Choat, S., C. Wolf, and S. O'Neill. 2023. Decolonising Economics and Politics Curricula in UK Universities. *Studies in Higher Education* 1–15.

Cook, L., and A. G. Opoku-Agyeman. 2019. Opinion: It Was a Mistake for Me to Choose This Field. *New York Times*, September 30.

Retrieved from https://www.nytimes.com/2019/09/30/opinion/economics-black-women.html.

Colander, D. 2005. The Making of an Economist Redux. *Journal of Economic Perspectives* 1(Winter):175–198.

Coyle, D. 2012. The Paradox of Popularity in Economics. *Journal of Economic Methodology* 19(3):187–192.

CSMGEP. 2019. *Report of the Committee on the Status of Minority Groups in the Economics Profession*. American Economic Association, December 2018. Retrieved from https://www.aeaweb.org/content/file?id=9030.

Darity, W. 2022. Alternatives to the Scarcity Principle. *The Journal of Economic Education* 53(4):340–347.

Dupas, P., A. Sasser Modestino, M. Niederle, and J. Wolfers, The Seminar Dynamics Collective. 2021. Gender and the Dynamics of Economics Seminars. *NBER Working Paper Series* 28494. Retrieved from http://www.nber.org/papers/w28494.

Dutton, C. 2025. In Trump's First Weeks, Dozens of Colleges Have Shut Down DEI Efforts. *The Chronicle of Higher Education,* 5 March. Retrieved from https://www.chronicle.com/article/in-trumps-first-weeks-dozens-of-colleges-have-shut-down-dei-efforts.

Eswaran, M. 2014. *Why Gender Matters in Economics*. Princeton: Princeton University Press.

Everett, S., and K. Linton. 2023. Decolonisation and Diversification of the Curriculum in UK Business Schools. Retrieved from https://charteredabs.org/decolonisation-and-diversi%EF%AC%81cation-of-the-curriculum-in-uk-business-schools/.

Exec. Order No. 14151. 2025. Retrieved from https://www.govinfo.gov/content/pkg/DCPD-202500118/html/DCPD-202500118.htm.

Exec. Order No. 14173. 2025. Retrieved from https://www.govinfo.gov/content/pkg/FR-2025-01-31/pdf/2025-02097.pdf.

Fourcade, M., E. Ollie, and Y. Algan. 2015. The Superiority of Economics. *Journal of Economic Perspectives* 29(1):89–114.

Fox, C. W., C. S. Burns, A. D. Muncy, and J. A. Meyer. 2017. Author-Suggested Reviewers: Gender Differences and Influences on the Peer Review Process at an Ecology Journal. *Functional Ecology* 31(1):270–280.

Freire, P. 1970. *Pedagogy of the Oppressed*. London: Penguin Random House.

Freire, P., and D. P. Macedo. 2014. *Pedagogy of the Oppressed*. Translated by Myra Bergman Ramos. 30th Anniversary ed. New York, NY: Bloomsbury Academic, an Imprint of Bloomsbury Publishing.

Gabster, B. P., K. van Daalen, R. Dhatt, and M. Barry. 2020. Challenges for the Female Academic during the Covid-19 Pandemic. *The Lancet* 395(10242):1968–1970.

Gamage, D. K., A. Sevilla, and S. Smith. 2020. Women in Economics: A UK Perspective. *Oxford Review of Economic Policy* 56(3):633–689.

González Stokas, A. 2023. Higher ed's DEI lip service. *The Chronicle of Higher Education*, May 4. Retrieved from https://www.chronicle.com/article/higher-eds-dei-lip-service.

Ghodsee, K. 2019. *Why Women Have Better Sex Under Socialism: And Other Arguments for Economic Independence.* London: Vintage.

Grady, J. 2015. Gendering Pensions: Making Women Visible. *Gender, Work & Organization* 22(5):445–458.

Guizzo, D. 2024. Inclusivity in Economics: The Role of Herstories in Economic Thought. *Contributions to Political Economy* 43(1):165–187.

Harter, C., and C. J. Asarta. 2022. Teaching Methods in Undergraduate Intermediate Theory, Statistics and Econometrics, and Other Upper-Division Economics Courses: Results from a Sixth National Quinquennial Survey. *The American Economist* 67(1):132–146.

Helmer, M., M. Schottdorf, A. Neef, and D. Battaglia. 2017. Gender Bias in Scholarly Peer Review. *ELife* 6:1–18.

Hengel, E. 2022. Publishing While Female. Are Women Held to Higher Standards? Evidence from Peer-Review. *The Economic Journal* 132(648):2951–2991.

Hooks, B. 1994. *Teaching to Transgress: Education as the Practice of Freedom.* New York: Routledge.

Kuiper, E. 2022. *A Herstory of Economics*. Cambridge: Polity Press.

Kvangraven, I. H., and S. Kesar. 2023. Standing in the Way of Rigor? Economics' Meeting with the Decolonization Agenda. *Review of International Political Economy* 30(5):1723–1748.

May, A. M., M. G. McGarvey, and D. Kucera. 2018. Gender and European Economic Policy: A Survey of the Views of the European Economists on Contemporary Economic Policy. *Kyklos* 71:162–183.

Mearman, A., D. Guizzo, and S. Berger. 2018. Whither Political Economy? Evaluating CORE Project as a Response to Calls for Change in Economics Teaching. *Review of Political Economy* 30(2):241–259.

Nelson, J. A. 2018. *Economics for Humans*, 2nd ed. Chicago: The University of Chicago Press.

OECD. 2017. *Systems Approaches to Public Sector Challenges*. Paris: OECD Publishing.

OfS. 2018. *Equality and Diversity Objectives for the Office for Students*. Retrieved from https://www.officeforstudents.org.uk/media/eed00cc0-ea32-4cca-9838-9b668cfe5e47/ofs-edi-action-plan-2019-22.pdf.

Paredes, V., M. D. Paserman., and F. J. Pino. 2023. Does Economics Make You Sexist? *The Review of Economics and Statistics*, July 24:1–47.

Porter, C., and D. Serra. 2020. Gender Differences in the Choice of Major: The Importance of Female Role Models. *American Economic Journal: Applied Economics* 12(3):226–254.

Power, M. 2004. Social Provisioning as a Starting Point for Feminist Economics. *Feminist Economics* 10(3):3–19.

Rugaber, C. 2023. Economics Website is Filled with Racist and Sexist Speech, Some Blame the Nation's Top Universities. *AP*. Retrieved from https://apnews.com/article/hate-speech-economics-website-posts-universities.

Santos, G., and S. D. van Phu. 2019. Gender and Academic Rank in the UK. *Sustainability* 11(11):3171.

Sarsons, H., K. Gërxhani, E. Reuben, and A. Schram. 2021. Gender Differences in Recognition for Group Work. *Journal of Political Economy* 129(1):101–147.

Shackelford, J. 1992. Feminist Pedagogy: A Means for Bringing Critical Thinking, and Creativity to the Economics Classroom. *American Economic Review* 82(2):570–576.

Small, S. F. 2023. Infusing Diversity in a History of Economic Thought Course: An Archival Study of Syllabi and Resources for Redesign. *Eastern Economic Journal* 49:276–311.

Stephen, J. S., N. D. Barnett, and A. A. Ben Ramadan. 2023. Diversity, Equity and Inclusion in Course Design and Instructional Material Development. In *Global Perspectives on Higher Education*, ed. J. S. Stephen, G. Kormpas, and C. Coombe, vol. 11, 147–161. Knowledge Studies in Higher Education. Springer.

Stevenson, B., and Zlotnik. 2018. Representations of Men and Women in Introductory Economics Textbooks. *AEA Papers and Proceedings* 108(May):180–185.

Strenio, J. 2023. Diversifying the "Great Economists": An Assignment to Promote Inclusivity and Belongingness in Introductory Economics Courses. *Review of Political Economy* 35(3):650–665.

Strenio, J., and Y. Rodgers. 2023. Integrating Gender Into a Labour Economics Class. *Advances in Economics Education* 2(1):26–44.

Sümer, S., and H. Elsen-Ziya. 2022. Academic Women's Voices on Gendered Divisions of Work and Care: 'Working Till I Drop…Then Dropping.' *European Journal of Women's Studies* 30(1):49–65.

University of Oxford. 2023. What is EDI and Why Does it Matter? Retrieved from https://edu.admin.ox.ac.uk/what-is-edi-and-why-does-it-matter.

Wu, A. 2018. Gendered Language on the Economics Job Market Rumors Forum. *AEA Papers and Proceedings* 108:175–79.

Place and Space for Feminist Economists? The Development and Maintenance of Feminist Economics Graduate Training in the United States

Sarah F. Small and *Teresa Perry*

1 Introduction

Feminist economics has a long history of being marginalized within the economics discipline and continues to be peripheral to mainstream economics (Pearse and Keane 2023). This trend partially reflects the marginalization of women and women's economic issues in the wider discipline itself. While several researchers have recently examined the role of women faculty in economics, feminist economists have long argued that the marginalization of women in the discipline has limited the methods and scope of economics research, policy, and teaching pedagogy (Cardel et al. 2020).

S. F. Small (✉)
Department of Economics, University of Utah, Salt Lake City, UT, USA
e-mail: sarah.small@utah.edu

T. Perry
Department of Economics, California State University San Bernardino, San Bernardino, CA, USA
e-mail: Teresa.Perry@csusb.edu

© The Author(s), under exclusive license to Springer Nature Switzerland AG 2026

V. Dolar and T. Perry (eds.), *Missing Voices in Economics*,
https://doi.org/10.1007/978-3-031-97180-8_7

Broadly, feminist economists suggest the questions economists ask are often very focused on a masculine experience. For example, feminist economists have challenged the mainstream's understanding of work, encouraging them to consider not just paid market work, but also unpaid care and socially reproductive work. Feminist economists have also long argued that economics' obsession with quantitative approaches is anti-feminist and obscures many important aspects of economic life (Tejani 2019).

Unlike other social sciences, economics has largely ignored the concerns of feminists in their own field (Pearse and Keane 2023). However, taking the concerns of feminist economists more seriously has the potential to attract more women to the discipline—a timely issue given economics' long-standing issue with including women in the field (Forget 2011). For this reason, we examine how feminist economists have started and sustained feminist economics within economics graduate programs across the United States.

Inclusion of feminist approaches in graduate training prepares future economists to take women's economic issues more seriously, perhaps making the field more relevant and inviting to women broadly. Courses about feminist economics highlight the importance of these approaches in the economic discipline and graduate teaching faculty who self-identify as feminist economists can mentor and advise dissertations on feminist economic topics, encouraging the next generation of researchers.

Since the institutionalization of feminist economics in the 1990s a handful of graduate economics programs in the United States have, at one point or another, included feminist approaches in graduate instruction (Espinel and Betancourt 2022). For example, the University of Utah, American University, Colorado State University, and the University of Massachusetts at Amherst currently have either PhD-level courses or certificates with feminist economics foci or have graduate teaching faculty self-identifying as feminist economists. Some master's level programs, like those at University of Massachusetts at Boston, Wright State University, the Levy Institute at Bard College, Denver University, and John Jay College CUNY, have also included feminist economic courses or self-identified feminist faculty teaching at the graduate level at one point or another in the past couple decades.

In this chapter we ask: how exactly do feminist economic approaches take root in economics graduate programs? And how do we keep them from losing their footing? Ultimately, through our oral history collection, we find that that feminist economics took root in graduate programs partially in tandem with heterodox economics: heterodox economics is a school of thought that embraces ideas outside of mainstream economic theory (for instance, Marxian, institutionalism, post-Keynesian, etc.). However, many also relied on support from gender studies departments and colleagues in labor economics. Patterns also emerged indicating that feminist economists have largely relied on one another across universities and cohorts to maintain the discipline's status in graduate programs, generating their own conferences, communities, and funding opportunities when their home departments provided minimal resources or support. We conclude with specific action items a faculty member might take to maintain or begin incorporating feminist economics in their department's graduate program.

2 Data and Methods

We collect and analyze oral histories from ten tenured or emeritus feminist economists with current or former affiliations with the aforementioned graduate programs. We consider an economist as a feminist economist if they indicate so on their university profiles or publications, or if they have published in the journal *Feminist Economics* at least twice. To ensure that they do not face repercussions within their field, university, or department, we keep participants anonymous and only interviewed scholars who were retired or who had tenure or emeritus status. Tenure is especially important for research such as this because it has traditionally protected academic freedom (Tiede 2018).

Oral histories were collected over Zoom or in-person over hour-long semi-structured interviews. We asked questions with an intent to understand how feminist economics has made its way into graduate-level economics programs in the United States and how it has been sustained or pushed out of such programs. Namely, we examined questions of hiring, retention, and tenure among feminist economics faculty within graduate-level economics departments. We also asked questions about broader institutionalization of feminist economics in the programs, including aspects of course and certificate development, relationships with gender studies departments, and funding to support graduate students. We began most interviews asking oral history narrators to describe how they came to feminist economics, which we begin with below.

3 How Faculty Came to Feminist Economics

Many of our interviewees began their careers before the founding of the International Association for Feminist Economics (IAFFE) in the early 1990s. For this group of scholars, they came to feminist economics largely because of their own interests as feminists, and then eventually applied it to economics with a coalition of their peers. Some came from more mainstream economics departments like Stanford while others came from traditionally heterodox departments like UMass Amherst. In both types of departments, many feminist economists faced barriers in pursuing work related to gender in their dissertations and ultimately many completed their PhD having done little writing on gender or feminism. Narrators suggested that the barriers often came from faculty, where they faced sexism on an individual level, and their research interests in feminism were often denounced as illegitimate. This is corroborated in Kim's (2023) recent work. However, many of those we interviewed emphasized that comradery with their fellow graduate students and interdisciplinarity in their training allowed them to pursue feminist economics on the side. Indeed, some explicitly noted classes or individual faculty outside the economics department were far more willing to support their interests in feminist economics.

Finding community was essential for many of our narrators, especially in the beginning of their careers. For example, one prominent feminist economist that we interviewed was roommates in graduate school with a woman who would also later become another important feminist economist. Combined, the two eventually worked as faculty in three PhD granting programs in the United States. As graduate students, the two young scholars spent many hours discussing material from their courses and applying feminist concepts to it, but struggled to find a home in their largely mainstream department:

> I was taking economics classes, she was two years ahead of me [in the program], but we ended up being roommates...and we were talking about women. And she introduced me to feminist theory—the very Western family theory books by Kate Millet and all that. So, it was very interesting for me to read about...That kind of opened my mind about looking at things with a different lens. Now that said, both she and I were taking mainstream economics. There was probably one heterodox economist there, but for the most part it was all mainstream. And when I expressed that I was interested in gender, I was told, 'Oh, you should take either

> health or population. I mean, if you're ever going to do economics, the only two areas that will be open to you would be health or population'. Well in these, women are thought of more as an instrument...So I said I'll just get my degree and do my [feminist] work after I get my degree. And that's basically what she and I did.

Other young feminist economists of the era were lucky to live in areas where feminist and activist groups were strong and found community in those spaces: one specifically mentioned lesbian activist groups in her state, while another noted women's organizations in her home country fighting Martial Law. For other scholars, they found spaces in economics through organizations like the Union for Radical Political Economy's (URPE's) Women's Caucus and the American Economic Association's Committee on the Status of Women in the Economics Profession (CSWEP), though many of them eventually left these organizations to begin IAFFE (Cohen 2019). Many narrators discussed the very first IAFFE meeting in Washington DC as a formative experience.

4 Getting Hired as a Feminist Economist

Ultimately, this is also how they built feminist economics in economics graduate departments: by creating their own community and networks and uplifting the profile of feminist economics through these connections. But first, they had to get jobs in PhD and masters granting departments.

Some scholars we interviewed secured positions in their departments through strong gender studies programs in their university at the time: two expressed that this swayed the intellectual identity of the university and upper administration in their favor during hiring and promotion. Another indicated that she began her career with a dual appointment in gender studies and economics before managing to move to the economics department full-time. Still, this came with its own set of challenges:

> Holding a joint appointment came with difficulties: attending two sets of faculty meetings, participating in curriculum issues, hiring in two departments. Another difficulty became apparent over time as my salary lagged behind Economics colleagues of the same rank. Due to the lower base salary and slower growth rate in the Women's Studies half of my salary...In 2009, as I was promoted to full professor rank, I requested to move to a full line in Economics, and this happened with the support from the Dean, the Department chair, and VP of Diversity, Director of Gender Studies.

Aside from this scholar, the rest of those we interviewed were initially hired in economics departments under listings for fields that were not explicitly feminist or gender economics. Namely, most feminist economists had been hired in these PhD and masters granting departments for their secondary interests like macroeconomics, development, finance, international political economy, labor, etc. In fact, we would be remiss if we did not note that many of these scholars, especially those in PhD granting departments, have scholarly expertise in macroeconomics. While it is possible that there are preferences for macroeconomists in such departments, our interviewers suggested some of their success can be traced back to the International Working Group on Gender, Macroeconomics, and International Economics (GEM-IWG).

In 1994, Nilüfer Çagatay, Diane Elson, and Caren Grown founded the International Working Group on Gender, Macroeconomics, and International Economics (GEM-IWG) (Elson and Grown 2023). At the time, Nilüfer herself was just three years into her role at the University of Utah after working at the New School earlier in her career: two departments which now have reputations for graduate work in feminist economics. Caren Grown was economist-in-residence and co-director of the Program on Gender Analysis in Economics at American University and was senior scholar and co-director of the Gender Equality and Economy Program at the Levy Economics Institute at Bard College. Between them, these two women were instrumental in institutionalizing feminist economics within four graduate-degree programs in economics. Then came the participants GEM-IWG's regular summer schools: multiple narrators indicated they had participated in the summer schools, which often took place at the University of Utah (sometimes with outside funding from the Ford and Macarthur Foundations) (Elson and Grown 2023). In fact, one narrator indicated that this group was the only safe space for her to think about issues of unpaid work, even in a department with others working on gender:

> The group Nilufer, Diane, and Caren put together in the early '90 s was actually a safe place for me to pursue this idea. I could not pursue it in the department. Nobody was supporting me there and there were not very many international organizations or agencies at that time interested in this topic. So even though it was focused on macro, Nilufer in particular saw there was an importance of bringing time unpaid work and linking it with macro.

Another narrator indicated that shortly after she was hired as faculty in her department, she attended one of the summer schools, met another macroeconomist in the field, and pushed for her hire just a year later. Indeed, this is often how hires were made when feminist economists could not convince their more mainstream colleagues to post listings explicitly for feminist or gender economics: they relied on connections made in IAFFE and GEM-IWG and rallied their support behind a feminist economist who might fit the bill of one another, agreed upon subfield listing. In fact, one narrator suggested that she has never been able to convince her colleagues to put out a call for nor hire a person labeled solely as a 'feminist economist' but has instead had to get them hired under a different subfield.

Many of the narrators suggested that, when they were hired or when they pushed to hire more feminist economists, heterodox colleagues in the department were often more open than mainstream colleagues:

> It was a pluralist department, so people were supportive. If it was a mainstream department, I never would've survived and would've just left.

Others noted that having women as department chairs or deans often helped the process along, as they were often interested in hiring more women in the department.

5 Getting Tenure as a Feminist Economist

> It was a big uphill struggle...Just being a woman, period, was a big problem, let alone the topic you chose to work on.

Marlene Kim has documented challenges feminist economists have faced getting tenure and staying in economics departments overall (Kim 2023). Our interviews with those in graduate-degree granting departments largely corroborated Kim's findings. Namely, some were denied tenure at their institutions and pursued legal suits to overturn the decisions, though this came with their own challenges and hostilities. A narrator who was able to win her tenure case said,

> Someone asked me, how can I return to a department with a chair that denied me tenure? I said, I am not going to waste my time on negative

> energy. There is so much work to be done on gender and all the problems of the world....There is time use data to be analyzed!...Eventually we all moved on.

Others noted that hostilities followed them throughout the time in their department, costing them their health and happiness, with one narrator even pointing to intra-department tensions as contributing to her feminist colleague's cancer diagnosis.

Some scholars were unsuccessful in overturning their tenure denials and jumped from department to department for decades. Though this job instability was a challenge for those individuals, they were able to plant feminist seeds in several economics departments, often establishing undergraduate and graduate courses that stayed on the books for years after.

Scholars we interviewed who were employed in heterodox programs often noted that their departments had a policy that journal rank and type were not important in the tenure process, which allowed them to publish interdisciplinarity and with a feminist focus. However, some noted that even if this was the policy on paper, colleagues often wanted the prestige of a top ten journal publication when junior faculty went up for review. Others summarily indicated that these types of metrics did not really matter at all at the end of the day: if the department did not want a feminist economist, they would find a way to deny tenure.

Still, many have argued that IAFFE's journal *Feminist Economics* provided and continues to provide a high-quality and high-ranked outlet in economics and has been instrumental in helping feminist scholars get tenure (Small and Braunstein 2024). Among our interviewees, many also noted journals like *World Development* and *Review of Radical Political Economics* as key outlets to publish feminist economics work. Some suggested that writing books also allowed them more intellectual freedom while still counting toward promotion and tenure.

Among those in more mainstream departments and those whose careers began before *Feminist Economics* was well established, their tenure strategy was often to publish twice as much as they needed to get tenure: half in feminism, half in mainstream. This way, even if their department and university just looked at the publications they felt were true 'economics' (as opposed to feminist economics), they would still win tenure:

> It was an all-male and fairly progressive department. But they basically said in the letter giving me tenure they had no idea what to do with this feminist stuff but on the basis of my more mainstream work, yes, they would give me tenure. So they were tolerant, they didn't seem to count it against me, but the department as a whole was not willing to take it as a contribution.

6 Making Feminist Economics Part of Graduate Programs in Economics

Ultimately, getting jobs in R1 and R2 universities and keeping those jobs through tenure have been half the battle for feminist economists looking to institutionalize feminist perspectives in economics graduate programs. The second half of the battle was establishing feminist economics in the graduate degrees through courses, certificates, formal field designations, and completed dissertations and theses.

Throughout our interviews, themes emerged which showed distinct differences in strategies among feminist economists in master's programs and in PhD programs. Namely, many of the terminal master's programs were newly established while our narrators were active in their departments: this is in line with recent research suggesting that university offerings of master's programs have exploded nationwide in the last several decades (June 2022). Many indicated that their terminal master's programs were designed with specific intent to be training spaces for students with an interest in progressive policy. In fact, one narrator explained that to establish and accredit the master's program in her department, the state's department of higher education required they show how the economics master's would be different from others in public universities across the state. In this case, the program's unique feature was that it was designed with a focus on social economics rather than just applied economics. This meant that political economy could be more easily integrated into the curriculum, though she noted that they have faced challenges maintaining the gender component of the program due to low enrollment.

How did gender and feminist approaches make their way into these new, often socially progressive, master's programs and into established PhD programs? Our interviews uncovered two main mechanisms: first, because they already had feminist economics faculty in the department and second, because those faculty had already successfully added undergraduate-level gender and feminist economics courses.

Institutionalizing feminist economics within doctoral programs was challenging. Among all our oral history interviewees, none had arrived at their programs before the department's doctoral program was established. Therefore, they had to alter the curriculum of the doctoral programs working with what was already the norm and without designing the graduate curriculum from scratch. In most PhD programs, this happened slowly and through several different strategies. One strategy was that feminist economics faculty would be assigned a course that was already on the books and would include feminist components in the syllabus. For instance, one narrator indicated they added a gender component when they took over a political economy course. In more mainstream departments, some specifically looked to labor economics courses to add gender components and then branch off new courses from there. As one scholar described, labor was one avenue in which her colleagues could most easily see why gender was relevant:

> [In 1988], it was being taught nowhere...There was a view that the only difference between men and women in the economy is in the labor force. That's it. Nothing else.

Another strategy was to team up with others doing work on inequality and create a related field. For instance, one narrator discussed how she partnered with a Marxist economist in her department to create a new two-course field for PhD students on political economy: including her course on race and gender and a Marxian approaches course. Two others indicated they had teamed up with fellow faculty working on labor to create a connected sequence of PhD-level electives on labor and gender. This is not especially surprising given that the research in feminist economics has tended to overlap with Marxist and labor economics: for instance, Hartmann wrote on the 'unhappy marriage' of Marxism and feminism, and more recently Brewer wrote on the intersection between stratification economics, labor economics, and feminist economics (Hartmann 1979).

Almost all the scholars we interviewed highlighted the success of their undergraduate gender economics courses as a pipeline for eventually motivating graduate-level courses. Most of the faculty were more easily able to get an undergraduate-level gender economics on the books, so they began there. Then, after the departments had seen the success of undergraduate courses on gender in the economy, and if they had the faculty to devote to a graduate-level class, many incorporated gender in their graduate curricula. Interestingly, the undergrad courses' enrollment was often supported by diversity initiatives either at the university or within higher education more broadly:

> ...[We] applied for a teaching grant at the University to attend a Diversifying the Curriculum workshop at Wellesley College in June 1995. This was a one-week workshop, the end product of which was our Political Economy of Race, Class, and Gender course, which [we] started offering in 1996. When the diversity requirement was introduced at the University, I recall doing the paperwork (justifications) for [the undergraduate course].

Indeed, enrollments were often a key component discussed by our narrators. University budget models often require high enrollments to offer a class and keep it on the books. Some enrollments in feminist economics classes, at both the undergraduate and graduate levels, have also been supported by cross-listing with gender studies programs, but our narrators indicated that this did little by way of actual support for the programs. Some explained that this was because gender studies programs were offering similar (and therefore redundant) courses. Some also perceived that gender studies departments were consistently under-resourced and unsupported by universities, so their cross-listing did little to boost support of the feminist focus in the economics department.

7 Funding Feminist Economics

When asked about how they maintained (or were unable to maintain) feminist economics as a pillar of the graduate-degree program in their departments, many of our narrators pointed to issues of university funding. Many noted funding from external sources was essential to sustaining graduate programs. For example, several programs specifically target grants and consultancies so that they could use the funds to cover graduate students' tuition and stipends. Many of these grants came from organizations like Hewlett, the Institute for New Economic Thinking (INET), the Ford Foundation, and even IAFFE.

Support from universities for feminist economics in graduate programs was few and far between. Some PhD granting programs offered feminist economics faculty support in the form of course releases or research assistantship funding when they held high-up roles in IAFFE such as journal editor or president. Others found support in diversity initiatives on campus but noted that these tend to flow with political currents, and very few resources are devoted to issues concerning gender with other pressing issues like racism and the environment taking the fore in scholarly funding.

8 Maintaining A Feminist…Or Gender… Or Labor Identity

Scholars in feminist economics are well aware of the distinction between gender and feminist economics: gender economics is often more influenced by mainstream methods and considers gender differences in a given economic context without more explicit examinations of power. Feminist economics always centers intersectionality, social provisioning (including unpaid work), and patriarchy and power (Power 2004; Small and Braunstein 2024). Given these differences, how do faculty and economics departments decide how courses should be labeled? When asked about whether they ever encountered debates over using 'feminist' or 'gender' in their course titles, very few indicated this was even a consideration. Given debates over gender versus feminist economics, we found this a bit surprising. However, as one faculty member explained, they wanted their program to be attractive globally, and with different interpretations of 'feminism', they thought 'gender' would be a more fitting in the courses and field title in their graduate program:

> When we began in 2008, the word feminism had a particular lens to it. A lot of the faculty at that time still thinking the feminist movement is like burning the bra, going for the pill kind of thing. And it's very Western: the word feminist also was not used very often in the gender and development field because the word 'feminist' seems to have come from the Western perspective. And a lot of women's groups in the South are very, you know, sort of very cautious in just adopting everything from the West. So, we wanted this to be international. We wanted the program to have an international focus and also to have an international presence. If we had used the feminist term at the beginning, we might not be able to open doors. We can't even talk to them, let alone convince them to come to our program. So, we decided to use 'gender'.

Reflecting on present day, the narrator commented that now feminist economics is more established and recognized, and she asserted that groups in the South have further developed their own understanding of what feminism means to them, so she was not sure whether this decision would stand if it were made today.

Broader systemic changes in the university have also forced the word 'feminist' out of course names. As one faculty put it, changes from upper administration budget models forced the feminist economics courses to be trimmed, lumped with labor economics, and renamed 'gender' from 'feminist':

> From the start, feminist economics was a two-course field, and we offered these courses every other year. In the early 2000s, due to the Dean's restriction of the size of admitted PhD students, the Department had difficulty in staffing certain PhD electives every other year. This led to the curriculum revision that cut some two-course fields to a one-course field or to combine related fields to create a new sequence. Feminist Economics was combined with Labor Economics. I believe it was at that point that the single feminist economics field course in the sequence was relabeled Gender...based on the notion that the gender focus was the shared content.

Indeed, many feminist economists we interviewed dealt with being lumped into labor economics, even if they did not study labor:

> I didn't teach a gender related course while I was there, but they put me on labor economics because any woman could teach labor economics, right? [laughs] I mean, it wasn't my field, but I worked some gender related stuff in.

However, in the experiences of our narrators, it was often the labor economists who were friendly to incorporating notions of gender and feminism into their courses and often sparked debates within departments that helped bring feminist economics into the fore.

Indeed, many of our narrators suggested that interplay and conversation with others in their department brought them over to feminist economics. One described it as 'feminism by osmosis', with another describing it like a 'lake effect':

> [They] said to me that in Wisconsin there some 'Lake Effect'...where because it was this institutionalist and fairly progressive graduate program, you went there and became like that even if you didn't start out like that. And I think that happens that happens here. We hire plenty of people weren't leftist, but then they come and I think they start asking better questions...We just had somebody who was really good and I remember when I interviewed her and told her that we have feminist economists here and she said, 'What? What is that? I've never heard of that, but I think I would like it.' And she did!

9 Threats on the Horizon

Many of our narrators expressed concern over looming crises in university funding and budget models. In fact, many of our narrators had the perception that their university was purely focused on money and had little interest in the intellectual project of feminist economics.

> They only look at this from a money-making kind of approach and didn't see the real value of the program to innovative knowledge construction and to training scholars in this area. So that remains a disappointment for me.

Another narrator noted that within the research arm of their department, the gender program was soft funded and relied on a steady flow of grants, while other aspects of research in the department were supported by the institution. Indeed, funding threats from increasingly neoliberal university budget models was a concern among many of our narrators, and seems to be a concern among scholars in feminism across disciplines (Acker and Wagner 2019). One narrator in particular also noted that the closing of small liberal arts colleges across the country was of concern, since many PhDs with feminist economics training are housed there.

This also speaks to issues of pipeline problems that many interviewees raised: with only a few PhD programs training feminist economists, will departments with graduate programs interested in maintaining their feminist identity be able to find economists to fill faculty positions? One interviewee whose department recently hired in feminist economics indicated this was a problem, and said it was confounded by her mainstream colleague's disinterest in hiring job candidates who do anything other than causal econometrics:

> The feminist identity [of the graduate program] is threatened by the fact that there aren't that many feminist economists to hire...[Whenever we tried to hire someone,] The 'straight' people in the department, who were very sympathetic to the project, would always find fault with their empirical technique because that's what they learned. That's what mainstream economics programs are teaching: technique. And that's all they care about. And it seems like all they care about is causality, which is like, are you kidding me?

Another narrator from a PhD granting department offered similar concerns:

> If we had [in the applicant pool] a feminist economist or Marxian doing causal inference, that would be the holy grail!

Because part of feminist economics' core tenants is to embrace methodological plurality, the economics' disciplines obsession with causal econometrics can make it difficult for today's feminist economists to find footing in graduate-degree granting programs (Nelson 1995).

Relatedly, throughout our interviews, several universities across the United States were listed as having once housed a feminist economist or two, but many were in mainstream departments and were eventually pushed out. In turn, some narrators expressed concern that if their department lost its heterodox identity, it would lose its feminist identity as well, with one narrator going so far as to say,

> I do not foresee threats [to feminist economics remaining in the graduate program], provided heterodox faculty strength remains.

However, maintaining a heterodox identity is no guarantee that feminist economics will also be maintained. Several of our narrators pointed to the New School as a prime example of this issue: a department with a strong heterodox identity, but for many years devoted no real resources to hiring a tenure-line feminist economist. Any course offerings in feminist economics within the department have been filled by a parade of visiting, temporary professors, ultimately offering no stability for the subfield in the program. Others also noted that heterodox faculty could still be sexist and against the feminist project. One even noted that founding feminist economists Barbara Bergmann once exclaimed that "socialists are all sexist pigs." Ultimately, it seems that having a heterodox identity can help institutionalize feminist economics in a graduate program, but this is not always the case.

In a similar vein, feminist economists often feel isolated based on their area of research and their individual identity. Hiring women and women of color was another challenge that many of our interviewees discussed. One narrator said, "I didn't fully understand how underrepresented I would be." Many departments make decisions based on votes, and as the narrator's colleague pointed out, "you're just one vote." For underrepresented groups within the economics discipline, and when researchers study in smaller fields, like feminist economics, they are often left feeling isolated and unsupported.

10 Action Items for Starting or Maintaining Feminist Economics in a Graduate Program

Given the wisdom from our oral history collection, what have we gleaned by way of action items for maintaining or beginning feminist economics in graduate programs?

First, building community is essential: many forged alliances in their department, in IAFFE, in GEM-IWG, across their university with gender studies faculty, and across the world with global partnerships. Several departments began or sustained their graduate program's focus in feminist economics by fostering ties within their departments, even among those not trained or publishing on gender. Indeed, some indicated that several faculty who were not trained or published in feminist economics were interested in participating: "We formed a gender working group for graduate students working on their dissertations... I was surprised that about seven faculty members joined."

Some projects and programs were designed specifically with spreading feminist economics to other graduate programs. One interviewee also noted Susan Feiner's traveling feminist economics course, which originated in 1997 with funding from the Ford Foundation and brought Feiner and other feminist economics faculty to a handful of PhD granting programs across the United States to offer a for-credit course in feminist economics. American University has also leveraged funding from the Open Society Foundation to partner with universities across Asia and Latin America to develop curricula for teaching gender analysis in economics in a developing country context.

Second and relatedly, finding external funding is essential. Given the American higher education budget structure, it is unlikely scholars will find much internal support from the university for the feminist economics project. Many of our narrators relied on funding from organizations like IAFFE, INET, Hewlett, Ford, NHS, and Open Society to support graduate students and graduate programs. For instance, American University has also built community with the Institute for Women's Policy Research (IWPR), establishing a fellowship and postdoctoral pipeline with the institute for feminist economics graduate students.

Third, improving the number of graduate students interested in pursuing feminist economics is pivotal. This is often accomplished by piquing interest among undergraduates through undergraduate-level gender economics courses. Evidence from our other chapter in this book also shows these courses improve the likelihood an undergraduate woman takes more economics courses, which has the potential to improve gender diversity in the field more broadly.

Fourth, given concerns from the mainstream about the validity of non-causal quantitative work and qualitative work, feminist economists hoping to elevate the discipline need to support such work in their reviewing and citing. Many narrators indicated that hiring feminist economists was sometimes difficult when they were not doing causal work. Citing and otherwise supporting non-causal feminist literature is one way to elevate the status of these candidates (Borgman and Furner 2002).

Fifth, mentoring and recruiting is an essential component of keeping the feminist economics project alive in graduate programs in the United States and beyond. Many of our interviewees indicated mentoring was an essential part of their initial success and their jobs thereafter:

> I have to mention: I had mentors along the way. I think you cannot do this on your own, you know, especially if you're challenging whatever is the ongoing thinking. Whether it be a pluralist department or a mainstream department, you need to have that kind of support for space for you to be able to pursue those ideas and not be told this stupid or not a priority.
> I really took seriously my role as a professor. The mentoring part is very important. And when I work with a PhD student, I don't accept one unless I am very sure I can give the time to help them. And so that's basically passing forward to the next generation.

Lastly, many narrators suggested scholars hoping to convince their colleagues to institutionalize feminist economics in their graduate programs should simply lean on the importance of feminist economics. Namely, convince fellow faculty and administration that it is an important component: one narrator indicated that it would be a disservice to students to exclude gender analysis from economic study and would give students an incomplete portrayal. Another specifically took the angle of convincing heterodox departments, saying, "If you want to be a good leftist department, you have to have someone working on gender."

11 Conclusion

Ultimately, incorporating and maintaining feminist economics within graduate programs is important for improving the 'leaky pipeline' of women in economics. Broadly, speaking to issues that concern women will help pique their interest in the discipline and make it more relevant, which has been shown to be an important aspect of improving diversity in economics (Bayer et al. 2020). It is also important for the sake of future economics education and policy. Our oral history interviewees indicated that many of the feminist alum from their master's programs worked in state and local government and that many of alum from PhD programs worked in liberal arts colleges across the world. For these reasons, infiltrating and maintaining feminist economics and feminist faculty in graduate degrees is a surefire way to help feminist economics permeate throughout higher education and public policy.

References

Acker, Sandra, and Anne Wagner. 2019. Feminist Scholars Working Around the Neoliberal University. *Gender and Education* 31(1):62–81. https://doi.org/10.1080/09540253.2017.1296117.

Albelda, Randy. 1995. The Impact of Feminism in Economics—Beyond the Pale? A Discussion and Survey Results. *The Journal of Economic Education* 26(3):253–273. https://doi.org/10.1080/00220485.1995.10844877.

Bayer, Amanda, Syon P. Bhanot, Erin T. Bronchetti, and Stephen A. O'Connell. 2020. Diagnosing the Learning Environment for Diverse Students in Introductory Economics: An Analysis of Relevance, Belonging, and Growth Mindsets. In *AEA Papers and Proceedings*, vol. 110, 294–298. 2014 Broadway, Suite 305, Nashville, TN 37203: American Economic Association.

Borgman, Christine L., and Jonathan Furner. 2002. Scholarly Communication and Bibliometrics. *Annual Review of Information Science and Technology* 36(1):1–53.

Brewer, Rose M. 2016. Theorizing Race, Class, and Gender: The New Scholarship of Black Feminist Intellectuals and Black Women's Labor. In *Race, Gender and Class*, 58–64. Routledge.

Cardel, Michelle I., Emily Dhurandhar, Ceren Yarar-Fisher, Monica Foster, Bertha Hidalgo, Leslie A. McClure, and Sherry Pagoto et al. 2020. Turning Chutes into Ladders for Women Faculty: A Review and Roadmap for Equity in Academia. *Journal of Women's Health* 29(5):721–733. https://doi.org/10.1089/jwh.2019.8027.

Cohen, Jennifer. 2019. The Radical Roots of Feminism in Economics. In *Including A Symposium on 50 Years of the Union for Radical Political Economics*, vol. 37, 85–100. Emerald Publishing Limited. https://doi.org/10.1108/S0743-41542019000037A007.

Elson, Diane, and Caren Grown. 2023. Nilüfer Çagatay 1955–2022 In Memoriam. *Feminist Economics* 29(3):3–9. https://doi.org/10.1080/13545701.2023.2221264.

Espinel, Camila Orozco, and Rebeca Gomez Betancourt. 2022. A History of the Institutionalization of Feminist Economics Through Its Tensions and Founders. *History of Political Economy* 54(S1):159–192. https://doi.org/10.1215/00182702-10085682.

Forget, Evelyn L. 2011. American Women and the Economics Profession in the Twentieth century. *Œconomia. History, Methodology, Philosoph* 1–1:19–30. https://doi.org/10.4000/oeconomia.1807.

Hartmann, H. I. 1979. The Unhappy Marriage of Marxism and Feminism: Towards a More Progressive Union. *Capital & Class* 3(2):1–33. https://doi.org/10.1177/030981687900800102.

June, Audrey Williams. 2022. Higher ed Added More than 9,000 Master's-Degree Programs in Less Than a Decade. *The Chronicle of Higher Education* 68(15):2. https://www.chronicle.com/article/higher-ed-added-more-than-9-000-masters-degree-programs-in-less-than-a-decade.

Kim, Marlene. 2023. Gender in Economics Fifty Years Ago and Today: Feminist Economists Speak. *Review of Radical Political Economics* 55(1):8–25. https://doi.org/10.1177/04866134221093095.

Nelson, Julie A. 1995. Feminism and Economics. *Journal of Economic Perspectives* 9(2):131–148.

Pearse, Rebecca, and Helen Keane. 2023. How Feminist Knowledge is Made in and Beyond Disciplines. *Gender and Education* 35(1):1–17. https://doi.org/10.1080/09540253.2022.2137105.

Power, Marilyn. 2004. Social Provisioning as a Starting Point for Feminist Economics. *Feminist Economics* 10(3):3–19. https://doi.org/10.1080/1354570042000267608.

Small, Sarah F., and Elissa Braunstein. 2024. Has the Feminist Economics Intellectual Project Lost its Way? An Analysis of the Journal's Evolution. *Feminist Economics* 30(1):1–39. https://doi.org/10.1080/13545701.2023.2283468.

Tiede, Hans. 2018. The Front Rank: On Tenure and the Role of the Faculty in the Defense of Academic Freedom. *History of Education Quarterly* 58(3):441–447. https://doi.org/10.1017/heq.2018.21.

Tejani, Sheba. 2019. What's Feminist About Feminist Economics? *Journal of Economic Methodology* 26(2):99–117. https://doi.org/10.1080/1350178X.2018.1556799.

Can Gender Economics Courses Attract More Undergraduate Women to Economics Departments?

Teresa Perry and Sarah F. Small

Women are underrepresented at every level in the economics discipline (Buckles 2019; Bayer and Wilcox 2019). One primary reason for this may be because the discipline and curriculum is masculine-centered and often ignores many economic aspects of women's lives (Nelson 1995). Dynan and Rouse (1997) find that undergraduate women are less likely to perceive economics as interesting, and Noble Calkins and Welki (2006) find that perceived interest in the subject is a key factor in determining the choice of undergraduate economics major.

Therefore, we suggest that an undergraduate introductory class focused on economics and gender has the potential to attract a more diverse pool of undergraduate majors than traditional economics courses. In this study, we examine how enrollment in a Gender in the Economy

T. Perry (✉)
Department of Economics, California State University San Bernardino, San Bernardino, CA, USA
e-mail: Teresa.Perry@csusb.edu

S. F. Small
Department of Economics, University of Utah, Salt Lake City, UT, USA
e-mail: sarah.small@utah.edu

© The Author(s), under exclusive license to Springer Nature Switzerland AG 2026

V. Dolar and T. Perry (eds.), *Missing Voices in Economics*,
https://doi.org/10.1007/978-3-031-97180-8_8

class relates to the likelihood that undergraduate students take more introductory economics courses in the future. Our data is from Colorado State University, a large, public land-grant university whose economics department offers an introductory-level Gender in the Economy class, which has no prerequisites. For many students, the Gender in the Economy class is their first introduction to economics. While the topics covered in the course vary by instructor, several core topics are covered in most sections of the class. These include the care economy (including unpaid care work), household bargaining models, the wage gap, and the economics of discrimination.

Using registrar data from the university, we begin with a simple descriptive analysis to examine what percentage of students take additional economics courses after taking Gender in the Economy, what those additional economics courses are, and the demographic information of those students. This data was approved by the IRB at Colorado State University (Protocol #4595) and is anonymous. We also consider the importance of instructor characteristics, such as instructor race, ethnicity, gender, and faculty status, in influencing whether students of similar backgrounds take additional economics courses, which studies have shown is impactful (Bettinger and Long 2005). Finally, we develop an econometric model to understand whether the Gender in the Economy class is successful in encouraging undergraduate students to enroll in more economics courses, compared to other introductory-level courses in the department. The main results suggest that the Gender in the Economy class is indeed successful at driving interest in economics courses and majors among undergraduate students.

The goal of this chapter is to determine if more gender-aware economics curricula are capable of increasing interest and retention among undergraduates. We suggest that studying gender economics provides broader representations of economic actors and focuses on issues of inequality and social policy, which will better engage economics students and increase enrollment in subsequent economics courses, particularly among underrepresented populations.

1 Literature Review

Women, African American, Hispanic, and Native American students are seriously underrepresented in the economics profession in the United States. There are leaks at every stage of the professional pipeline, but increasing diversity among economics undergraduates is an important step toward ultimately increasing diversity in the economics profession. Bayer and Wilcox (2019) find that women and some students of color major in economics at a third of the rate of White, non-Hispanic men. The literature offers several explanations for—and possible solutions to—this underrepresentation.

Rask and Tiefenthaler (2008) use data from a liberal arts college to show that women are more responsive to their relative grades in economics than men. In other words, women who get lower grades in economics compared to their typical GPA are less likely to major in economics than men with similar experiences. Another study finds that students of color perform less well in introductory economics courses than their White counterparts and suggests that these relatively poor grades might discourage students from continuing their studies in economics (Emerson and English 2016). Some researchers blame inadequate math preparation for economics courses, often proxied by students' SAT/ACT scores or survey questions that ask students about their comfort level with math. However, others have found that math confidence explains a negligible part of the underrepresentation in economics by women and students of color (Emerson et al. 2012; Bayer and Rouse 2016).

Women and students of color may also feel excluded from the economics major due to underrepresentation among economics faculty. Carrell et al. (2010) analyze data from the US Air Force Academy, where students are randomly assigned to professors. They find that women students perform significantly better in introductory math and science courses if they are taught by women faculty, and these students are subsequently more likely to pursue majors in science, technology, engineering, or math. Fairlie et al. (2014) find similar effects for underrepresented students of color at a large community college. Similarly, Lusher et al. (2018) find that students perform better in the course when they have a teaching assistant of their race or ethnicity. Hale and Regev (2014) find that a larger share of women faculty leads to more women students entering economics PhD programs. Diversity in faculty also suggests diversity in modes of teaching and social ideology. For instance, Paredes et al. (2020) find that exposure to women faculty attenuates some of the sexist biases held by male economics students.

Curriculum redevelopment may also make economics more relevant to women and students of color. According to research by Dynan and Rouse

(1997), women are less likely to perceive economics as interesting. Noble Calkins and Welki (2006) argue that perceived interest in the subject is a key factor in determining the choice of undergraduate economics major. Bayer et al. (2020) find that women and students of color are more likely to report coursework being irrelevant.

The lack of interest in economics might result from the values explicitly or implicitly promoted in undergraduate economics courses. Jackstadt et al. (1985) find that introductory economics courses tend to make students more conservative than other university introductory courses. Paredes et al. (2020) find that incoming economics students in Chile hold more gender biases than other students and that this difference grows as students' progress through the program. Similarly, Fischer et al. (2017) show that students studying economics in German universities have more pro-market political attitudes than their peers. Other studies have examined whether economics makes students more selfish, with most studies concluding that economics students do behave more selfishly than other students (Gerlach 2017; Bauman and Rose 2011). Given the experiences of discrimination and inequity that many women and students of color face, it is possible that women and students of color are drawn more to studies of social issues in economics than men and White students. Studies suggest that broadening the curriculum in undergraduate economics courses may play a crucial role in the growth mindset of undergraduate students about economics.

The literature on gender economics courses specifically is sparse and many universities do not offer gender in the economics courses. However, Burnett (1997) found that institutions with a large economics department and a large female cohort were the most likely to offer economics courses with a focus on gender. Further, Bosshardt and Walstad (2017) examine the proportion of economics courses taken by economics majors: gender economics courses are so uncommon that they do not show up on their list. There is growing research about how to better incorporate gender into different economics courses (Berik and Rodgers 2022; Strenio and Rodgers 2023; Mukherjee 2018; Nelson and Goodwin 2009), but these are not stand-alone courses on gender or feminist economics alone. Therefore, this study intends to examine how a stand-alone gender economics course affects future course enrollment.

2 Data and Methods

This study investigates how a course that focuses on economic issues of gender, gender economics, and feminist economics might influence student's preferences to take future economic courses. Given the topic of the class and the lack of diversity in economics as a discipline, we also focus on how the Gender in the Economy course might impact future enrollment for other underrepresented minorities.

Colorado State University (CSU) is a land-grant public university located in Fort Collins, Colorado, with 26,559 undergraduates and 7,437 graduate students in the fall semester of 2020 (Institutional Research 2020). Most undergraduates (84%) are full-time students, and 53% of undergraduates identify as women. A large majority of CSU's undergraduates (70%) identify as White, although the University has increased its share of students of color in recent years. In 2020, 14.7% of the undergraduates identify as Hispanic or Latino, 2.8% identify as Asian, 2.4% identify as Black or African American, and less than one percent identify as American Indian, Alaskan Native, or Native Hawaiian. Another 4.7% of students identify as more than one race or ethnicity. We refer to the 29% of students who identify as Black, African American, Hispanic, Latino, Asian, or American Indian, Alaskan Native, Native Hawaiian, or multiple races as "students of color." This aggregation of course obfuscates the diverse experiences of students of varying racial and ethnic backgrounds, but it still offers a useful comparison to the hegemonic White group.

The Gender in the Economy course (ECON 211) at Colorado State University is defined in the course catalog as, "an introductory course which takes an interdisciplinary approach to examining ways in which gender, as a culturally defined concept, affects the economy." The course is offered in-person and online in an asynchronous format. There are no prerequisites for the course and many students across majors take it. The majority of students take Gender in the Economy courses in a class of 30 to 40 students. Students attend two weekly 75-minute lectures or three weekly 50-minute lectures with their instructor. The COVID-19 pandemic caused the sections in the Spring of 2020 to be moved online, but courses remained in person (with social distancing measures) starting in the Fall of 2021. Table 1 highlights the most common five majors in the Gender in the Economy course at CSU during our sample time.

While the course is not a prerequisite for the economics major, it counts as an elective for the major. Students from other majors take the

Table 1 Top 5 Majors in the gender in the economy course

Major	*Percentage (%)*
Economics	15.59
Animal science	6.46
Equine science	4.19
Psychology	3.71
Business administration	3.43

course because of word-of-mouth recommendations, third-party course and professor ranking websites, academic counselors, students who need to meet a GT-pathways general education requirement for the state of Colorado or the AUCC requirement for Diversity, Equity, and Inclusion, and scheduling. During this period, feminism experienced a resurgence in popular culture. For example, the #MeToo movement, which began in 2017, encouraged survivors of sexual assault and violence to share their experiences online (Quan-Haase et al. 2021). Although this study does not directly address such social movements, it is important to acknowledge that these events could have also influenced student interest in enrolling in the Gender and the Economy course.

Instructors have freedom in course design, but certain topics are often covered, including theories of gender, the neoclassical perspective, feminism, and feminist economics, labor markets in a gender context, social reproduction and care work, gender and poverty in the US, and women and globalization. The instructors for the course are overwhelmingly PhD students, with only 6% of students taking a Gender in the Economy course with a faculty member. Further, 55% of students took Gender in the Economy courses taught by female instructors and 63 took Gender in the Economy with instructors of US nationality. Of the students who took Gender in the Economy, 57% were taught by White instructors, less than 1% were taught by Black instructors, 25% were taught by Asian instructors, and 18% were taught by Hispanic instructors.

Table 2 reports the percentage of students who are women, students of color, first-generation college students, and Pell Grant recipients in economics courses, including the Gender in the Economy course as well as in Introductory and Intermediate Microeconomics and Macroeconomics courses. A similar percentage of students of color and Pell Grant students take the Introductory Microeconomics course and the Gender in the Economy course at CSU.

Table 2 Summary statistics

	Total	*Percentage (%)*
Gender in the economy		
Students of color	2912	26
Pell grant	2912	18
First generation	2912	29
Women	2912	64
Introductory microeconomics		
Students of color	10,467	25
Pell grant	10,467	15
First generation	10,467	22
Women	10,467	40
All economics courses		
Students of color	30,156	25
Pell grant	30,156	15
First generation	30,156	23
Women	30,156	42

Note This data is from the dataset used in this paper which consists of any student who has taken an economic course from Fall of 2016 to the Spring of 2022

However, the number of women students is significantly higher in the Gender in the Economy class than in the Introductory Microeconomics class. 60% of the students who take Gender in the Economy are women, while only 40% of the students in the introductory microeconomics course and 42% of students in any economics course are women. Therefore, simply having a gender economics course at Colorado State University has caused more women students to learn about economic theory. There are also about 6% more first-generation students that take the Gender in the Economy class over other economics courses.

We utilize a simple treatment strategy to analyze the effect of the Gender in the Economy class on the continuation of students in other introductory courses. We focus on other introductory courses because upper division economics courses require more prerequisites which students have not met if they have only taken one introductory economics class. The treated group is any student who took Gender in the Economy as their first economics course and the control group is any student who took one of the following courses as their first economics course: Racial Inequality and Discrimination, Issues in Environmental Economics, or Working with Data. Along with Gender in the Economy, these courses do not require any prerequisites and are available for any student at the university to take. Students who first took Introductory Microeconomics or Introductory Macroeconomics were excluded from the control group because most students who take Introductory Microeconomics are required to take it in conjunction with Introductory Macroeconomics for their major. Both courses are required for several majors and their inclusion biases the sample.

The dependent variable is a binary variable, which is 1 if a student takes another introductory economics course after their initial introductory class, and 0 if they took any introductory course at CSU but no additional economics course. The other introductory classes are Introductory Microeconomics, Introductory Macroeconomics, Gender in the Economy, Race Inequality and Discrimination, Issues in Environmental Economics, and Working with Data. These are all of the introductory economics courses offered at Colorado State University. The latter four courses do not require any course prerequisites. To take Introductory Microeconomics students must complete a math course at a certain level and the prerequisite for Introductory Macroeconomics is the same level of math and Introductory Microeconomics. We examine the effect of taking the Gender in the Economy class on the probability of taking a second economics course within three terms. The dependent variable measures the likelihood that students will take another economics course. Control variables vary by the empirical specification but include student demographic variables, term fixed effects, instructor fixed effects, whether the student is an economics major, and GPA and SAT scores. A probit model with robust standard errors is performed to understand the effect of the treatment on the likelihood that a student will take another economics course. The marginal effects are presented in all reported results.

3 Results

Before presenting the regression results, we first show the percentage of students who take another economics course after an introductory course. We only include students who are not economics majors when they take ECON 211 in Table 3 because all economics majors will take additional economics courses.

Table 3 highlights the number and percentage of students that take an additional economics course after taking an introductory course.

Table 3 Percentage of students that take another economics course

	All students		*Undergraduate women*		*Undergraduate men*	
	Percentage	*Observations*	*Percentage*	*Observations*	*Percentage*	*Observations*
Gender in the economy	12.82	1911	10.80	1334	17.47	578
Issues in environmental economics	6.32	570	3.70	270	8.67	300
Racial inequality and discrimination	13.55	155	15.79	95	9.84	61
Working with data	7.55	53	0	16	10.81	37
Introductory microeconomics—not including macroeconomics	2.65	7540	3.77	3373	1.75	4167
Introductory microeconomics—including macroeconomics	38.74	11921	37.39	5181	39.80	6801

Notes Table is based on student registrar data from Fall of 2016 to Spring of 2022. The sample includes any student who took an introductory economics course

The most popular economics course is Introductory Microeconomics, followed by Gender in the Economy and Issues in Environmental Economics. Racial Inequality and Discrimination has only been offered since Spring of 2020 and Working with Data has been offered since the Spring of 2019. Of the 155 students who take Racial Inequality and Discrimination and who are not economics majors, 13.55% go on to take another introductory course. For Gender in the Economy, 12.82% take another economics course. This percentage is higher than Issues in Environmental Economics and Working with Data.

Undergraduate men are more likely to take a second introductory economics course after Gender in the Economy and undergraduate women are most likely to take a second introductory economics course after Racial Inequality and Discrimination. Both courses discuss economic topics that are unorthodox to introductory microeconomic or macroeconomic neoclassical economic theory. These two courses also emphasize the importance of the interconnection between inequality, economics, and identity. Both courses provide promising evidence that they inspire students enough to encourage them to take more economics courses.

In Table 4, we analyze the impact of the Gender in the Economy course on the probability of taking another economics course. Students enrolled in Gender in the Economy were 4.2% more likely to take another economics course after controlling for student demographic controls, term fixed effects, and GPA and SAT scores. These results are positive and statistically significant across all four regression specifications. Instructor-fixed effects are also included because graduate student instructors may have a positive or negative impact on student retention. Note that a substantial portion of the sample is missing their SAT scores in the registrar data and are dropped in regression (4).

When we separate the regressions by gender, the results indicate that undergraduate men and women both have a higher probability of taking another economics course after Gender in the Economy than other introductory economics courses. Undergraduate men are between 5.6% and 8.1% more likely to take an economics course after Gender in the Economy than other introductory economics courses. The evidence also suggests that Gender in the Economy is successful in encouraging undergraduate women to take another economics course as compared to other introductory economics courses.

These results highlight that the Gender in the Economy course is successful in encouraging students to take more economics courses for

Table 4 Effect of gender in the economy on taking a future economics course

	(1)	*(2)*	*(3)*	*(4)*
All students				
Gender in the economy	0.063***	0.069***	0.068***	0.042**
	(0.013)	(0.013)	(0.017)	(0.019)
Observations	3526	3526	3398	2356
Women students				
Gender in the economy	0.049***	0.058***	0.058**	0.03
	(0.018)	(0.017)	(0.023)	(0.024)
Observations	1950	1950	1901	1342
Men students				
Gender in the economy	0.078***	0.081***	0.080***	0.056*
	(0.019)	(0.019)	(0.025)	(0.03)
Observations	1576	1576	1492	1009
Student demographic	Yes	Yes	Yes	Yes
Term fixed effects	No	Yes	Yes	Yes
Instructor fixed effects	No	No	Yes	Yes
GPA and SAT scores	No	No	No	Yes

Notes Table is based on student registrar data from Fall of 2016 to Spring of 2022. The sample includes any student who took an introductory economics course. The marginal effects are posted here

both undergraduate women and men. This result is especially important for any departments with decreasing enrollment in economics courses. Universities could offer a similar course if they want to attract more students to economics.

To get a better picture of how Gender in the Economy impacts undergraduate women, Table 5 presents an intersectional approach. We analyze how the course impacts different groups for women by race, ethnicity, Pell Grant status, and first-generation status. Unfortunately, the sample is very small for some groups and they had to be excluded from our analysis. Only 47 Black women exist in the sample, with 40 of them having taken Gender in the Economy. Of the 62 students who identify as Asian women, the 24 who took a different introductory class than Gender in the Economy didn't take any other economics courses. There are only 3 Hawaiian students in our sample, 16 Native American students in our sample, and 83 students who identify as multiracial and women. While our sample wasn't large enough to examine the effect by these different identities, it is an important avenue for further research.

Table 5 Intersectional analysis of the effect of gender in the economy on taking a future economics course

	(1)	(2)	(3)	(4)
Hispanic women students				
Gender in the economy	0.140**	0.170***	0.150**	0.211**
	(0.061)	(0.059)	(0.064)	(0.084)
Observations	283	278	275	189
White women students				
Gender in the economy	0.040*	0.040*	0.030	0.005
	(0.021)	(0.021)	(0.028)	(0.028)
Observations	1330	1286	1252	932
Pell and women students				
Gender in the economy	0.034	0.048	0.079*	0.068
	(0.036)	(0.035)	(0.041)	(0.044)
Observations	447	447	439	258
Non Pell and women students				
Gender in the economy	0.055***	0.062***	0.057**	0.031
	(0.020)	(0.020)	(0.027)	(0.028)
Observations	1504	1504	1463	1036
First generation women students				
Gender in the economy	0.070*	0.085**	0.098**	0.047
	(0.037)	(0.037)	(0.041)	(0.043)
Observations	570	570	563	338
Non-first gen women students				
	0.044**	0.049**	0.040	0.018
	(0.020)	(0.020)	(0.027)	(0.028)
Observations	1381	1381	1339	982
Student demographic	Yes	Yes	Yes	Yes
Term fixed effects	No	Yes	Yes	Yes
Instructor fixed effects	No	No	Yes	Yes
GPA and SAT scores	No	No	No	Yes

Notes Table is based on student registrar data from Fall of 2016 to Spring of 2022. The sample includes any student who took an introductory economics course. Marginal effects are reported

Table 5 provides more insight into who is taking more economic courses after Gender in the Economy. Hispanic women are one of the groups that are most likely to take future economics courses after taking Gender in the Economy. Hispanic women who took Gender in the Economy are between 14% and 21.1% (depending on the regression specification) more likely to take other economics courses as compared to Hispanic women who take other introductory courses in economics. The effect for undergraduate women who are Pell recipients is not particularly strong. First-generation students and non-Pell recipients who are women are also more likely to take future economics courses, but this result is not statistically significant in the last specification.

We next examine the impact of the Race, Inequality, and Discrimination course on the likelihood of taking another economics course. Our goal is to examine if the two separate courses have separate effects. Table 6 highlights the effect of Race, Inequality, and Discrimination on taking another economics course. Across all students, there is no statistically significant effect of the course on taking future economics courses. This is also true for undergraduate men and women. However, it is important to note that the sample size for this course is much smaller as it was only introduced in 2020. Given more time, the Race, Inequality, and Discrimination course may have effects like Gender in the Economy.

Ultimately, Tables 4, 5, and 6 show that introductory courses have different effects on students. In other words, the first economics course

Table 6 Effect of a race, inequality, and discrimination course on taking a future economics course

	(1)	*(2)*	*(3)*	*(4)*
All students				
Race, inequality, and discrimination	0.011	−0.005	−0.009	0.037
	(0.025)	(0.026)	(0.032)	(0.035)
Observations	3526	3526	3398	2356
Women students				
Race, inequality, and discrimination	0.059**	0.042	0.040	0.056
	(0.028)	(0.031)	(0.037)	(0.039)
Observations	1950	1950	1901	1342
Men students				
Gender in the economy	−0.059	−0.076*	−0.097*	−0.007
	(0.043)	(0.045)	(0.056)	(0.064)
Observations	1576	1576	1492	1009
Student demographic	Yes	Yes	Yes	Yes
Term fixed effects	No	Yes	Yes	Yes
Instructor fixed effects	No	No	Yes	Yes
GPA and SAT scores	No	No	No	Yes

Notes Table is based on student registrar data from Fall of 2016 to Spring of 2022. The sample includes any student who took an introductory economics course that a student is exposed to matters. While this chapter focuses on differences by gender, future research should examine variation in taking future economics courses by race, ethnicity, Pell Grant status, first-generation status, and more. Because students were not randomly assigned to courses, the sample may be subject to selection bias. Given this empirical limitations we are cautious in interpreting these results as causal. Future studies that employ random assignment can provide more robust evidence on the relationship between gender economics courses and students' willingness to continue their studies in economics.

4 Conclusion

Understanding the reasons for the leaky pipeline in economics is critical for performing and producing better and more robust economic research. This chapter attempts to understand if a Gender in the Economy class inspires undergraduate students to take more economics classes because the pipeline starts at the undergraduate level. The course is a semester-long class, taken in person or online, and offered at Colorado State University. The summary statistics highlighted that undergraduate women are much more likely to take a Gender in the Economy course compared to other introductory economics courses. Regarding taking additional economics courses, the main results indicate that the Gender in the Economy class does encourage more students to take economics courses over other introductory classes including Issues in Environmental Economics, Race, Inequality, and Discrimination, and Working with Data. The course has positive effects on both undergraduate men and women taking future economics courses. It is possible that the Gender in the Economy class recruits a different group of students than other introductory classes to economics and can expose a whole different generation to economics.

Our study is the first that we know of to examine how an undergraduate Gender in the Economy course impacts future course enrollment. Future research must explore these dynamics in more detail so that we better understand the impact of economics courses on women's retention in the subject.

References

Bauman, Yoram, and Elaina Rose. 2011. Selection or Indoctrination: Why Do Economics Students Donate Less than the Rest? *Journal of Economic Behavior & Organization* 79(3):318–327. https://doi.org/10.1016/j.jebo.2011.02.010.

Bayer, Amanda, Syon P. Bhanot, Erin T. Bronchetti, and Stephen A. O'Connell. 2020. Diagnosing the Learning Environment for Diverse Students in Introductory Economics: An Analysis of Relevance, Belonging, and Growth Mindsets. *AEA Papers and Proceedings* 110:294–298.

Bayer, Amanda, and Cecilia E. Rouse. 2016. Diversity in the Economics Profession: A New Attack on an Old Problem. *Journal of Economic Perspectives* 30(4):221–242. https://doi.org/10.1257/jep.30.4.221.

Bayer, Amanda, and David W. Wilcox. 2019. The Unequal Distribution of Economic Education: A Report on the Race, Ethnicity, and Gender of Economics Majors at U.S. Colleges and Universities. *The Journal of Economic Education* 50(3):299–320. https://doi.org/10.1080/00220485.2019.1618766.

Berik, Günseli, and Yana van der Meulen Rodgers. 2022. Teaching Development Economics from a Gender Perspective. *The Journal of Economic Education* 54(1):60–75. https://doi.org/10.1080/00220485.2022.2144571.

Bettinger, Eric P., and Bridget Terry Long. 2005. Do Faculty Serve as Role Models? The Impact of Instructor Gender on Female Students. *American Economic Review* 95(2):152–157. https://doi.org/10.1257/000282805774670149.

Bosshardt, William, and William B. Walstad. 2017. Some Lasting Effects of Undergraduate Economics on Retirement Planning. *American Economic Review* 107(5):650–654.

Buckles, Kasey. 2019. Fixing the Leaky Pipeline: Strategies for Making Economics Work for Women at Every Stage. *Journal of Economic Perspectives* 33(1):43–60. https://doi.org/10.1257/jep.33.1.43.

Burnett, Nancy J. 1997. Gender Economics Courses in Liberal Arts Colleges. *The Journal of Economic Education* 284:369–376. https://doi.org/10.2307/1183420.

Carrell, Scott E., Marianne E. Page, and James E. West. 2010. Sex and Science: How Professor Gender Perpetuates the Gender Gap. *The Quarterly Journal of Economics* 125(3):1101–1144. https://doi.org/10.1162/qjec.2010.125.3.1101.

Dynan, Karen E., and Cecilia Elena Rouse. 1997. The Underrepresentation of Women in Economics: A Study of Undergraduate Economics Students. *The Journal of Economic Education* 28(4):350–368. https://doi.org/10.1080/00220489709597939.

Emerson, Tisha L. N., and Linda English. 2016. Classroom Experiments: Is More More? *American Economic Review* 106(5):363–367.

Emerson, Tisha L. N., KimMarie McGoldrick, and Kevin J. Mumford. 2012. Women and the Choice to Study Economics. *The Journal of Economic Education* 43(4):349–362.

Fairlie, Robert W., Florian Hoffmann, and Philip Oreopoulos. 2014. A Community College Instructor Like Me: Race and Ethnicity Interactions in the Classroom. *American Economic Review* 104(8):2567–2591. https://doi.org/10.1257/aer.104.8.2567.

Fischer, Mira, Björn. Kauder, Niklas Potrafke, and Heinrich W. Ursprung. 2017. Support for Free-Market Policies and Reforms: Does the Field of Study Influence Students' Political Attitudes? *European Journal of Political Economy* 48:180–197. https://doi.org/10.1016/j.ejpoleco.2016.07.002.

Gerlach, Philipp. 2017. The Games Economists Play: Why Economics Students Behave More Selfishly Than Other Students. *PLoS ONE* 12(9):e0183814. https://doi.org/10.1371/journal.pone.0183814.

Hale, Galina, and Tali Regev. 2014. Gender Ratios at Top PhD Programs in Economics. *Economics of Education Review* 41:55–70. https://doi.org/10.1016/j.econedurev.2014.03.007.

Institutional Research, Planning and Effectiveness. 2020. Common Data Set 2019–2020. Colorado State University. Accessed at http://irpe-reports.colostate.edu/pdf/cds/cds1920.pdf.

Jackstadt, Stephen L., Jerry Brennan, and Scott Thompson. 1985. The Effect of Introductory Economics Courses on College Students' Conservatism. *The Journal of Economic Education* 16(1):37–51. https://doi.org/10.2307/1182183.

Lusher, Lester, Doug Campbell, and Scott Carrell. 2018. TAs Like Me: Racial Interactions Between Graduate Teaching Assistants and Undergraduates. *Journal of Public Economics* 159:203–224. https://doi.org/10.1016/j.jpubeco.2018.02.005.

Mukherjee, Sucharita S. 2018. Challenges and Pedagogies for Teaching Inequality in Undergraduate Development Economics. *International Journal of Pluralism and Economics Education* 9(1–2):69–80.

Nelson, Julie A. 1995. Feminism and Economics. *Journal of Economic Perspectives* 9(2):131–148. https://doi.org/10.1257/jep.9.2.131.

Nelson, Julie, and Neva Goodwin. 2009. Teaching Ecological and Feminist Economics in the Principles Course. *Forum for Social Economics* 38(2–3):173–187. https://doi.org/10.1007/s12143-009-9033-1.

Noble Calkins, Lindsay, and Andrew Welki. 2006. Factors That Influence Choice of Major: Why Some Students Never Consider Economics. *International Journal of Social Economics* 33(8):547–564. https://doi.org/10.1108/03068290610678707.

Paredes, Valeria A., Muriel D. Paserman, and Fernando Pino. 2020. Does Economics Make You Sexist? Working Paper No. 27070, National Bureau of Economic Research. https://doi.org/10.3386/w27070.

Quan-Haase, Anabel, Kaitlyn Mendes, Dennis Ho, Olivia Lake, Charlotte Nau, and Darryl Pieber. 2021. Mapping #MeToo: A Synthesis Review of Digital Feminist Research Across Social Media Platforms. *New Media & Society* 23(6):1700–1720. https://doi.org/10.1177/1461444820984457.

Rask, Kevin, and Jill Tiefenthaler. 2008. The Role of Grade Sensitivity in Explaining the Gender Imbalance in Undergraduate Economics. *Economics of Education Review* 27(6):676–687. https://doi.org/10.1016/j.econedurev.2007.09.010.

Strenio, Jacqueline, and Yana van der Meulen Rodgers. 2023. Integrating Gender into a Labour Economics Class. *Advances in Economics Education* 2(1):26–44.

Trans*ing the Economic Lens

Justine Dombrowski

1 Content Warning

This chapter will include discussion of racism, sexism, ableism, transphobia, and negative health outcomes, but only to the extent that I think it is illustrative. Trans people do not need to perform suffering. This chapter will also include discussions of the power of being trans and of coming from a trans perspective, as well as the joy inherent in transness itself.

2 It's a Trans World After All

First and foremost, this is not a primer on trans people. Below I discuss some concepts and abbreviations that are relevant to the rest of this piece. However, I don't fully "cislate," or translate for the main purposes of cis audiences, my work (Nicolazzo and Jourian 2020). This is partly because I don't want to, because I want to speak directly in solidarity with my TGD economists and researchers, and partly because I think that cis academics and economists have to become more comfortable with their

J. Dombrowski (✉)
University of Utah, Salt Lake City, UT, USA
e-mail: justine.dombrowski@utah.edu

© The Author(s), under exclusive license to Springer Nature Switzerland AG 2026

V. Dolar and T. Perry (eds.), *Missing Voices in Economics*,
https://doi.org/10.1007/978-3-031-97180-8_9

ignorance on gender. I also want to state upfront that this is an analysis that centers the experience of trans individuals in the imperial core, particularly in the so-called United States. Analysis that is NOT US-centric is an absolutely vital addition to this work, but is best done by others who have lived experience in those regions. As I am born and raised in the imperial core, this is where I will center my work.

For the purposes of this piece, I'll use Trans and Gender Diverse (TGD) to describe the wide umbrella of gender identities that are not cis (gender identity that aligns with the gender assigned at birth). Other acronyms will be limited to SGM (Sexual and Gender Minority) and SM (Sexual Minority). Kimberlee Crenshaw, among others, participated in the popularization of the theory of intersectionality which has been used and reshaped and reapplied in the 30 + years since its inception in an immense number of areas of study. Crenshaw "highlights the need to account for multiple grounds of identity when considering how the social world is constructed," centering Black women in her analysis of the conversation surrounding violence against women (Crenshaw 1991). This theory, and the centering of Black women, is vital to an understanding of transing economics. First, Black women and Black TGD folks have been central to organizing and theorizing about identity in contrast to violent norms, both societally and within academia. Second, it highlights the complexities of increased violence that over-policed, under-resourced, and marginalized peoples face, and provides a framework through which to analyze these nuances. Implicit in my writing is an underlying prioritization of intersectionality, though I can always do better to apply and recognize intersectionality and other theories' impact on and implications for my work, and how my work impacts the material world.

There are many forms of gender diversity—I can't and won't cover them all here. That's not my goal. There are beautiful pieces of work where people talk about their identities and what they mean to them and their community, and this piece is specifically looking at gender diversity as an abstract and liberatory concept within economics and research. I'll do this through my own lenses, elaborated further on in my positionality section. I try to be specific where authors have specified what population within the trans/not cis sphere they are discussing, but often all trans people are lumped together with gender diverse, gender non-conforming, non-binary, and even LGBQ people. So, as you read further, consider when a statistic is mentioned for trans people, why might that be different for different trans people? Race? Gender performance? Gender transgression? Gender conformity? Gender legibility? Disability? Age? Citizenship? Nation of origin?

I want desperately to talk about this in a way that is only full of trans joy. But that's hard to do, given the realities of the systems in which we live. In the following section, I hope to contextualize some of the differences that those within our community experience, hopefully not with a deficit-centered perspective (though perhaps intent is less important than impact in this regard). I hope in future years I will come more into my own and find bigger and more joyful ways to talk about my experience in economics.

2.1 *The Trans Experience*™

Some TGD people seek to pass, or be assumed to be a specific gender upon first glance by strangers. Some TGD people do not seek to pass (Goldberg, Kuvalanka, and Dickey 2019). Some TGD people cannot pass, given some external constraints (money, physical safety, etc.). Some TGD people seek transitions that will align their body more with their gender identity, presentation, or variety of other features of how they perceive themselves in relation to gender. Some TGD people do not wish to transition in any way, and some TGD people cannot. The trans experience is not a homogenous one, and doesn't encompass all extra-binary gendered experiences or experiences that are outside or reject the concept of gender innately. Much like any other identity, transness is inherently experienced and interpreted through the lens of our other identities, and as such can amplify marginalization trans people experience in other parts of their personhood. Race itself is a vital factor in understanding trans experiences in the world. In line with research across disciplines, it is evident that trans men and women of color experience more discrimination than white trans folks pretty much across the board (Suárez et al. 2022). So, implicit in our coming understanding of gender must be the idea that gender across culture and across race, even within the same culture, will hold different meanings, marginalizations, and privileges. Further, as economists, I hope it is no shock that class, income, and wealth affect this experience. Data indicate that trans women with lower social and wealth class, integrally connected to race and education, are at greater risk for experiencing discrimination than trans women in higher income brackets (Suárez et al. 2022). For trans men, these statistics slightly differ and are also differently complex; trans men with higher levels of education attainment seemed to experience reduced levels of discrimination, while trans men in higher income brackets did not (Suárez et al. 2022).

Binary trans and non-binary trans people have different experiences, but are often collapsed into one group (Goldberg, Kuvalanka, and Dickey 2019; Platt 2020). I may experience depression, isolation, reduced capacity for work, and more in relation to my gender within economics, but trans women, and particularly trans women of color, statistically have a higher likelihood for being targeted for harassment, discrimination, and violence than the average population and myself. For me, passing to be femme generally increases the frequency I'm misgendered. For a trans woman, passing to be femme can be vital not only to their mental health, but their physical health and safety as well. It's also possible for TGD identities to be labeled as not "legible" or "gender non-conforming," regardless of if they identify with binary gender labels of "man" and "woman" or not. Onlookers may be unfamiliar with someone's gender or gender presentation, and might be able to better place a "passing" binary trans person or misgender a non-binary trans person to fit within their (usually binary) understanding of gender. But then "passing" binary trans folks are also subject to increased pressures to conform to the expectations of that gender (Goldberg, Kuvalanka, and Dickey 2019). In this way, and others, "illegible" or "gender non-conforming" identities challenge the gender binary "related to having one's gender invalidated, unacknowledged, or questioned by others explicitly due to existing in a society where a binary understanding of gender is imposed on all" (Puckett et al. 2023, 119).

2.2 *Positionality*

There is a myth within research that perpetuates that removing the personal from science will somehow remove bias from our work. I think the reality lies somewhere in the opposite direction. By attempting to obscure or remove indications of our own identity from our research, we lose insight into the research methods, process, analysis, and conclusions, as well as continue to perpetuate the idea that we can actually remove ourselves from our work. I think it's important to write about who I am, and positionality and reflexivity statements are becoming more frequent in spaces that embrace their state as a social science, like psychology, sociology, and education research.

Some people feel trapped by gender. Some people feel liberated by gender. Some people don't think about their gender at all. I, at some points of my life, have been in all of these camps. Many of these identities, such as my race, my generational education and access to resources, and perceptions of my gender and sexuality, allow me into spaces more safely and with fewer issues than others in the TGD community (Maughan, Natalier, and Mulholland 2022). Some identities are double-edged swords, like being constantly misgendered and constantly assumed to be straight, but they still provide me with advantages and access to resources within economics and society at large (Maughan, Natalier, and Mulholland 2022). All of this means I bring a very specific lens to this research, but it is just that—only one of many lenses. I encourage all those reading these pages to carefully consider what it is I might have missed, glossed over, or not given enough wordcount to because of my specific identities, marginalizations, privileges, and blindspots.

3 The Gender Question

The way we study gender frames it in the way the researchers implicitly see it, and without challenging that framework we will continue to uphold this conceptualization of gender: inflexible, binary, fixed, and biological (Jordan 2021). As scientists with perhaps too much sway in policy, law, and government, what economists research and how we research it matters. While there is empirical evidence that contradicts the gender binary, mainstream research of all persuasions continues to tailor their questions to just two of those genders (men and women) (Cameron and Stinson 2019). And, when someone's gender is not so straightforward or is unknown, their data may either be shoved into the binary through arbitrary means or even dropped altogether (Garvey et al. 2019). This exclusionary data standard is encouraged and upheld by academic institutions and publishing journals alike.

Like many identities that are important to a person or groups of people's lived experiences, economists treat gender as an "add in" variable, when in reality it's a complex identity that impacts all areas of a person's life. Continuing to use "male" and "female" erroneously equates sex and gender, and continues to misrepresent sex and gender in research (Garvey et al. 2019). Part of transing economic methods is centering people and experiences who are not the "norm" (Robinson

2022). Norms, in this case, might include "rationality and scarcity, maximization and equilibrium, commodities and exploitation, [that] embody historically specific visions of normative masculinity, femininity, whiteness, and heterosexual orientation" (Rands 2019, 66). Instead of perpetuating the false belief that the concepts we build our models and assumptions on are completely objective, it is vital for economists to understand that the questions we choose to ask, how we ask them, how we collect data, how we clean and analyze data, and how we present our results inherently have our own values and norms imbedded within them (Rands 2019).

Most of the work I see frames the trans experience in very specific ways. First, much of the research focuses on inequity, and how trans people are affected by transphobia in direct and indirect ways. A majority of the papers I've read, in several fields of study, review similar characteristics on repeat: barriers to healthcare, high risk of attempt of suicide, high rates of mental illness, and high rates of harassment and discrimination (Holloway 2023). This is valid and necessary work, and I appreciate those folks who do it. AND it's a deficit-based approach to the study of being trans and how that transness interacts with the larger society and economy; there is so much more to being trans. Second, a majority of research and raw data seems to rest on gender essentialist principles, such as categories of gender that are binary and "biologically" based, as well as that each gender has unique and mutually exclusive attributes that the other does not (Vargas and Farquhar-Leicester 2023).

Part of trans liberation is the reframing of rigid and binary concepts of gender in all areas of life—and this includes research. It takes more than just studying what happens to trans people, it takes radical imagination to theorize other systems, it takes the patient and painstaking unworking of internalized gender norms, it takes the intentional study of gender by people who think it doesn't affect them, and it takes the complete and total acceptance of transness as an identity in research. How do we shift the narrative from pathologizing TGD folks to framing research around trans joy, hope, dreams, visions, and futures (Holloway 2023)? If we're including gender in studying transness specifically, is our narrative playing into the "tragic trans trope?" Are you reinforcing dominant narratives about gender (Holloway 2023)? Economic researchers, particularly those who use feminist methodologies, must disrupt the dominant narrative around trans people that portrays us as "broken," and, maybe most importantly, center hope (Holloway 2023).

So how should researchers actually measure gender? Like many questions posited in this paper, there really isn't one, homogenous answer. There are a few (relatively) agreed upon points though, including having more than two answers to the question "what is your gender," separating gender, sex, and gender identity questions, and being critical as to why exactly they are asking questions about gender in the first place (Lindqvist, Senden, and Renstrom 2021). Fundamentally, "[t]he use of gender and sex either synonymously or without clear differentiation is a symptom, not a root, of the problem. We believe that researchers have not seriously taken on the task of defining gender (or sex) in their analyses" (Garvey et al. 2019, 7). Some researchers argue that queering and transing research in and of itself requires that we move away from strict and static classification schemes (Ruberg and Ruelos 2020). This, obviously, is more work than making a "male" or "female" checkbox on a survey.

But just because something is difficult to research or incorporate into research doesn't mean it is not worth the time and energy to do so, and further, working with data is already heterogeneous and messy. How researchers codify the world is important, and in order to meaningfully have TGD people participate and have agency in our research, we must understand how the process of binarily gendering research upholds systems of transphobia inside and out of academia. In doing this work, I've also found principles of research that benefit me outside of research strictly about gender—transing research is more than checkboxes. Transing research is rejecting static categorization, transing research is moving outside of the classical constraints that economics traditionally imposes, transing research is historical and tangible and imaginative. That's part of the beauty of being trans. Once you've begun to understand gender as a social construct, you can create the world that fits you. While society makes this difficult and, for many, physically dangerous, the radical imagination to separate gender identity, gender presentation, and the vast number of other aspects of gender has the potential to provide immense freedom.

3.1 *Who's the Default?*

I have been both the minority and the majority in pretty much every space I have occupied in academia. It's no secret that economics is overwhelmingly composed of white, cis, hetero men (as I'm sure other chapters in this book will review), and while I share privileged identities with this group, my gender has never been the norm in the classroom. Further, no one is teaching a graduate OR undergraduate economics class about trans issues, let alone even including TGD people in readings, discussion, datasets, or projects. Important to note, however, are all the dimensions of who is the default, or who is expected to be in a space beyond even what I mention below. Yes, white, cis, hetero men are often dominant spaces in academia, but it's also vital to consider aspects of class, citizenship, ability, and other factors that can and do contribute to professional and academic outcomes.

3.2 Race

My understanding of the concept of a "default" that society sees, values, and caters to is fundamentally shaped by race scholars and critical theory, such as intersectionality, Critical Race Theory, and its offshoots, such as QueerCrit and Queer of Color Critiques. These last two, in particular, "support this dimension by centering lived realities among queer and trans* people of color as valid knowledge sources for disrupting intersectional oppressions." (Leyva, McNeill, and Duran 2022, 83) One of the major issues in researching TGD people of color is that datasets just don't contain enough people in these categories to make statistically significant findings. Further, a lot of the research relating to TGD folks of color is also focused around racialized and medicalized issues like HIV and poverty (Farvid et al. 2021). By not including TGD people of color in analyses and narrowing the research that is relevant to them, researchers severely limit our knowledge of TGD people and the ways in which we interact with the world.

We also know that trans women have vastly different experiences than other TGD individuals, particularly along identity lines such as race (Biello and Hughto 2021). We struggle to capture this difference because, by and far, white trans people are better represented in data than trans folks of other races and ethnicities (Suárez et al. 2022). Biello and Hughto (2021) cite recent evidence: "relative to White transgender women, transgender women of color in this study were twice as likely to report having a transgender identity instead of a female identity; thus, the use of gender identity to explore the impact of intersectional stigma may have contributed to differential misclassification by race."

3.3 Cisnormativity

"Cisnormativity is the assumption that it is "normal" to be cisgender" (Worthen 2016, 31). Cisnormativity is not just part of the layperson's world. Research as we know it is based on cisnormativity. Every study that represents gender as a binary perpetuates this. Every study that does not discuss transness or other gender identities besides "man" and "woman" perpetuates this. The default is cisgender, but a growing body of research is indicating that younger generations are feeling less bound to the strictness of cisgenderism (Goldberg, Kuvalanka, and Dickey 2019). Cisnormativity is more than taking a specific set of gender identities as the default in research; it also requires continuing narratives within research and education that other trans people, such as through tropes of trans deviance.

In order to uphold and maintain cis as "normal," transphobia has to operate at many different levels, including structural, theoretical, interpersonal, and individual. This can be done through legislation, practices stemming from laws, social settings and structures, gendered architecture, and more. Cisnormative research also upholds binaries in viewing and understanding TGD peoples' lives (Nicolazzo and Jourian 2020). Further, when TGD folks participate in cisnormativity they can internalize it and repeat the process of non-affirmation, but within themselves (Puckett et al. 2023).

3.4 Trans-Erasure

I edited this piece at an "interesting" time—in the first few months of Donald J. Trump's second term of presidency, in which he has made about 9 executive orders relating to trans people in the first month. I will not discuss the specific attacks and rhetoric used there—but it is interesting to note that while all this attention is focused on legislation that is aggressive toward trans people, the government is systemically trying to erase them from research and historical records. The NYT paraphrases the CDC itself in correspondence with funding recipients, informing them "that any vestige, remnant, or renamed piece of diversity programs funded by the federal government are immediately, completely, and permanently terminated" (Rabin and Mandavilli 2025). Trans people are among the most-targeted in this "anti-DEI" attack, though among those at risk for funding are grants containing words like "woman," "Gulf of Mexico," "Black," and "clean energy" (Yourish et al. 2025; Heidt 2025).

States and institutions are already caving to erasing transness before some of Trump's executive orders have even gotten through the courts—one might call it premature or over-compliance (Closson, 2025). And it only serves to make erasing trans people seem normal and right. For example and following the CDC's lead, Stonewall National Monument recently (verified as of 2/25/2025) erased all major mention of trans people from their website, despite the fact that some of the most prominent activists in the gay rights movement and this particular scuffle were trans (Stonewall National Monument; Kim 2025). There remain some pictures of these prominent figures scattered throughout the website, mentioning that they were part of STAR, but focusing their efforts on work for the "LGB" community (Virtual Fence Exhibit-Stonewall National Monument). Notably, most of the pages attributed to the monument note "last edited" dates in 2024 or before—except the pages noting the history of the actual monument and movement, which were all updated on February 13, 2025. Trans people, as mentioned elsewhere here, are already understudied. Pretending we don't exist while aggressively legislating us to the shadows only serves to further endanger the already violently oppressed among us and enable the stifling of trans futures in research and the world at large.

3.5 Gender = Women

In the areas I operate, I have had to learn that when people say gender, they usually mean women. In trying to research TGD identities in our field, many of the papers that purported to be about "gender in economics" were, in fact, about women in economics. In talking about diversity and inclusion within the department, the topic of conversation is usually about women (Reggiani, Gagnon, and Lunn 2023). The study of women in economics is exciting and necessary! And by only highlighting women's experiences in relation to men's while calling it "gender," we reinforce the otherness that almost all, if not all, gender diverse people experience. In fact, the reason I came out for the first time as an academic was that I was continuously being invited to a Women in Economics group at my department. While its purpose serves to create a space for minority gender identities in economics, grouping me with the Women of Economics implicitly and constantly misgenders me, and makes it more likely that I'll be read strictly as a cis woman within these spaces. This experience might have been affirming for another TGD individual! But it wasn't for me.

3.6 LGBQ + T

TGD people are inherently interwoven within the LGBTQ+ community. We were fundamental to its progress, we benefit from its triumphs, and we can often find common ground with our siblings who queer the world around them. Further, conceptions of gender are innately intertwined with the LGBQ + struggles, and our scholarly pursuits benefit from their queering of research. It is also true that much of SGM research focuses on the SM portion of the audience, sometimes only including 2 binary options in relation to gender (Marsh 2018), and often may not even have enough TGD people in their sample to make any statistically significant commentary.[1] In many cases, this can remove TGD from a study's findings altogether, making it much less of LGBTQ + study and much more of a LGBQ + study (Marsh 2018; Cook et al. 2020). LGBQ + research is vital and exciting. And we can also recognize that it often does little to validate and provide resources, relief, or insight for TGD bodies and experiences (Marsh 2018; Farvid et al. 2021). TGD folks have strengths and struggles that are distinct from their SM siblings', so continuing to only lump them together is inadequate in addressing the material lives of TGD people as well as SM people (Farvid et al. 2021).

It's also true that TGD people can and do have SM identities as well as their TGD ones, and that these identities are interconnected with one another. As evidenced at the beginning of this chapter, it's also vital to recognize in our work that those who straddle multiple identities in marginalized and liminal spaces experience different effects of stigma and discrimination (Farvid et al. 2021). Economists must sit within the dialectic that more than one apparently contradictory thing can be true at once. We can be inherently interconnected to LGBQ + struggle, and also not be represented in that struggle by the current discourse and research. In cases such as this, study design must include methods that

[1] Statistics are an important part of analysis, but not the only valuable method. This paper discusses some of the barriers to making statistically significant commentary about TGD individuals and their experiences, but does not mean to imply that quantitative analysis is somehow superior or more necessary than other methods.

will attract a significant number of TGD people AND TGD data must be disaggregated from LGBQ + data.

4 Trans in the Academe

Academia is a very gendered space, particularly research. In my first year of my graduate degree, I had a well-meaning colleague ask me how I knew I was trans when I came out to my cohort. For cis people, this seems to be a reasonable question: how would one actually know if their gender wasn't what they were told it was? While not all trans folks devote time and energy to studying gender at an academic level, their personal inquiry into their own gender is embodiment of this theoretical practice and it highlights a specifically trans experience. One of the most powerful aspects of the trans experience is the, by necessity, investigation into gender in society, in relationships, and within ourselves. For cis individuals, this does not seem to be as frequent an experience.

For many TGD folks, including myself, we have had to compress ourselves to fit into what economics and the academe want to see. We're TGD only when it's convenient to have TGD people on posters, panels, or the department website, and all other times our experiences and identities are ignored. I'm not sure that I think any place within the academic institution can be "transformed" but I do think shifting the view of gender to a more expansive and fluid concept is necessary at a scientific as well as cultural level, along with many other measures such as prioritizing indigenous research methodologies, landback, reparations, universally inclusive design, and more. None of this happens in a vacuum, but we can all begin the process of challenging our own static perceptions of education, knowledge, and research—and gender is one piece of this process.

4.1 *The Physical Reality of Academia*

Physical violence against trans people is not an unknown phenomenon, and not the central focus of this piece. But, there are often-overlooked aspects of physical health specifically relevant to the trans experience in higher education that are important here. Even the structures of departments and campuses reflect gendered ideas of who will be on campus, or who deserves to be on campus. The most vulnerable and private places, such as bathrooms, healthcare facilities, recreation centers, and dorms, are gendered in an almost exclusively binary fashion (Knutson et al. 2022). TGD people don't have spaces to change or rest or receive healthcare or, if they're on campus, live and sleep. In fact, I'd argue that academia is more architecturally gendered than most workplaces, where the only gendered space might be the bathroom.

For example, according to the 2015 US Transgender Survey, research has indicated that somewhere around 59% of trans people will not use public restrooms for fear of gender-based violence or discrimination (Vargas and Farquhar-Leicester 2023). An important detail in this research is that about 32% of trans people will avoid eating or drinking in public spaces just for the purpose of not having to use the restroom in public (Baril, Sansfacon, and Gelly 2020), and about 8% have reported suffering medical affliction from this practice, most prominently kidney or urinary tract-related infections and bladder pain syndrome.[2] This is one of many examples of how physical and public space is not only gendered, but violently cisnormative (Baril, Sansfacon, and Gelly 2020). The physical, tangible way in which our world binarizes us is emblematic of something that, to me, is important about trans identity; it's not transness that brings about dysphoria and psychological distress and poor health outcomes, it's the institutions that confine and punish transness.

4.2 Mentorship + Representation

There are no statistics on genderqueer and trans economists. If a gender that is implicitly recognized, womanhood, is still overtly and explicitly not treated equitably in our field, what hope do trans economists have of being hired, paid appropriately, being funded, and being valued within the profession?

It should go without saying that the relationship with their advisor is important to graduate students, as they often have quite a bit of contact throughout the completion of the graduate degree, they can influence career and academic outcomes (Goldberg, Kuvalanka, and Dickey 2019), and they are perhaps the most tangible symbol of the power dynamics between faculty and students (Knutson et al. 2022). Mentors and advisors are evidenced to have a large amount to do with career outcomes. They have been linked to "self-efficacy, career interest, and

[2] Think again—WHO among TGD people is the most at risk in these situations? WHO is experiencing this distress disproportionately?

professional outcomes, among minority students in particular" (Goldberg, Kuvalanka, and Dickey 2019, 48) Not having role models could also hamper career prospects (Reggiani, Gagnon, and Lunn 2023). In the context of a transphobic or trans-silent department, however, non-disclosure can be the best strategy for TGD graduate students to get the most out of their relationship with their advisor because it takes less emotional energy than educating, informing, or arguing (Goldberg, Kuvalanka, and Dickey 2019). Departments have power relations, and the choices made about graduate students shape our everyday and material lives (Bonner-Thompson, Mearns, and Hopkins 2021). Those decisions include stipends, teaching load, class load, progress in the degree, qualifying exams, and a wide array of other factors. All of this can be dependent on relationships within the school, and decisions by faculty have material ramifications on our quality of life. When we add in intersectionalities like nation of origin and citizenship, these decisions that departments make have even more impactful ramifications.

TGD people, in most areas of our lives, have to practice "strategic self-disclosure" (Parsons 2023, 111). Some TGD and LGBQ people can decide to disclose their identities. This is not true across the board of TGD people, and a true, in-depth discussion of self-disclosure should include discussions of passing and gender legibility (Parsons 2023). Some trans people don't have the choice to come out. Some have very real fears of violence, and some know that they "appear trans" because of the ways in which they transgress their gender assigned at birth, whether they want to or not.

All of these considerations are the choices TGD people (and many other violently marginalized groups) have to make, balancing feeling and being seen as who we are, against our safety, our jobs, our academics, and our relationships. Should I come out or not? Should I engage in activism or not? Should I just do my job (perhaps being complicit in my own oppression) or risk my job, but stand true to my identity (Weiser, Wagner, and Lawter 2018)? A TGD student might ask themselves if the only reason they're in a program is because they've been tokenized and if the department and field even truly see value in their skillset (Holloway 2023), or if they've only been put on a research project for optics or to increase access to the trans community to benefit the PI's research, but maybe not the community or the TGD student themselves (Nicolazzo and Jourian 2020).

As much as representation is a superficial issue that institutions cling to in order to "prove" that they are equitable and diverse, there is something to be said for seeing someone like you in your field. But asking trans economists to come out makes them potentially open to excess criticism, violence, economic and social destabilization, and increased anxiety. When I reflect on my experiences in academia, I can see the ways and places that having out trans professors would have made a big difference in my life and research. So being out and outspoken in academia is a burden many people holding marginalized identities willingly take on as a sort of responsibility to each other and to incoming generations. Community, mentorship, and representation are vital to survival, and also to intergenerational trans knowledge generation.

4.3 *Trans-Silence*

Cisnormativity in research isn't always explicitly insidious. It can also look like encouraging a student in general, but not specifically around their study of trans people, or pointedly ignoring the mention of trans people in discussion, or by suggesting that a research question would be "easier" if the model was shrunk to a binary understanding of gender. Not explicitly discouraging research is not the same as actively encouraging and celebrating trans research. And trans research does deserve to be celebrated. My experience of being NB or GD in economics has been very "don't ask, don't tell." I'm lucky to be able to say that I don't feel that I have ever been explicitly dissuaded from researching trans issues. But that is not to say that I have been encouraged. No one has said no to my trans research, but only recently has anyone taken the time to move outside their own wheelhouse and find resources and opportunities for me to do my research. While I have recently found this support, I've spent much of my time in academia feeling that if I want my research to be read, evaluated, and given meaningful feedback I have to write about cis people.

Some of the many ways that queer and trans topics are othered in academia is by relegating these topics to self-contained courses, not including them in requisite material because they're "not part of the core curriculum," labeling them as "controversial" or "sensitive" topics, and by not providing clear and explicit support to those who invest in these topics (Maughan, Natalier, and Mulholland 2022). I could write this same sentence about studying race, disability, and a whole host of other identities relegated to the margin. Through my graduate education there has been little to no discussion of TGD issues: no classes, very few, if any, sections within other classes, and certainly almost no discussion around framing gender in an econometric sense.

Vitally, education requires educators to teach not only the material, but why students are learning it (Rands 2019), which I can say, from personal experience, is not a question departments seem to want to answer. My department is heterodox, and what we're taught is rarely adequately applied to more modern theories surrounding gender, something that Marxist and historical-materialist methods are uniquely cut out for (Rands 2019). Departments nation-wide need to review the current curriculum of their entire department, from mandatory classes to electives, and at all course levels, to ensure that gender (AND race, ability, etc.) is being taught in a continuous and critical matter—not just ignoring TGD folks or teaching the trope of tragedy for transness (Holloway 2023). Transness isn't a "sensitive topic," it's a lived experience, and departments that call themselves pluralist or feminist or heterodox need to actually address the transphobia, racism, ableism, and sexism in their local communities and in the nation. Trans people live real lives and experience real things. As mentioned above in Trans-Erasure, ignoring trans people doesn't change that they are there. Queer and TGD education should not be controversial—the continued erasure and "sensitization" of these topics reinforce the narrative that they don't fit in with acceptable curriculum, and thus they could be subject to censorship or jeopardize funding (Maughan, Natalier, and Mulholland 2022). (I actually wrote this paragraph in 2024 but am submitting this manuscript in 2025—now we're seeing this happen in real time (Kozlov and Mallapaty 2025).)

In reality, there is no subject that doesn't include trans people or these other identities. Economists study populations, and populations inherently have TGD people within them. Curriculums and syllabi may also have exclusionary language or emphasize exclusionary practices like referring only to "men" and "women" or "male" and "female" with no discussion of why this was done, if there are alternatives, and the effect it has on the research and findings (Knutson et al. 2022). Similarly, when faculty bring students to work on their projects, implicit in how they design and implement research is their framing of gender (Knutson et al. 2022)—something I and I suspect many trans students are hypervigilant about.

5 Trans Futures

While I'm currently a graduate student, it won't be long until I enter the job market and experience a related, but different, slew of minefields when it comes to being trans. Sometimes being trans in academia is immensely liberating. I count myself lucky to be within a demographic that necessitates the nuanced understanding of identity as a social construct and, therefore, mutable. One of the burdens of holding any marginalized identity, however, is wondering if any progress would be made toward, in this case, trans liberation in this space without your own presence and constant, constant effort (Boustani and Taylor 2020). Generally, it's just TGD people who are trying to make the changes and, much like folks who have advocated for their own marginalized identities such as race and disability, they are often unrewarded for doing that work (Leyva, McNeill, and Duran 2022). I didn't start thinking I wanted to do gender research specifically—but it feels like that research won't be done if I'm not the one to do it. Maybe that's thinking too much of myself, but too frequently I see questions of gender pushed aside or binarized for ease over and over and over again in my field.

As is true in all areas of solidarity and activism, there isn't one thing or a list of things to do that will suddenly make you supportive of a group of marginalized people or confer your status as an "ally." There isn't an end line. Being gender celebratory means more than just having better questions and more trans respondents. Some TGD folk want more/better questions around gender and sex in your questionnaires, and some think that this further boxes gender into something measurable and quantifiable. Economics as a discipline has to build up reflexivity and positionality as important and critical. If we don't, then we are continuing to reinforce normality and default-ness of majority populations (Leyva, McNeill, and Duran 2022). TGD identities are increasing in frequency, with a large share of people who identify as non-binary being currently under the age of 29 (including myself!) and some studies indicating that as many 10% of youth identify in some way as GD (Burnette et al. 2021).

There are also plenty of cultural climate factors that departments and universities should consider. One of the most commonly used "inclusive" practices around gender is sharing one's pronouns upon meeting. While pronoun sharing can be a good practice, it can also force TGD students to be out in a space where maybe they don't want to be (Siegel 2019). Further, if you ask for someone's pronouns, you have to actually use the right ones (Wilson 2020); using they/them pronouns for a trans woman, when you know she uses she/her pronouns, is still misgendering her, and a common phenomenon in neoliberal spaces. Misgendering people and other trans-exclusionary behaviors are hurtful, isolating, and can make TGD folks feel like they have to keep experiences like their transition to themselves. There's true psychological distress and uncertainty while trying to be a researcher; big life things change for trans people and cis people will refuse to acknowledge the events or their impacts (Junkers 2019).

It's also hard for TGD folks to feel welcome in space where transphobic events, on campus both locally and nationally, are either promoted or just not addressed. In my tenure as a graduate student, there have been actively transphobic events on campus, one of the most restrictive gender bills in the nation passed at our state legislature, and the murder of trans folks both nationally and locally. My department has said nothing. That doesn't make me feel welcomed in a space, that doesn't make me feel valued in a space, and that certainly doesn't make me feel safe or supported.

Other methods of creating a pro-trans environment include the prioritization of how researchers and professors treat gender in departmental standards and hiring procedures, hiring more TGD PIs and faculty (and encouraging them to do TGD research), and including serious discussion of gender in curriculum. However, as discussed in the Mentorship & Representation section, just having TGD faculty is not enough. Representation should increase, but departments should be careful to avoid tokenizing TGD students and faculty, reinforcing pathologization, reproducing trauma, and insisting that TGD students and faculty perform education or gender for their cis colleagues (Leyva, McNeill, and Duran 2022). Being trans-celebratory is work. Being trans-celebratory and actively engaging with their own gender conceptions removes burdens from trans folk (Holloway 2023). Good intentions alone are not enough.

In my opinion, the goal is not more and better checkboxes for gender in surveys, the goal is a broadening understanding of gender as socially constructed, mutable, personal, and time-based within economics (Garvey et al. 2019). As has been mentioned over and over and over again in solidarity work and critical education pedagogies, in order to be able to relate to a global struggle, we have to see where we fit in it. I'd like to see cis economists asking themselves more questions about their own gender—what is it that makes you a man or a woman?

Is that important to you? Do you think those characteristics are necessary for anyone to call themselves a man or a woman? How has gender affected your life? Could you be TGD? Why or why not? How would your research change if you took a different assumption, rather than the assumption of two genders, to be true? Why, against all evidence, do you take the assumption of two genders to be true? It's ok if your answer is that it's easier—but when we make that decision, we have to reckon with that.

Transing economics is more than increasing the number of trans economists or the number of pieces written about trans people. Transing economics is about a fundamental shift of how we think about, view, and research gender as a whole. Transing economics requires resetting what we think of as the default and, instead, recognizing the vast ways in which identities defy binaries and shift over months, years, and generations. Most importantly, a transed economics has to be celebratory of trans people and research, not just tolerant and not just using right pronouns (Holloway 2023). A TGD celebratory economics needs to be radical and interdisciplinary (Kersey and Voigt 2021). It has to protest economic and social norms, be anti-gender-essentialist, resist labels and static identities, and break TGD folks and their study out from women and LGBQ folks (Kersey and Voigt 2021). There isn't one right lens of gender to use—there are plenty of people even within the TGD community that have very different lenses, all valuable in their own right. Instead, question whatever lens you're using, listen to TGD voices, and do the work of unlearning the gendered way in which you operate in the world and, as a result, the gendered way in which you do research.

Acknowledgements This analysis would not have been possible without the generations of activism and solidarity work that people of color have done, particularly the theorizing and organizing of Black Trans and Gender Diverse (TGD) folks and women. I also want to thank the TGD scholars who have gone before me and paved the way to be able to speak about these issues in light of day.

References

Baril, Alexandre, Annie Pullen Sansfaçon, and Morgane A. Gelly. 2020. Digging Beneath the Surface: When Disability Meets Gender Identity. *Canadian Journal of Disability Studies* 9(4):1–23. https://doi.org/10.15353/cjds.v9i4.666.

Biello, Katie B., and Jaclyn M. W. Hughto. 2021. Measuring Intersectional Stigma Among Racially and Ethnically Diverse Transgender Women: Challenges and Opportunities. *American Journal of Public Health* 111(3):344–346. https://doi.org/10.2105/AJPH.2020.306141.

Bonner-Thompson, Carl, Graeme William Mearns, and Peter Hopkins. 2021. Transgender Negotiations of Precarity: Contested Spaces of Higher Education. *The Geographical Journal* 187(3):227–239. https://doi.org/10.1111/geoj.12384.

Boustani, Karim, and Kirk A. Taylor. 2020. Navigating LGBTQ+ Discrimination in Academia: Where Do We Go from Here? *The Biochemist* 42(3):16–20. https://doi.org/10.1042/BIO20200024.

Burnette, Timber, Riley Dehority, Román Ramos Báez, and Lars Howell. 2021. Nonbinary Scientists Want Funding Agencies to Change How They Collect Gender Data. *Scientific American*, August 30, 2021. https://www.scientificamerican.com/article/nonbinary-scientists-want-funding-agencies-to-change-how-they-collect-gender-data/.

Cameron, Jessica J, and Danu Anthony Stinson. 2019. Gender (Mis)Measurement: Guidelines for Respecting Gender Diversity in Psychological Research. *Social and Personality Psychology Compass* 13(11):e12506. https://doi.org/10.1111/spc3.12506.

Closson, Troy. 2025. Columbia Agrees to Trump's Demands After Federal Funds Are Stripped. *The New York Times*, March 21, 2025, sec. New York. https://www.nytimes.com/2025/03/21/nyregion/columbia-response-trump-demands.html.

Cook, Tiffany E., Oscar E. Dimant, Rebecca Novick, Adetoro Adegbola, Uché Blackstock, Carolyn B. Drake, Mason E. Patenaude, Joseph E. Ravenell, Asa Radix, and Richard E. Greene. 2020. Gendered Expectations: Strategies for Navigating Structural Challenges in Support of Transgender and Nonbinary Trainees in Academic Medicine. *Academic Medicine* 95(5):704–709. https://doi.org/10.1097/ACM.0000000000003202.

Crenshaw, Kimberle. July1991. Mapping the Margins: Intersectionality, Identity Politics, and Violence against Women of Color. *Stanford Law Review* 43(6):1241. https://doi.org/10.2307/1229039.

Curtin, Nicola, Janet Malley, and Abigail J. Stewart. 2016. Mentoring the Next Generation of Faculty: Supporting Academic Career Aspirations Among Doctoral Students. *Research in Higher Education* 57(6):714–738. https://doi.org/10.1007/s11162-015-9403-x.

Farvid, Panteá, Thomas A. Vance, Samantha L. Klein, Yekaterina Nikiforova, Lisa R. Rubin, and Felix G. Lopez. 2021. The Health and Wellbeing of Transgender and Gender Non-Conforming People of Colour in the United States: A Systematic Literature Search and Review. *Journal of Community & Applied Social Psychology* 31(6):703–731. https://doi.org/10.1002/casp.2555.

Garvey, Jason, Jeni Hart, Amy Metcalfe, and Jennifer Fellabaum-Toston. 2019. Methodological Troubles with Gender and Sex in Higher Education Survey Research. *The Review of Higher Education* 43:1–24. https://doi.org/10.1353/rhe.2019.0088.

Goldberg, Abbie E., Katherine Kuvalanka, and Lore Dickey. March 2019. Transgender Graduate Students' Experiences in Higher Education: A Mixed-Methods Exploratory Study. *Journal of Diversity in Higher Education* 12(1):38–51. https://doi.org/10.1037/dhe0000074.

Heidt, Amanda. 2025. 'Mind-Boggling': US CDC Orders Gender-Related Terms Cut from Scientific Papers. *Nature*. https://doi.org/10.1038/d41586-025-00367-x.

Holloway, Brendon T. 2023. Highlighting Trans Joy: A Call to Practitioners, Researchers, and Educators. *Health Promotion Practice* 24(4):612–614. https://doi.org/10.1177/15248399231152468.

Jordan, Mark. 2021. How to Write Gender Questions for a Survey. Alchemer. https://www.alchemer.com/resources/blog/how-to-write-survey-gender-questions/.

Junkers, Tanja. 2019. Being Trans in Academia. *Chemistry World*, October 24, 2019. https://www.chemistryworld.com/opinion/being-Ðtrans-in-academia/4010489.article.

Keegan, Cáel M. 2020. Getting Disciplined: What's Trans* About Queer Studies Now? *Journal of Homosexuality* 67(3):384–397. https://doi.org/10.1080/00918369.2018.1530885.

Kersey, Elizabeth, and Matthew Voigt. 2021. Finding Community and Overcoming Barriers: Experiences of Queer and Transgender Postsecondary Students in Mathematics and Other STEM Fields. *Mathematics Education Research Journal* 33(4):733–56. https://doi.org/10.1007/s13394-020-00356-5.

Kim, Juliana. 2025. Park Service Erases 'transgender' on Stonewall Website, Uses the Term 'LGB' Movement. NPR, February 14, sec. National. https://www.npr.org/2025/02/14/g-s1-48923/stonewall-monument-transgender-park-service.

Knutson, Douglas, Em., Matsuno, Chloe Goldbach, Halleh Hashtpari, and Nathan Grant Smith. 2022. Advocating for Transgender and Nonbinary Affirmative Spaces in Graduate Education. *Higher Education* 83(2):461–479. https://doi.org/10.1007/s10734-020-00673-5.

Kozlov, Max, and Smriti Mallapaty. 2025. Exclusive: NIH to Terminate Hundreds of Active Research Grants. *Nature* 639(8054):281–282. https://doi.org/10.1038/d41586-025-00703-1.

Leyva, Luis A., R. Taylor McNeill, and Antonio Duran. 2022. A Queer of Color Challenge to Neutrality in Undergraduate Stem Pedagogy As a White, Cisheteropatriarchal Space. *Journal of Women and Minorities in Science and*

Engineering 28: 2. https://doi.org/10.1615/JWomenMinorScienEng.2022036586.

Lindqvist, Anna, Marie Gustafsson Sendén, and Emma A. Renström. 2021. What is Gender, Anyway: A Review of the Options for Operationalising Gender. *Psychology & Sexuality* 12(4):332–344. https://doi.org/10.1080/19419899.2020.1729844.

Marsh, Tracy G. 2018. Supporting Transgender Students in Higher Education: Opportunities for Mental Health Professionals. *Journal of Social, Behavioral, and Health Sciences* 13:1. https://doi.org/10.5590/JSBHS.2018.12.1.14.

Maughan, Lizzie, Kristin Natalier, and Monique Mulholland. 2022. Institutional Transphobia: Barriers to Transgender Research in Early Years Education. *Gender and Education* 34(6):721–737. https://doi.org/10.1080/09540253.2022.2057930.

Millar, Krystina, and Caroline V. Brooks. 2021. Double Jeopardy: Minority Stress and the Influence of Transgender Identity and Race/Ethnicity. *International Journal of Transgender Health*:1–16. https://doi.org/10.1080/26895269.2021.1890660.

Nicolazzo, Z., and T. J. Jourian. 2020. 'I'm Looking for People Who Want to Do Disruption Work': Trans* Academics and Power Discourses in Academic Conferences. *Gender and Education* 32(1):56–69. https://doi.org/10.1080/09540253.2019.1633461.

Parsons, Mikay. 2023. We Don't Do That Here: Investigating and Expanding Instructional Communication by 'Transing' the Communication Classroom. *Kaleidoscope: A Graduate Journal of Qualitative Communication Research* 21(1). https://opensiuc.lib.siu.edu/kaleidoscope/vol21/iss1/9.

Platt, Lisa F. 2020. The Presenting Concerns of Transgender and Gender Nonconforming Clients at University Counseling Centers. *The Counseling Psychologist* 48(3):407–431. https://doi.org/10.1177/0011000019898680.

Puckett, Jae A., Alix B. Aboussouan, Allura L. Ralston, Brian Mustanski, and Michael E. Newcomb. 2023. Systems of Cissexism and the Daily Production of Stress for Transgender and Gender Diverse People. *International Journal of Transgender Health* 24(1):113–126. https://doi.org/10.1080/26895269.2021.1937437.

Rabin, Roni, and Apoorva Mandavilli. 2025. Health Resources Vanish Following DEI and Gender Orders. *The New York Times*, January 31.

Rands, Kai. 2019. Mathematical Inqueery: Queering the Theory, Praxis, and Politics of Mathematics Pedagogy. In *Queer Pedagogies: Theory, Praxis, Politics*, ed. Cris Mayo and Nelson M. Rodriguez, 59–74. Critical Studies of Education. Cham: Springer International Publishing. https://doi.org/10.1007/978-3-030-27066-7_5.

Reggiani, Marco, Jessica Dawn Gagnon, and Rebecca Jane Lunn. 2023. LGBT + Academics' and PhD Students' Experiences of Visibility in STEM: More than

Raising the Rainbow Flag. *Higher Education*. https://doi.org/10.1007/s10734-023-00993-2.

Robinson, Brandon Andrew. 2022. Non-Binary Embodiment, Queer Knowledge Production, and Disrupting the Cisnormative Field: Notes From a Trans Ethnographer. *The Journal of Men's Studies* 30(3):425–445. https://doi.org/10.1177/10608265221108204.

Ruberg, Bonnie, and Spencer Ruelos. 2020. Data for Queer Lives: How LGBTQ Gender and Sexuality Identities Challenge Norms of Demographics. *Big Data & Society* 7(1):2053951720933286. https://doi.org/10.1177/2053951720933286.

Siegel, Derek P. 2019. Transgender Experiences and Transphobia in Higher Education. *Sociology Compass* 13(10):e12734. https://doi.org/10.1111/soc4.12734.

Stonewall National Monument (U.S. National Park Service). Accessed 10 April 2025. https://www.nps.gov/ston/index.htm.

Suárez, Mario I., Guadalupe Marquez-Velarde, Christy Glass, and Gabe H. Miller. 2022. Cis-Normativity at Work: Exploring Discrimination against US Trans Workers. *Gender in Management: An International Journal* 37(6):716–731. https://doi.org/10.1108/GM-06-2020-0201.

Vargas, Jacob E., and Alexander Farquhar-Leicester. 2023. 'Only 2 Genders': Implications of Virtual Transphobia for Transgender Mental Health. *Journal of Ethnographic & Qualitative Research* 17(1) (Spring):77–98.

Virtual Fence Exhibit—Stonewall National Monument (U.S. National Park Service). Accessed April 10, 2025. https://www.nps.gov/ston/learn/photos multimedia/virtual-fence-exhibit.htm.

Wang, Hansi Lo. 2025. Census Bureau Stopped Work on Data for Protecting Trans Rights, Former Director Says. NPR, February 21, sec. Politics. https://www.npr.org/2025/02/21/nx-s1-5305265/census-lgbtq-sogi-data-robert-santos.

Weiser, S. Gavin, Travis L. Wagner, and Myles Lawter. 2018. Double Jeopardy: (Trans)Versing Higher Ed as Queer Trans Advocates. *Journal of Curriculum and Pedagogy* 15(3):323–39. https://doi.org/10.1080/15505170.2018.1542359.

Wilson, Jo D. 2020. They're Crying in the All-Gender Bathroom: Navigating Belonging in Higher Education While First Generation and Nonbinary. *The Vermont Connection* 41(1). https://scholarworks.uvm.edu/tvc/vol41/iss1/17.

Worthen, Meredith G. F. 2016. Hetero-Cis–Normativity and the Gendering of Transphobia. *International Journal of Transgenderism* 17(1):31–57. https://doi.org/10.1080/15532739.2016.1149538.

Yourish, K., A. Daniel, S. Datar, I. White, and L. Gamio. 2025. These Words Are Disappearing in the New Trump Administration. *The New York Times*, March 7. https://www.nytimes.com/interactive/2025/03/07/us/trump-federal-agencies-websites-words-dei.html.

Florence Edler: The "Indispensable Collaborator" of Raymond De Roover

Olivia M. Young

When economic historians think about the late medieval and early modern worlds, the name of Raymond de Roover is practically synonymous with their field of study. His contributions on the bill of exchange, economic doctrines of scholasticism, just price, the School of Salamanca, and the Medici bank, among other subfields, are still widely cited and taught today, and have been for decades since their publication (Decock 2009; Rubin 2010; Van Houdt and Monsalve 2021). Classed by Odd Langholm as one of the preeminent representatives of a revisionist view, which, superseding Weber and Tawney, eventually became "the conventional interpretation" of the economic thought of medieval churchmen, De Roover has become a scholar whom others must engage with, a classic of the historiography (Langholm 1998). Even though biographical explorations of his life, or total summations of his oeuvre, are relatively thin on the ground, he has continued to be the topic of intense attention, including in the popular realm (Chafuen 2003). However, the woman once referred to as his "indispensable collaborator", his wife, has been relegated to the realm of the occasional, obligatory mention or single

O. M. Young (✉)
Department of History, University of Chicago, Chicago, IL, USA
e-mail: omyoung@uchicago.edu

© The Author(s), under exclusive license to Springer Nature Switzerland AG 2026

V. Dolar and T. Perry (eds.), *Missing Voices in Economics*,
https://doi.org/10.1007/978-3-031-97180-8_10

footnote, the gender bias motivated obscurity she faced during her professional life continuing decades after her death (R. de Roover 1974, 13). Florence Edler de Roover is an important scholar, both under her own name and as a collaborator with her husband, the motivating force and research powerhouse behind his famous monographs. Her biography, though, is a prime example of the way missing voices in economics were silenced in the first place, her findings and analysis needing the imprimatur of a male scholar in order to be taken seriously in the early and mid-twentieth-century American academe.

Before attempting to understand the depth and breadth of Edler's importance as an economic historian, it is essential to provide a brief biographical sketch of her life, in order to understand the circumstances under which she operated. Born December 14, 1900, in a suburb of Chicago, Illinois, Florence Edler studied for her BA, MA, and PhD all at the University of Chicago, specializing in philosophy, history, and romance languages (F. Edler de Roover n.d.a). She spent much of the 1920s and 1930s abroad, traveling and studying in England, France, Italy, Switzerland, Germany, Spain, Belgium, Holland, Austria, Hungary, Turkey, Greece, Morocco, Tunisia, and Algeria, among other locations (F. Edler De Roover n.d.b). Among the linguistic competencies she was known to possess during the time of her dissertation was Italian, French, German, Spanish, Dutch, Flemish, and Latin (medieval and vulgar), with multiple specializations in geographical and time variants of these languages (F. Edler De Roover n.d.c).

She held multiple teaching positions during her MA and PhD study (roughly 1922 to the end of the doctoral degree in 1930) and published numerous articles (F. Edler De Roover n.d.c). After her marriage to Raymond de Roover in 1936, whom she met on an archive trip to Antwerp funded by the Belgian American Foundation two years prior, her output declined precipitously, though never fully stopped (Graves and Stevelinck 1988). De Roover, four years Edler's junior, emigrated to the United States after their marriage, obtaining an MBA from Harvard in 1938 and a PhD from the University of Chicago in 1943 (Graves and Stevelinck 1988). He held various positions at Boston College, University of California at Berkley, Illinois University, and Wells College, but his uncollegial nature made it hard for him to hold onto a long-term posting, and he did not find a long-term professorship until his hiring by Brooklyn College (1961–1972) (Graves and Stevelinck 1988). Florence supported her husband financially and intellectually through his student period and taught herself at Cedar Crest College and MacMurray College, the former of which she was head of department at for a year. (F. Edler De Roover n.d.a). After her husband's death in 1972, she relocated to Italy, intending to finish a book project which she had begun before their marriage, but was unable to continue after suffering a stroke in 1983, and died in Florence four years later (University of Chicago Library 2017).

In the introductory biography she provided for lectures (she spent two years presenting her dissertation at various universities and learned societies), she wrote that she was "a specialist in the economic history of Italy during the Middle Ages and the Renaissance. She is well known as the author of A GLOSSARY OF MEDIAEVAL TERMS OF BUSINESS: ITALIAN SERIES (1200–1600), and of numerous other publications, such as essays in cooperative volumes, periodical articles in several languages, and numerous book reviews. She has lectured in a number of art museums, colleges, and universities, and before historical societies in the East, South, and Middle West. Her most popular lecture is an illustrated one 'Lucca, Medieval City of Silks,' [her dissertation topic] which is also the title of a book that will appear in 1951" (F. Edler De Roover n.d.d). Although her dissertation appears to have received some form of publication when it was finished in 1930, it was never released as a book.

Despite this, Edler's solo works constitute an important contribution to economic history. Her dissertation, for example, was a topic of constant correspondence with other economic historians, even decades after she finished the project. The eminent Yale-based economic historian Robert Sabatino Lopez, who corresponded with both Mr. and Mrs. De Roover, asked Florence on multiple occasions for sources she had used in that dissertation so that he could utilize them into his own publications, and looked to her to read and critique chapters he had written on Italian economic history and economic history more generally (F. Edler De Roover 1946). The aforementioned *Glossary of Mediaeval Terms of Business,* which the Medieval Academy of America commissioned her to write, was published in 1934 and met with overwhelmingly positive reviews (Picard 1934). Prominent French legal historian and politician Roger Picard marked it out as a "rich" work deserving of "nothing but praise" (Picard 1934). It helped to give scholars the vocabulary to understand what they were reading and researching in medieval account books, letters, etc., and to explain it, so that greater comprehension and comparison was possible (Littleton 1935). The book continues to be cited as a valuable resource today (Goldthwaite 2015).

Edler also made important contributions to the history of marine insurance. Sabine Go holds her as a revolutionary figure in the field (Go et al. 2009). Her research and monographs led scholars to see that marine insurance was not a Greek or Roman invention, as was the consensus early in the twentieth century, but something, like bills of exchange and double entry bookkeeping, which emerged from the commercial revolution of 1275–1325 in the "Italian mercantile city states" (Go et al. 2009, 13–4). This was a key point in tracing the history of early modern capitalism as "marine insurance…facilitated the development of long-distance trade" which was one of the backbones of it (Go et al. 2009, 13). Challenging consensus was a running theme of her work, and she was unafraid to question the work of more established scholars, arguing in a multitude of languages and bringing both qualitative and quantitative analyses to bear (Edler 1937).

The most important work that Edler did, though, is that which few, if any, scholars recognize as hers at all. But before exploring that work, and how her essential role in it has been obfuscated, the scope and importance of the work itself must be more fully explained. In particular, his prominence in the literature on medieval and early modern economic history, scholastic economic thought, and bills of exchange, the high regard in which he was held by many of his colleagues, and the frequency with which he continues to be referenced today.

The "historian sans pair of medieval business and banking institutions", Raymond De Roover declared in 1942 that, "in any economic system, whether medieval or modern, 'money, banking, and credit,'" are so closely connected and interwoven that they cannot be separated" (R. de Roover 1974, vii; R. de Roover 1948a, 2). Certainly, De Roover's work shows a deep sensitivity to the connections between those three realms, and more generally an eagerness not just to present the history of banks or banking institutions, but to show how they functioned in their time. The bank that De Roover's name is associated with more than that of any other is the Medici Bank, on which he wrote two books and published a multitude of articles. (His own history with the bank, and the actual break-down of the work done in both books, is tied to larger questions about the amount of credit due to Florence Edler in the work they pursued together. This will be more fully explicated later)

While the Medici bank had been studied by other historians before, Richard Goldthwaite considered De Roover's *The Rise and Decline of the Medici Bank* to be a "model business history" and wrote that, in conjunction with Federigo Melis' work on the subject, "little more need be said...on the banking techniques and internal history of the Medici bank" (Goldthwaite 1987, 4–5).

1948's *The Medici Bank* was De Roover's first book length effort on the subject, though it was mainly composed of the text of three previously published articles (R. de Roover 1948a). In the book, he shows how Florentine bankers operated as traders as well as bankers, and uses a lawsuit tried in a Bruges court in 1455 to shed light on how the Medici bank functioned as an organization (R. de Roover 1948a). With his "unusual combination of practical European commercial training and formal education by some of America's most outstanding professors", he was able to translate very fragmentary records into a holistic portrait of a functioning organism, and not simply a snapshot, but a moving picture of the bank's functioning through time (R. de Roover 1948a, viii). The focus of the last chapter was on the downfall of the bank, especially why that downfall came about. He ends up his study citing, and agreeing with, a 1943 article on the banker Sassetti by Florence Edler, concurring that "'the downfall of the Medici banking house cannot be traced to a single cause, but to a complex of circumstances and a combination of interacting factors'", though he places the largest amount of blame in those multivariate factors on tendency of merchant bankers to "drift" from private to government finance (R. de Roover 1948a, 59–66).

Although it may seem like the Medici story may be one of limited academic interest, De Roover marked it out as important to the history of banking as a whole because the family "did not innovate", but the relative abundance of their records allowed one to see contemporary business practice in action and to compare between families, regions, and times (R. de Roover 1948a, 31). His much longer and more archivally engaged *The Rise and Decline* therefore presented not only a more complete picture of the Medici operation, but gave other scholars a wider range of areas where they could compare their own work, and possibly see how certain banking practices spread and were, or were not, adapted for new places and times.

It is worth noting that Florence Edler's *Glossary on Mediaeval Terms of Business, Italian Series, 1200–1600*, published in 1934, would have been of assistance in the execution of the Medici studies and other economic histories of the period and beyond. Prominent French legal historian and politician Roger Picard marked it out as a "rich" work deserving of "nothing but praise" (Picard 1934, 442). It helped to give scholars the vocabulary to understand what they were reading and researching in medieval account books, letters, etc., and to explain it, so that greater comprehension and comparison was possible (Littleton 1935). The main 300 pages of text were taken up with this endeavor, but that is not all which the book contained. 100 pages of appendices gave "valuable information regarding Medici partnerships, Medici accounts and bookkeeping methods, and the Florentine woolen industry", as well as a "fascinating" 44-page study of bookkeeping practices in the fourteenth and fifteenth centuries, particularly with regard to merchant banking (Littleton 1935, 153–4).

The couple's contributions to the history of banking, though, must be viewed in light of those to the entire history of the development of early modern capitalism, especially with regard to bills of exchange. Lettres de change were financial instruments invented in Italy that came into widespread use around the mid-thirteenth century and functioned as currency exchange mechanisms (allowing merchants to make purchases in a local currency without carrying that money with them), short-term credit extensions, and trade facilitators (making trade easier and more profitable as transporting specie could cost 8–12% of its total value) (R. de Roover 1963; Rubin 2010). De Roover conceived of these as one of the most important spurs to early modern capitalism and the development of a complex banking system.

By requiring the presence of agents in different cities to affect the changes in currency, bills of exchange helped encouraged banking houses to establish the permanent foreign branches, a development assisted by the gradual dissipation of the Champagne Fairs (R. de Roover 1970). Bills of exchange also caused fairs, mostly for the purpose of credit transactions, to pop up in cities like Lyon and Besaçon, spurring interregional commerce, diffusing the use of complex financial institutions, and helping those cities become commercial and financial centers, albeit not as powerful as many of the ones that existed in Italy (R. de Roover 1970).

Florence Edler's work, before her marriage and after, displayed no less sensitivity to how particular financial and legal instruments, and patterns of commerce, contributed to the development of capitalism. In her PhD thesis, Edler made detailed explanation of the legalistic nature of the medieval economy in Lucca, showing how contracts and law bound practices affected everything from insurance contracts to the way of choosing silk export carriers, and from that the development of the larger commercial world (Edler 1930). That work did not cease when she married, nor was it considered unimportant. The eminent Yale economic historian Robert Sabatino Lopez, who corresponded with both Mr. and Mrs. De Roover, asked Florence on multiple occasions for the sources she had used in that dissertation so that he could incorporate them into his own publications, and looked to her to read and critique chapters he had written on Italian economic history and economic history more generally (F. Edler de Roover 1946).

Edler is held in particular regard by scholars of marine insurance, some of whom, like Sabine Go, view her as a revolutionizer of the field (Go et al. 2009). Her research and monographs led scholars to see that marine insurance was not truly a Greek or Roman invention, as was the consensus early in the twentieth century, but something, like bills of exchange and double entry bookkeeping, which emerged from the commercial revolution of 1275–1325 in the "Italian mercantile city states" (Go et al. 2009). This was a key point in tracing the history of early modern capitalism as "marine insurance…facilitated the development of long-distance trade" which was one of the backbones of it (Go et al. 2009, 13).

Throughout his career, De Roover was praised for his ability to marry the practical workings of economic history with the thought that surrounded and, in some cases, undergirded it (R. de Roover 1974). This was especially apparent in the study of usury, and scholastic economics more generally. In the early twentieth century, the dominant strain of thought on the scholastics, following Weber and Tawney, was that they had held back the development of capitalism in Western Europe, clinging to an Aristotelian theory of value and a positive perception of guilds as medieval "welfare agencies" which sought to keep everyone from going above or below their proper place in society, and/or that their pronouncements were simply ignored by bankers and merchants (R. de Roover 1958, R. de Roover 1967). De Roover broke decisively from this view.

Digging into the works of prominent Schoolmen like Saint Bernardino of Sienna, he showed that usury was a more complex concept than was often understood. Usury was not any interest demanded above the legally or socially acceptable rate, but excess "above the principal of a mutuum, or loan, exacted by reason of the loan itself" (R de Roover

1967, 258). Leases, loans of objects, and other contracts were not under the usury prohibition (R de Roover 1967). This was reflected in the way that bills of exchange were structured, as they were not created with the guarantee of a profit or loss, so they did not constitute a mutuum, and the opportunity cost which was implied within became a justification for profit (R de Roover 1967). "Scholastic usury doctrine", he wrote, "decisively affected the development of credit and of banking institutions" (R de Roover 1971, 92). As De Roover was able to show, economic thought and economic innovation were in constant conversation; when the concept of dry exchange came about as a method of hiding loans, thinkers like Bernardino roundly condemned it, learned enough in the operation of financial instruments to see it for what it was (R. de Roover 1955).

On the topic of scholastic theories of value, De Roover was arrayed similarly against the Weber-Tawney conception and shed light on the writings of quite a few scholastic thinkers to defend his position. Although some figures, like Langenstein and Duns Scotus, advocated a labor theory of value, the mainstream of scholastic thought, from Aquinas and Bernardino to the School of Salamanca, favored the market as the determiner of just price (R. de Roover 1955). His influence on this issue was such that Odd Langholm wrote he was a thinker, "like Weber", that one had to take a position on when explaining the Scholastic theory of value (Langholm 1998).

But De Roover did not stop at refuting the idea of schoolmen as unrepentant followers of Aristotle, or even at explaining how scholastic economic ideas influenced, and were influenced by, law and on the ground commercial reality (R. de Roover 1958). He made an effort to draw lines of intellectual lineage between the scholastics and later economists, tracing how something like an anticipation of consumer preference scales in John Buridan, or market price as a just price in Aquinas and Bernardino, made its way into the work of the Salamanca schoolmen, continental thinkers like Antonio Serra, seventeenth- and eighteenth-century legal scholars like Pufendorf and Grotius, and finally, though Francis Hutcheson, Adam Smith (R. de Roover 1955). (Though this is a gross over simplification of the complex paths which De Roover presents.) Therein, he validates his thesis, that "like other sciences, economics grows slowly by accretion" (R. de Roover 1955, 190).

Here, it would be instructive to compare De Roover's work to that of Joseph Schumpeter, done almost simultaneously, and with "fundamental agreement on various points", but tackled from quite different angles (R. de Roover 1955, 161–2). Schumpeter, in his chapter on "The Scholastic Doctors and The Philosophers of Natural Law", also saw a greater degree of continuity than was then commonly acknowledged between the scholastics and the classical economists (Schumpeter 1986). But he saw them as having a "detachment from the immediately practical issues of economic policy", far from De Roover's presentation of them as men knowledgeable about day-to-day economic practice so that they could offer sufficient guidance to the merchants and bankers in their flock (Schumpeter 1986, 137). Schumpeter does praise the "little monographs" on topics like the wool trade which Luis de Molina, seeking to understand the economic phenomena he wrote about and provided guidance on, produced (Schumpeter 1986, 137). But he himself largely fails to merge theoretical occurrences with on the ground facts or patterns, unlike trained accountant De Roover, as a consequence of which his analysis of scholastic thinkers often lacks any solid grounding in their motivations for writing as and what they did on economic topics.

This merging of thought and theory with practice, as well as his willingness to bring social and legal history into the mix, is a consequence in part of the fact that De Roover was trained as a historian, and even beforehand working in a time, when the Annales School was ascendant in France and influential over the rest of Europe and in the United States (Hexter 1972). The "concern to bring History into close relations with social sciences, especially human geography, economics, and sociology" and focus on the medieval and early modern Mediterranean world which characterized the fathers of the school is very present in his work (Hexter 1972). Indeed, one of his earliest academic articles was published in the famed *Annales d'histoire Économique et Sociale* and Fernand Braudel provided an introduction to his book on bills of exchange (R. de Roover 1937; R de Roover 1953).

By the same token, Florence Edler's work is marked by a very clear attempt to synthesize economics with art, legal codes and concerns, and geography in history. A short article on Hans Memling's "The Last Judgement", a fifteenth-century triptych, explores not only the creation and artistic value of the piece, but the real-life figures who appear in it, its relation to larger theological trends, its place in the history of the Medici bank, and how it fit into patronage culture and early modern international legal disputes (F. Edler de Roover 1945). Likewise, in a later article, "financial, warehousing, and marketing problems" intersected with the physical creation and intellectual content of books in the fifteenth and sixteenth centuries (F. Edler de Roover 1953). For both husband and wife, economic history existed in a larger intellectual framework, and by surveying, for instance, the actual methods of double entry bookkeeping and the economic tracts of men like Bernardino of Sienna or Cardinal Cajetan together, they were able to illuminate these intersections and provide a fuller portrait of both.

This partnership did not have a promising start, though, and the anxieties of those close to Edler about de Roover would turn out to be prescient. When Edler chose to marry de Roover in the mid-1930s, a multitude of her contemporaries and advisors, who included such prominent economists and economic historians as Jacob Viner, Frank H. Knight, and John Ulric Nef, warned her against marrying the at that time an obscure scholar (University of Chicago Library 2017). According to Julius Kirshner, who studied informally under the couple while working toward his PhD at Columbia in the late 1960s, De Roover garnered a lot of ill will among those who knew her as a student because they felt he "dominated" her and stood in the way of her clear potential to become a "top scholar" (Kirshner 2021, 20:30). Their fears were proved true in very short order. The downturn in Edler's rate of publication coincided not just with an uptick in her husband's, but a total shift in focus. Before their marriage, the vast majority of De Roover's work focused on northern Europe, mostly Belgium and the Netherlands, of which he was a native (Espinas 1931). His original training was as an accountant, and his articles were small-scale studies of bookkeeping practices in Annales publications (Espinas 1931).

After the wedding, his work transformed seemingly overnight. Where before his focus had overwhelmingly been on practice, there was a sudden shift to questions concerning the intellectual underpinnings of economic practices and tools (R. de Roover 1937). An even more radical change occurred over the next ten years, as his geographic focus went from northern Europe to Italy and the Mediterranean more broadly, Florence's area of expertise. His first book publication, in fact, was also his first Italian work and probably his most famous: *The Medici Bank: its organization, management, operations and decline* (1948). Edler's 1934 *Glossary*, in addition to the 300 pages of main text it devoted to defining terms, contains 100 pages of appendices gave "valuable information regarding Medici partnerships, Medici accounts and bookkeeping methods, and the Florentine woolen industry", as well as a "fascinating" 44-page study of bookkeeping practices in the fourteenth and fifteenth centuries, particularly with regard to merchant banking (Littleton 1935, 153–4).

The *Glossary* is cited a handful of times in *The Medici Bank,* but it is the book's introduction which gives a startlingly clear story of Florence's role in its inception and creation. Kirshner explains that "the research for that [book] was done by his wife because that's the way things were done in those days. Wives didn't get credit but they often did a lot of the research and rewriting" (Kirshner 2021, 14:42). De Roover, who briefly mentions Florence as a "scholar in her own right", merely credits her with pushing him to photograph the account books of Francesco Sassetti, which provided him with a document of "the greatest value" (R. de Roover 1948b).

A substantially expanded and revised version of the study, published in 1963 as *The Rise and Decline of the Medici Bank,* also contains a forward which goes into vastly more detail on Florence's contributions to the book. She summoned him to the Medici archives in 1949 because there was so much material that had been neglected by earlier historians, "took charge of all the research involved in this new scheme", went systematically through "the inventory of the Medici Archives prior to the Principate" in order that they could navigate the papers, and "discovered the secret account books of the Medici Bank in a mislabeled bundle (No. 153)" (R. de Roover 1966, xii). Asserting in a jocular tone that she has refused co-credit because of her dislike for any work "bristling with statistical tables", he goes on to assure the reader that "her horror of them is unjustified…I prepared and typed all the tables, leaving to her the easier job of the regular text, the footnotes, and the bibliography" (R. de Roover 1966, xii). He treats any assertion that she should be given co-credit in a similarly flippant manner, opining that her name "should perhaps" appear on the title page (R. de Roover 1966, xii). A huge number of the primary source documents for all of his projects, especially those on scholastic thought, were written in Latin, but, as De Roover's comprehension of the language was somewhere between poor and non-existent, it fell on Edler to do all of the translation (Kirshner 2021). An undated missive from De Roover to Edler opens "I expect you to read this letter with care" and contains a laundry list of demands, from footnotes he wanted created for his upcoming publications to notes on secondary sources and translations of primary (R. de Roover n.d.). De Roover continued publishing into 1971, and none of his articles or books ever contain co-author credit with his wife, even where she is cited extensively.

Robert Sabatino Lopez, writing on the occasion of Raymond de Roover's election as Fellow of the Medieval Academy, congratulated Florence on her husband's achievement, briefly expressing a wish that there were "matrimonial slots" in the organization before dismissing such an idea with the apparently obvious observation: "but it was necessary to bet on only one member of the De Roover family, and some of our colleagues are obdurate anti-feminists" (Lopez 1970). The opinion that Edler's contribution was something on the level of secretarial work, and so did and does not deserve equal recognition with De Roover's, or anything approaching the acknowledgment of a co-author, persists, couched in the argument that, "She was a very good scholar, but she didn't have the imagination that De Roover did" (Kirshner 2021, 15:52). That his work only shows a substantial turn to the intellectual after their marriage, never mind greater sensitivity to matters of government, politics, material culture, and conflict, gives lie to such an argument. It is not a minor point, either, considering Kirshner himself admitted he had "no intention…of claiming that de Roover's insight was singularly novel", but instead that De Roover's "unique" contribution was providing an explanation which married the theoretical and the practical with equal depth (R. de Roover 1974, 19).

A look at Florence Edler de Roover's life and career is also a view into an academe dominated by sexism, where female scholars constantly struggled not just to publish independently, but to be taken seriously at all (Madden 2002). It is a dynamic which replicates itself in a multitude of ways, large and small, again and again. Despite almost always signing herself in professional correspondence as "Dr. Florence Edler de Roover" or "Professor Florence Edler de Roover", institutions from her sometimes publisher, McGraw-Hill, to Museum of Fine Arts Boston insisted on referring to and addressing her as "Mrs. de Roover", and her lectures were pigeonholed as being best suited to a female audience (Mcgraw-Hill n.d.; Museum of Fine Arts Boston 1946).

A letter written to her nephew, Robert, in 1958 gives perhaps the most insightful view into Edler's own cognizance of this and both how she felt about and dealt with her reality. She begins by enquiring about her relative's significant other, showing concern about the younger woman's education heightened by the similarities they share:

Neither you nor your parents had mentioned Nancy's major before your last letter. I am glad she is an historian. Where is she teaching; in the upper grades or a high school? How intellectual and ambitious is she? By that I mean, does she have any desire to do graduate work herself? An M.A. would help her to earn more as a teacher even in public schools (F. Edler de Roover 1958).

Commenting on her nephew's career prospects, she moves to reflect on her own marriage as a female historian:

> "If you think you have found a congenial life companion and are determined to get married soon, nothing I or Raymond may say will make any difference, so we shall not waste time, ink or paper. Whether you go on in History or chance to Law alters the picture for the next few years very little: your wife will have to continue to work to help support you. I used to say I was making a long term investment in Raymond, which I expected to pay well in the end. Raymond thinks I should be satisfied since I have a "famous" husband. I have my dubious moments, but probably would do it all over again, though with my eyes open to some of the problems I could not foresee before experiencing them" (F. Edler de Roover 1958).

A latter comment, added in pen with an arrow pointing to the words "a 'famous' husband", specifies "the advantageous or disadvantageous of a famous husband R. d. R." (F. Edler de Roover 1958). The subtext of her comment appears to be an awareness that the expectations of contemporary society and the institutional structures of academia were always going to cast her in a supporting role, and that her way of both navigating them and getting her work into the world for a serious hearing was to use her husband as a conduit, at the price of any substantial credit to herself for her ideas or her scholarship.

The dissatisfaction which she hints at in the letter, likewise, shaped the rest of her life. Probate paperwork provides a dry but telling narrative of Florence's life after her husband's death in March of 1972.

> "The decedent and her husband moved to Brooklyn, New York, where her husband was employed by Brooklyn College until his death March 14, 1972; that shortly thereafter decedent sold her Brooklyn home, shipped a good many of her possessions (books, furniture, etc.) to this Affiant's home in Rock Island to be stored, completely terminated her residence in Brooklyn, and moved to Florence, Italy for the expressed purpose of completing a book dealing with the Florentine silk Industry - a book which

> she had started before her marriage - a book which required research in the Florence museums and archives in the surrounding towns" (Circuit Court of the Fourteenth Judicial Circuit Rock Island County 1987).

Although ill health hampered her goal, she planned to use the closing years of her life to establish her independent reputation as a scholar in her own right, returning to the work she had commenced more than four decades before and beginning to disentangle her own legacy from that of her husband.

Richard Goldthwaite's characterization of Florence Edler as the "indispensable collaborator" of Raymond de Roover, "historian sans pair of medieval business and banking institutions", which might seem a generous or even overblown conclusion to those who know the standard story of de Roover's life, instead now appears to be an understatement (R de Roover 1974, vii–13). Without Florence Edler, there would have been no "famous" de Roover, and the accountant who dabbled in Annales style bookkeeping history by night likely would have stayed just that for the rest of his life. Florence Edler's work, that published under her name and that which she did for her husband to garner credit alone, has much of import to say about the medieval and early modern economic world, in both its practical and its intellectual manifestations, and their numerous and important overlaps and influences.

But her life itself is an interesting and essential window into the experiences of women in economics and economic history in the twentieth century, in the various challenges they faced and the strategies they used to navigate an overwhelmingly patriarchal sphere where their success was by no means taken for granted. It is a salient one in part because of the common themes it reveals. One of her most important contemporaries, and an occasional correspondent of herself and her husband, Marjorie Grice-Hutchinson, was the victim of multiple acts of plagiarism by the Spanish economic historian Francisco Gomez Camacho, who reproduced significant sections of her work in his articles and chapters without credit for years (Ballor 2014). While the methods by which their work was coopted were different, the essential underlying ethos and lack of serious respect for female contributions to the field were the same. By refocusing attention on both the work and the stories, scholars can make a step toward combating that erasure and making the academic world a richer one.

References

Ballor, Jordan J. 2014. Editorial: Plagiarism in a Digital Age. *Journal of Markets and Morality* 17(2):349–352.

Biographie Nationale de Belgique, vol. 40 (supplement 12). Brussels: Établissements Émile. Bruylant, 1977.

Braun, Harold Ernst, Erik De Bom, and Paolo Astorri. 2021. *A Companion to the Spanish Scholastics*. Leiden, The Netherlands: Brill.

Circuit Court of The Fourteenth Judicial Circuit Rock Island County, Illinois: Estate of Florence E. De Roover, Deceased (No. 87 P427), Papers, [Box 3, Folder 1], UChicago Special Collections.

Chafuen, Alejandro Antonio. 2003. *Faith and Liberty: The Economic Thought of the Late Scholastics*. Studies in Ethics and Economics. Lanham, Md.: Lexington Books.

Decock, Wim. 2009. Lessius and the Breakdown of the Scholastic Paradigm. *Journal of the History of Economic Thought* 31(1).

Day, John. 1987. *The Medieval Market Economy*. Oxford: Basil Blackwell.

De Roover, Florence Edler (n.d.a), "Curriculum Vitae of Florence Edler de Roover", Papers, [Box 2, Folder 7], Hanna Holborn Gray Special Collections Research Center, University of Chicago Library.

De Roover, Florence Edler (n.d.b). "European Travel of Florence Edler de Roover", Papers, [Box 2, Folder 7], UChicago Special Collections.

De Roover, Florence Edler (n.d.c), "Curriculum Vitae of Florence Edler de Roover: Courses Taken at the Universities of Chicago, Florence, Harvard, and Toulouse", Papers, [Box 2, Folder 7],UChicago Special Collections.

De Roover, Florence Edler (n.d.d), "Introduction to Florence Edler de Roover: Head of Department at Cedar Crest College", Papers, [Box 2, Folder 7], UChicago Special Collections.

De Roover, Florence Edler. *Florence Edler De Roover to Robert Sabatino Lopez, March 9, 1946.* Letter. From Yale Manuscripts and Archives, *The Robert Sabatino Lopez Papers, 1932–1987.*

De Roover, Florence Edler. 1945. A Prize of War: A Painting of Fifteenth Century Merchants. *Bulletin of the Business Historical Society* 19(1):3–12.

De Roover, Florence Edler. 1953. New Facets on the Financing and Marketing of Early Printed Books. *Bulletin of the Business Historical Society* 27(4):222–230.

De Roover, Florence Edler. 1934. *Glossary of Mediaeval Terms of Business, Italian Series, 1200–1600*. Cambridge, MA: Mediaeval Academy of America.

De Roover, Raymond. 1937. Aux Origines d'une Technique Intellectuelle: La Formation et l'expansion de La Comptabilité à Partie Double. *Annales d'histoire Économique et Sociale* 9(44):171–193.

De Roover, Florence Edler, *Florence Edler de Roover to Robert Weber, November 16, 1958*, Papers, [Box 3, Folder 1], UChicago Special Collections.

De Roover, Raymond. 1974. In *Business, Banking, and Economic Thought* ed. Julius Kirshner. Chicago: University of Chicago Press.

De Roover, Raymond. 1971. *La pensée économique des scolastiques: doctrines et méthodes*. Montréal: Inst. d'études médiévales.

De Roover, Raymond. 1953. *L'évolution De La Lettre De Change, XIV-XVIII Siècles: Avant-propos De Fernand Braudel*. Affaires Et Gens D'affaires; 4. Paris: Libraire. Armaud Colin.

De Roover, Raymond. 1970. Le Marché Monétaire Au Moyen Age Et Au Début Des Temps Modernes. Problèmes Et Méthodes. *Revue Historique* 244(1[495]):5–40.

De Roover, Raymond. 1948a. *Money, Banking and Credit in Mediaeval Bruges: Italian Merchant Bankers, Lombards and Money-Changers, a Study in the Origins of Banking*. Cambridge, MA: Mediaeval Academy of America.

De Roover, Raymond. 1948b. *The Medici Bank: Its Organization, Management, Operations and Decline*. New York: New York University Press.

De Roover, Raymond. 1955. Scholastic Economics: Survival and Lasting Influence from the Sixteenth Century to Adam Smith. *The Quarterly Journal of Economics* 69(2):161–190.

De Roover, Raymond. 1958. The Concept of the Just Price: Theory and Economic Policy. *The Journal of Economic History* 8(4):418–434.

De Roover, Raymond. 1963. "The Organization of Trade." Chapter. In *The Cambridge Economic History of Europe from the Decline of the Roman Empire*, ed. M. M. Postan, E. E. Rich, and E. Miller. The Cambridge Economic History of Europe. Cambridge: Cambridge University Press.

De Roover, Raymond. 1966. *The Rise and Decline of the Medici Bank: 1397–1494*. New York: W.W. Norton and Company.

De Roover, Raymond. 1967. The Scholastics, Usury, and Foreign Exchange. *The Business History Review* 41(3):257–271.

Edler, Florence. 1937. Eclaircissements à Propos Des Considérations De R. Davidsohn Sur La Productivité De L'argent Au Moyen âge. *Vierteljahrschrift Für Sozial- und Wirtschaftsgeschichte* 30(4):375–380.

Edler, Florence. 1931. The Monastic Scriptorium. *Thought (New York)* 6(2):181–206.

Edler, Florence Marguerite. 1930. *The Silk Trade of Lucca During The Thirteenth And Fourteenth Centuries*. ProQuest Dissertations Publishing.

Espinas, Georges. 1931. Revue de Quelques considérations sur les livres de comptes de Couard de Marke par Raymond de Roover. *Revue Historique de Droit Français et Étranger (1922–)* 10(4):741–743.

Florence Edler de Roover Papers. Hanna Holborn Gray Special Collections Research Center, University of Chicago Library.

Go, Sabine, Sadik Harchaoui, Halim El Madkouri, and Baukje Sijses. 2009. *Marine Insurance in the Netherlands 1600–1870: A Comparative Institutional Approach.*

Goldthwaite, Richard, "The Practice and Culture of Accounting in Renaissance Florence", (*Enterprise & Society* 16, no. 3 (2015)), 629–645.

Goldthwaite, Richard A. 1987. The Medici Bank and the World of Florentine Capitalism. *Past & Present* 114:3–31.

Grabill, Stephen J. 2007. Raymond De Roover's Enduring Contribution to Economic History. *Journal of Markets and Morality* 10(1).

Grice-Hutchinson, Marjorie. 1993. *Economic Thought in Spain.* Brookfield: Edward Elgar Publishing.

Graves. 1988. Oliver Finley and Stevelinck, Ernest. Raymond De Roover (1904–1972) Business historian. *Accounting Historians Notebook* 11(2), Article 11:14–16.

Guide to the Florence Edler de Roover Papers 1933–1978", The University of Chicago, 2017.

Herlihy, David. 1972. Raymond De Roover: Historian of Mercantile Capitalism. *Journal of European Economic History* 1(3)(Winter):755.

Hexter, J. H. 1972. Fernand Braudel and the Monde Braudellien. *The Journal of Modern History* 44(4):480–539.

Kirshner, Julius. 2021. Interview by Olivia Young. Interview on Raymond De Roover. Zoom, October 18.

Lane, Frederic C., ed. 1953. *Enterprise and Secular Change: Readings in Economic History.* London: George Allen and Unwin.

Langholm, Odd. 1992. *Economics in The Medieval Schools: Wealth, Exchange, Value, Money and Usury according to the Paris Theological Tradition 1200–1350.* New York: E.J. Brill.

Langholm, Odd. 1998. *The Legacy of Scholasticism in Economic Thought.* Cambridge: Cambridge University Press.

Littleton, A. C. 1935. Review of Glossary of Medieval Terms of Business-Italian Series, 1200–1600. *Italica* 12(2):152–154.

Lopez, Robert Sabatino, *Robert Sabatino Lopez to Florence de Roover, February 12, 1970, Letter, From Yale Manuscripts and Archives, The Robert Sabatino Lopez Papers*, 1932–1987.

Madden, Kristen K. 2002. Female Contributions to Economic Thought, 1900–1940. *History of Political Economy* 34(1):1–30.

Mathews, Harry. 1999. *The Sinking of the Odradek Stadium.* Normal, IL: Dalkey Archive Press.

McGraw-Hill Book Company Correspondence (Undated)" & "Museum of Fine Arts Boston: May 1946 Program", Papers, [Box 2, Folder 7], UChicago Special Collections.

Picard, Roger. 1934. Revue de Edler, Glossary of Medieval Terms. *Revue d'histoire Économique et Sociale* 22(3/4):442.

Reinert, Sophus A., and Robert Fredona. 2020. Political Economy and the Medici. *Business History Review* 94(1):125–127.

Rubin, Jared. 2010. Bills of Exchange, Interest Bans, and Impersonal Exchange in Islam and Christianity. *Explorations in Economic History* 47(2):213–227.

The Robert Sabatino Lopez Papers, 1932–1987. Yale University Manuscript and Archives.

Schumpeter, Joseph A., *History of Economic Analysis,* (New York: Oxford University Press, [1954] 1986), 136–7.

Van Houdt, Toon, and Fabio Manslave, "Chapter 18: Usury and Interest" in *A Companion to the Spanish Scholastics*, (Leiden, The Netherlands: Brill, 2021), 475–497.

Doing the "Bad Job" to Make a Living and Expose Men: Economic Critique Voiced in Folktales by Marginalised Women

Irene Sotiropoulou

1 Introduction

The chapter presents the connection between economics and folk literature and explores how collectively created narratives are able to transmit economic information and to discuss burning topics of economic importance. Folk literature can grasp economic ideas generated by marginalised groups, like worker women or sex workers, that otherwise do not find a route to be disseminated through formal publishing or academic routes. Economics is unfortunately a patriarchal hierarchical discipline that keeps silencing or disdaining women economists marginalised within the field, and even more women economists belonging at the same time to various marginalised communities, designated by class, race, gender and sexual orientation identities, ability or ethnicity. The economic ideas of women in marginalised groups outside academia are even more erased, if not perceived as inexistent, in the academic discourse following the general epistemological pattern of considering the knowledge about the economy as something produced in academia by academics.

I. Sotiropoulou (✉)
Southport, United Kingdom

© The Author(s), under exclusive license to Springer Nature Switzerland AG 2026

V. Dolar and T. Perry (eds.), *Missing Voices in Economics*,
https://doi.org/10.1007/978-3-031-97180-8_11

By "women" in this chapter I mean all women, irrespective if and despite the fact that certain forms of patriarchy reduce them to a set of biological traits, or if other forms of patriarchy demand more of the performative part of (a certain) femininity to categorise them. After all we must be able to think outside patriarchal categories. I write in English for communication purposes but translating "woman" from Greek language does not even transmit the cultural connotations or the social struggles the word means. Taking the example of Cretan folk tales, I do not define women because this is not necessary to be able to talk about ourselves. Here I very much tell stories about women, in order to discuss how much patriarchy imposes on us irrelevant or impossible standards that are very much mobile according to what suits patriarchal hierarchies in each case. Hence, patriarchy can ask for one more requirement to be fulfilled, while we struggle to survive very material situations like poverty, hunger, violence, forced migration or social exclusion.

This study contributes to the discussion about what sources we use in economics and which of them can represent women's voices and which women's voices exactly. For the purposes of this study, I use a folktale from the island of Crete, Greece. The folktale falls under the generic rubric of a love story and discusses various economic issues, ranging from slave trade to non-remunerated support to people who need to flee for their lives and it focuses mostly on sex work that is performed by the protagonist for her to survive and expose her lover who forgot her.

The analysis is conducted through a feminist lens, taking grassroots economics as a framework of the analysis. By grassroots economics, I mean economic theory and practice which exist among everyday people and communities, in spaces that are more informed by everyday communal life and/or social movements than by established economic thinking. The next section presents the theoretical background of the study while the presentation of the case-study folktale takes place in section three. The folktale is discussed in detail in section four while the question of how such a tale came to survive in Crete for centuries is examined in section five. Conclusions are presented in the final section.

2 Theoretical Background of the Study

The paper is part of a larger research programme concerning grassroots economics. Grassroots economics recognises that people outside academia, in particular people who belong to social groups that are facing discrimination and exploitation, have economic knowledge which may be very much accurate in terms of descriptive power, holistic in terms of analytical power, and critical in terms of positionality towards economic activity. This is an approach developed in collaboration with Dr Ferda Dönmez-Atbaşı (University of Ankara) when we became aware of the impasses stemming from the formal economic knowledge, which is historically and socially specific to the societies in which that knowledge has been produced. It is specific people, with specific class, gender, ethnic and educational backgrounds who create or validate formal economic knowledge. We therefore want to draw attention to sources which are not shelved in the economics or business sections of the library.

The emancipatory potential of everyday collective practices is situated with their ability to inject past social experiences into contemporary debates. Everyday practices and folklore are no doubt capable of promoting the political aims of one or another group in society. Indeed, as critical folklore studies have shown (Briggs 2012; Gencarella 2009, 2010a, 2010b, 2011; Kousaleos 1999; Limon 1983, 1984, 2010; Lipsitz and Rodriguez 2012; Paredes 1963; Lopez Morin 2006), there is need to explore the positionality of popular artistic practices, and to critically examine which social group(s) is/are "speaking" or which social groups' aims and interests are articulated and promoted through specific popular practices. The work done by Jack Zipes (1993, 2001, 2006) on analysing folk and fairy tales through historical materialist perspectives has served as an example of how to analyse folktales as creations linked to specific time, space and historical conditions.

For this reason, feminist theory is equally important for grassroots economics and its analysis. I understand patriarchy as a social system which integrates certain economic structures which are common to patriarchal societies. Thus, I seek to analyse patriarchy in this paper as an economic system in its own right. Consequently, capitalism is perceived as a form of patriarchy (Agathangelou 2004; Fraser 2013a, 2013b; Federici 2013; Ehrenreich and English 1978; Bennholdt-Thomsen et al. 1988; Barker and Kuiper 2003; Eisenstein 1979).

The Cretan communities from which the folktale comes, constitute(d) a capitalist economy, at least during the time that the folktales were collected, transcribed and published by the collectors. Moreover, not all economic structures that are not capitalist are necessarily relics from the past or irrelevant to capitalism. Indeed, anything that is not capitalist in the economy may be coeval with capitalism, may co-exist, may be complementary or antagonistic, if not actually resisting capitalist arrangements in a straightforward manner.

Moreover, capitalism is not identical with patriarchy, because patriarchy as an economic system has various forms. Patriarchal economic arrangements existed before capitalism just like patriarchal economic arrangements appear even in economies that are not capitalist—or try not to be—today. This is why it is important to see, through folk literature, how non-capitalist arrangements may also be patriarchal or not. It is also necessary to investigate how people understand the patriarchal nature of capitalism, exactly by promoting their own understandings of what is fair to happen in the economy. This is particularly the case concerning social groups, such as women, who are exploited or discriminated in the mainstream/dominant economy. The patriarchal character of capitalism might be missed in mainstream academic economic theory but those who live in this economic system are very vocal about it.

The Cretan storytellers, in particular the ones who cooperated with the folktale collectors, might have had access to their contemporary critical ideological streams, like Marxism, feminism, anarchism, at least through press and mass media or through discussions in their communities. A class- or gender-aware position may have many influences that belong to both oral and written ways of transmission of a narrated story (Bottigheimer 2009). Especially about Crete, we know that press was available since very early compared to other regions in Greece and emancipatory ideas could be disseminated through print media too. One should also consider that class or ethnic or colonial divisions do not necessarily prescribe the access to information for people who might form other types of alliances, beyond the divisions designed for them by their society's authorities.

Folktales, therefore, are one among the many sources someone can use for learning and understanding grassroots economics. Just like other forms of folk literature and culture, they are tools or methods of the traditional or popular educational system which transfers knowledge from generation to generation and from one person to another. This popular educational system runs parallel and/or in opposition to the formal structures of knowledge dissemination in each society (Antoniou 2010; Mejia 2015; Vargas 2018).

No doubt, folktales are not historical narrations and they are not expected to be. Some of them have patterns that are quite old or ancient, and some have introduced features that refer clearly to a specific era, like the folktale I analyse in this chapter. However, we know for sure that they existed or were created or modified during the last centuries. Therefore, we cannot assume that folktales have not been informed or affected by capitalism before and after they have started to be transcribed or recorded by collectors the previous decades. We know that other types of literature the last centuries contain vast information about the economic activity of women in capitalism narrated by women artists (Henry 2018, Rutterford and Maltby 2009). It would be absurd to disdain sources because of the genre of the art.

In terms of economic education, the concrete incidents described in each folktale allow an understanding about the economy without losing the social characteristics of the people involved in the economic activity. In the case-study folktale "Fiorentinos and Dolcetta" (Φιορεντίνος και Ντολτσέττα) we do not have an economic agent, or an economic man, but a poor peasant, the pirates, the bad king, the king's daughter, the poor old woman, and many other people who represent social groups or attitudes. Class, gender and ethnicity, plus professional backgrounds of the main characters, are clearly visible and affect the plot.

The anonymity and the allegories along with the indefinite time and space of folktales provide an opportunity for the storytellers to describe and/or criticise economic behaviours that otherwise might be dangerous to talk about. Folktales are a low-cost route to disseminate ideas that in a formal capitalist setting would require significant amounts of capital to be transmitted (Antoniou 2010). Having access to official outlets of ideas dissemination also requires a degree of indoctrination or acceptance of the formal discourse frameworks that informal sharing does not have to compromise with (based on a comment by Justine Dombrowski, 3.6.2024, personal communication).

It is also absurd to say that women's particular ways of economic exploitation or money access were not known to the storytellers just because the folktale does not use contemporary economic terminology like "feminism" or "wage labour" or "sex work". To the contrary, most important capitalist institutions (like private property, the state, wage labour combined with unpaid women's labour or the commodity) existed before capitalism. Therefore, a folktale may also be a source of what everyday people thought of and did while the capitalist articulation of economic structures was taking place (Zipes 2001, 160). People in small communities or in discriminated social groups may have a very sophisticated picture of their societies, even if they might not consciously constitute themselves as a class in the way this is expected by (Western) revolutionary theory (Meraklis 1984, 69–77; Meraklis 1988, 23–38; Taussig 1980, 60–67).

The paper is also concerned with the question of which folktales survive and are narrated to the collectors to be published, and why. As a researcher of grassroots economic practices, I have witnessed this phenomenon of the community persistently promoting a certain set of ideas to be saved and documented by an outsider and/or researcher: participants avoided telling me about non-monetary practices that may be exploitative although those practices exist today in Crete, so the data persistently were "promoting" only the egalitarian non-monetary practices (Sotiropoulou 2013).

In other words, societies are not static or unable to understand what is happening in their economies. Much less are they passive to the changes of the economy when they are under colonial rule like the Venetian one was. The long history of revolts and riots in Crete (Detorakis 1994) should always be taken into account when asking questions whether people understood very well their historical context. It is just that various social groups did not have easy access to academia and to the press industry and they could not formally publish their ideas. Consequently, they expressed their views about the economy within other social activities (Beverley 2004; Meraklis 1988, 5–12; Zipes 2001, 29–38).

3 *The Folktale Used as Case Study: "Fiorentinos and Dolcetta"*[1]

The folktale is the first presented in the collection by Maria Mavredaki (2006, 11–23) "Fiorentinos and Dolcetta—Cretan folktales for grownups and little ones". I have not found yet any other version of it in other Cretan folktale collections, although Cretan folktales often have a progressive stance concerning women's freedom and sexual life (Kapsomenos and Papaderou 2014; Sotiropoulou 2016). Mavredaki informs us (2006, 172–173) that this folktale along with many other tales

[1] Unless otherwise stated, all translations of quotes and excerpts of the original folktale from Greek to English are done by the author.

in the same collection has been narrated to her by Olympia Charokopaki-Pontikaki, a storyteller who lived in Chania, Greece, and died in 1981 (the tale was narrated "some years before" 1981). The title of the tale consists of the names of the protagonists.

From the title one understands that this might have been an Italian folktale or a folktale with very strong Italian influences. Crete island has been a colony of Venice for more than 400 years (1204, while effective rule starts in 1211, to 1669, although effective rule gets limited in 1645 with the occupation of Chania by the Ottomans) (Detorakis 1994). A lot of traits in the culture of the island still bear influence from the Venetian era.

To facilitate the analysis and discussion of the tale, I provide below a brief summary of the story line and I examine content and literary details in the next sections. To avoid tiring the reader with using examples of story-telling discourse from multiple parts of the folktale to support my interpretation of the economic ideas in the story, I follow the structure of the tale. To do this, I used each major episode or scene of the tale as a set of economic ideas that the storyteller conveys to us. I focus on those episode-based ideas in order to show first, how systematic the storyteller has been in her political-economic analysis; and second, to enable the reader to see the sophistication of the economic ideas transmitted through the folktale. For a more general comprehensive analysis, I use the fifth section where the folktale is analysed on a second level as an economics educational/learning instrument.

The folktale has been one of those stories for adults to be narrated for more than an hour during gatherings and it is many pages long (imagine how long it would take to narrate it with all the pauses, enactments or imitations of characters). Moreover, this is not a very widely known story, like the Snowwhite family/type of folk and fairy tales, about which everyone has a main idea about the story line and the analyser can skip the plot details. On the other hand, I also wanted to follow the educational path that the storyteller chose. I suspect that both the storyteller of this version and the initial creator of the tale had some strong ideas about the economy and the role of women in it, but they did not opt for a didactic speech or a moralistic argumentation the usual way it is done by academics. This is a learning method on its own right and I believe that the readers might find it easier to follow the ideas if those are carefully linked to action and characters, just like the story presents them, instead of theorising abstractly about economic issues.

The storyline is as follows: Dolcetta is a 15-year-old princess in a kingdom where the king gets ill with psoriasis. No-one can help him heal apart from a magician who advises him to kill a child and use its blood as medicine. The servants of the king find a supposedly orphaned boy, Fiorentinos, who is 15 years old and whom they must buy as a slave from his pirate capturers. Dolcetta falls in love with him and reveals her parents' plan. The two youths decide to flee the country and the queen tries to stop them, initially with arguments, and then with a curse that the queen casts upon them, that when Fiorentinos is kissed by his mother, he will forget Dolcetta.

The two protagonists travel to reach the kingdom where Fiorentinos originates from. At the border, he leaves to get to the city and Dolcetta waits for him, but in vain as the curse took effect and Fiorentinos does no longer remember Dolcetta.

Dolcetta decides to go to the capital city to find him, and settles with a poor old woman. Dolcetta devises a plan so that she and the old woman have enough to eat: she will announce that she is doing the "bad job", i.e. that she is a prostitute-courtesan and will be receiving clients from now on following a strict procedure of appointment and prepayment of services.

The three princes of the kingdom try to make an appointment with her, prepaying high prices in zecchini (Venetian golden ducats) but she finds ways to avoid them all while keeping the money. For this, she is tried for fraud by the king. During the trial she reveals what has happened. Fiorentinos remembers her and wants to kill himself out of despair, but the other people stop him, and the young couple is again together (with the folktale-typical end-of-story marriage).

4 Patriarchy, Its Trades and Its Discontents

4.1 Child Sacrifice, Apprenticeship as Slavery and the Slave Trade

The first part of the story takes place at the kingdom where Dolcetta is a princess (*vassilopoula/βασιλοπούλα*).

For a non-lethal illness of the king (psoriasis), the magician advises that a child needs to be killed so that its blood can be used as a cure. The illness of the king is a top secret, because the king is afraid that the other kings will laugh at him. The servants of the palace go to another country (*πολιτεία/republic*) to find a child for the sacrifice, hinting that the king does not risk having a child from his own country killed for his illness. Moreover, it seems easier to tell a terrible lie to people who live far away, like the lie that the king's servants tell: they are looking for a young boy to be raised and trained in their palace and become a high-ranking officer, under the only condition that his parents will not meet him again.

Despite the lies, the two families whom the servants approach refuse to give their children away. The king's servants search then for an orphan and there Fiorentinos appears to say that he is without a family. Fiorentinos is a captive of pirates who demand to be paid a high price for the slave. The servants try to persuade them that the bright prospects of the kid are enough a payment but the pirates insist in being paid a money sum. They are all brought before the king who buys Fiorentinos from the pirates. At this point, everyone seems to be happy with the arrangement: Fiorentinos has been released by the pirates, the king has a kid to be killed for his cure and the pirates have a good sum of money at hand.

It is very interesting to see how the cure-by-sacrifice is not debated at all by the royalties who decide to proceed with killing a child for curing the non-lethal illness of the king. Not that if the illness was lethal, the solution of killing would be more justified. However, by keeping the seriousness of the illness moderate, the story blatantly displays the ruthlessness of the powerful.

In this episode, two economic practices are mentioned and interconnected: slave trade and apprenticeship in the royal palace. Apprenticeship of youth beside royalty is presented as sacrifice or killing/death of the youth for the benefit of the powerful. It is not a coincidence that the first two children's families refuse to give their children away, and the king's servants start searching for a family-less child to take. Slave trade provides a good solution for them, because, although Fiorentinos has a family, by being captured by the pirates-slave traders, he is deemed to be an orphan. It is also interesting to note that the pirates were not selling the child until they saw there was demand for it by the royal officers.

The story line is more than clear that slave trade is induced by the demand of royalties who want to dispose of unprotected children at will. Neither the pirates nor the families of children buy into the argument of a fabulous career for the selected child. Fiorentinos, on the other hand, is forced to exchange one slavery with another, getting actively involved with the king's envoys to get rid of the pirates. In that sense, he (thinks he) exerts agency upon his situation although he does not know what fate awaits him at the king's palace.

4.2 *The Mother-Daughter Conflict*

Princess Dolcetta takes care of the newcomer, washing his hands which are swollen because they were tied by the pirates with rope. She makes friends with him, and they fall in love with each other. Fiorentinos reveals to her that he is a prince who was taken hostage by the pirates three years ago.

The queen does not like her daughter's close friendship with the slave boy and she tries to stop her by telling her that the real purpose of this slave purchase was to cure the king's illness. Dolcetta reveals this plan to Fiorentinos and they both decide to flee the country. The queen attempts to stop them. Initially, she tries to remind her daughter of her love for her father, and then she claims that there is no other way to cure the illness of the king. Dolcetta is not persuaded and then the queen reminds her of her duty to be the first to obey the king because she is his daughter. Dolcetta reminds her mother that the royal couple obeys a magician, and the last argument by the queen is now that Dolcetta will never become a queen. Dolcetta does not care about the loss of the throne either. Fiorentinos intervenes in the discussion threatening that the young couple will kill themselves if they are prevented from fleeing. The queen lets them go but curses both of them "You may have my curse, that his mother kisses him and that he forgets you".

In this episode, the storyteller makes the two protagonists meet and confront the true nature of their meeting. First, the queen mother does not like Dolcetta getting close with a slave. To show her how useless a friendship with a slave is, she reveals to her daughter that the boy will be soon killed to cure the king. The revelation and future killing of Fiorentinos, instead of deterring Dolcetta, turns her into a rebel. She defies all rules and escapes with Fiorentinos.

It is ideologically very illustrative that the story transmits the dialogue between mother and daughter in detail. Dolcetta refuses to be manipulated by her love for her father, by pity for his illness, by her duty to obey the king-father, and by her "birthright" to the throne. She has an answer to all queen's arguments: she points out the injustice of killing an innocent person; the possibility of seeking other physicians from abroad; the fallacy of obeying a king who obeys a child-sacrifice supporting magician; and the indifference to be a queen as long as she will be with someone she loves.

Fiorentinos threatens that the young couple will kill themselves and the queen must let them go. Fiorentinos’s life combined with Dolcetta’s life is now precious enough for the queen to accept that the king might not be cured. However, the queen mother wants to destroy this love that effectively made herself and the king appear powerless. She curses the kids to be separated by oblivion (“that he forgets you/να σου ξεχάσει”) once the love of Fiorentinos’ mother interferes. Dolcetta is cursed to love someone who will not remember her as punishment for defying her royal parents’ decisions and power. The contrast between the mother who becomes implementer of patriarchal violence and her daughter who tries to stop this violence practically becomes the catalyst of the story line.

4.3 *The Kindness of the Strangers—part I*

During their trip, the two teenagers find support and shelter wherever they can. They literally live on the generosity of the people whom they meet while travelling until they reach the borders of the kingdom where Fiorentinos is from. Even in the palace of Dolcetta, the ironsmith had given a gift to Fiorentinos: a sword, which is used by Fiorentinos to show that he and his sweetheart are ready to die if not let free. Contrary to the “generosity” of the ill king, who just wanted to kill a child to cure himself, and the “righteousness” of the queen who finds the entire arrangement normal and demands obeisance, the commoners seem to be ready to sustain the two teens who are fleeing. Dolcetta is left at the border of Fiorentinos’ homeland to stay with the commoners in order to wait for Fiorentinos, until he comes back to take her following all honour etiquette that a princess like her deserves.

The unremunerated support that the two young escapees receive from strangers in foreign countries is in huge contrast with the fake generosity that they have experienced in the royal palace, much more with the violence that they are escaping from. It is also important to note that Dolcetta, having left her homeland and royal residence, is no more than an unknown commoner girl with no means of survival at hand. Dolcetta is dependent on Fiorentinos now, just like he was dependent on her while he was a stranger slave boy.

4.4 *The Mother-Son Relationship*

Fiorentinos reaches his palace, and everyone is happy to see him again, alive, safe and grown up. Fiorentinos asks the palace servants to prepare a royal chariot with musicians and soldiers for the following morning to go and take the princess who is waiting for him at the border of the kingdom. However, when he wakes up the next morning, he does not remember why he asked for the chariot and custody. He has forgotten Dolcetta: “I must have dreamed of it, seems to me. I do not love anyone!” he declares.

The reason is that the curse of Dolcetta’s mother has taken effect. Although Fiorentinos promises to his loved one that he will not let his mother kiss him, and he literally prevents his mother from kissing him, his mother kisses his forehead while he is asleep. She does not know about the curse, of course.

The most important issue in this episode is that Fiorentinos does not say anything to his mother about the curse that binds him and his loved one. It seems that he is confident that his refusal to be kissed by his queen mother is enough for the curse not to take effect..

There is a parallel situation here with the first and second episodes: the exercise of power on an unwilling person under various pretexts or justifications. The foreign king has the pretext of his need to be cured, and the mother of the protagonist has the pretext of her love for her son. Both stances, though, lead to very negative results: the boy is “used” for the royalties’ own purposes even if his life is in danger or damaged by that “use”. In both cases, Fiorentinos is not aware of what is happening. He thinks that he exerts agency by letting the king’s officers know that he is a captive by pirates, and he thinks that he exerts agency by not letting his mother kiss him. Agency may be an illusion when one confronts the powerful, says the tale—lethal in the first case, very damaging in the second case.

4.5 *The Kindness of the Strangers—part II*

Dolcetta has been left to wait for days at the border of the kingdom. “Since he did not come back on the third day, she understood what has happened. She decided to ride on her horse and go to the big city”.

Dolcetta is now a foreign girl in a kingdom where no-one knows her. The curse of her mother deprived her of the only person who loved her and knew her in this foreign country. She has no money and the only valuables she possesses are her horse and the silk dress she took with her while leaving home. Once she is at the city outskirts she donates the horse to a poor peasant who cries because his horse is dead and cannot help him with ploughing. "I can give you my horse to plough, I do not need it", she says and when the peasant wants to thank her, she asks for the favour to stay somewhere for the night. He agrees to host her at his family home and Dolcetta reaches the city the very next morning, visits the market (*pazari/παζάρι*) and then finds the palace. Fiorentinos with one of his brothers leave the palace in a chariot, wherein Fiorentinos sees her but does not recognise her. The despair of Dolcetta does not prevent her from finding a temporary solution: she stays with a poor old woman who lives near the palace, but she has not enough food for the two of them.

It is very interesting to see that Dolcetta takes the risk of entering a foreign country and going to the capital city in order to find Fiorentinos. She is 15 after all and a total stranger. She continues refusing to enter the market by selling her horse or the silk dress she took with her—both would have achieved a good price at the market. Instead, she prefers to keep the dress with her and to donate the horse to a peasant and then ask a favour for one night's stay at his place. She could have bought many nights' stay by selling the horse or maybe she could have bought provisions for her to survive. However, just like all people who helped her, she gives away the horse and asks only for what she needs.

Dolcetta continues to stay away from the market even when she meets the old woman who lives near the palace. The old woman, despite being very poor, is happy to have Dolcetta at her place but she has no means to acquire adequate food supplies for two women. It is Dolcetta's turn to find a solution for this.

4.6 New Courtesan in the City

"How does a whirlwind swirl? Such a swirl Dolcetta's mind took, too—so it seemed to her—and there came up to her mind, a crazy, a very crazy idea, and she says to the old woman:

- *I, my aunt, will say that... I do the bad job, to make money for us to eat what we want!*
- The old woman was hitting her knees with her hands and saying:
- *No, no, no, my little child, God may not allow it!*

– *You did not understand, my little aunt! I will say it like this, but I will not do it!*
– *And, aren't you afraid of the bad people?*
– *I have my plan! Be patient and you will see!"*

Dolcetta put on her silk dress, and sat at the house balcony "and was stunning like the sun—she was that much beautiful". There was heard in the neighbourhood that "a foreign woman came and does the bad job for a living". No-one wondered how the courtesan could wear a silk dress, given that wealthy courtesans were able to copy noble women's fashion (Sperling 1999).

The folktale describes in detail only four cases of clients asking for the new courtesan's services. The first client is a commoner, and Dolcetta makes an appointment with him a month later. He insists to go that very same night but she explains the terms and conditions of her service provision: "Because I accept only one lad per evening and I make the agreement one month in advance... I am a foreigner and in my homeland we have this as a custom. Am I going to change [ways] now that I am here? Go!".

The folktale says that "she was turning everyone away" without giving us any more information, until the princes appear as clients.

The turn that the story takes in this episode is "unexpected", in the sense that this is a complete plot twist or "subversion"[2] of the character of Dolcetta. Instead of the romantic, indifferent to money and power teenager, she becomes all of a sudden not only a businesswoman but also a quite smart one, with a business plan that will allow her to have access to money.

The dialogue between the two women is illustrating that both women know very well what they are talking about and what the dangers for Dolcetta will be. The dangers are not related to the reputation of Dolcetta or her social status but to the "bad people" who might abuse her and/or put her life in danger, as it was happening to the prostitutes in Venetian Crete (Van Gemert 1980). Physical violence is their only worry (main danger for sex workers in general) and Dolcetta seems to have devised a plan to minimise the risks.

[2] In Greek, the literary phenomenon of plot twist is called "ανατροπή" (anatropi), translated literally as "subversion".

Although prostitution-courtesanship is named in the story as "bad job", there is nowhere any moralist argument concerning whether Dolcetta or any other women should or should not do this type of work. The old woman mentions God as the entity that should not allow Dolcetta to do this job, but there is no God that intervenes in the story. As it typically happens in Cretan folktales, God is summoned to avoid a bad situation, but the bad situation is avoided by the wit of the protagonist or by other creatures, human or non-human (Sotiropoulou 2016, 2019).

Dolcetta does work as a courtesan in the sense that she declares herself as such and enters in contracts with clients as such. That she finds ways to avoid providing her services is considered by everyone (apart from herself and the old woman) as a breach of contract, but this does not make her less of a courtesan. The non-provision of services and the measures she takes against the "bad people" is something very internal to her plan, something that she decides to do despite being a courtesan and because she is one.

What does Dolcetta do to protect herself and make money without having sex she does not want to have? First, she stays with the old woman, avoiding being isolated as a courtesan. Second, she creates rules for her clients and the transactions she will enter into, and she insists on those rules. Third, she uses her foreign origin as an explanation for the strict rules she imposes, claiming to have enough experience in the sector abroad and to treat those established rules as equivalent to a tradition of her business. Courtesans working in various cities that were not their original ones seem to have been common in Renaissance Italian cities in general and in Venetian Crete too (Mantioni 2016; Van Gemert 1980). Being "foreign" is a double-edged sword for a sex worker, just like for Dolcetta: the "foreigner" might have/negotiate her own way because she is already in a disadvantaged position in an unknown place where her safety is in danger at any moment (Rossiaud 2013). Finally, she insists in being prepaid, even one month in advance, making sure she can gain money and time for her and the old woman, but also for her quest to make Fiorentinos remember her.

4.7 *The Foreign Courtesan and Her Royal Clients*

The eldest son of the king asks for an appointment after he learns from the old woman that the beautiful woman at the balcony is a foreigner who does the "bad job" so that she and the old woman can survive. He promises one hundred (100) "*tsikinia*"*(τσικίνια)*/zecchini for her to accept him. He meets her in person, but she makes him get down under the balcony again and send her the gold coins with a basket she throws from the balcony. Contrary to what she said to the commoner, the appointment is made for the same evening, at nine o' clock. Dolcetta makes clear that he must be punctual, otherwise she will not open her door.

He arrives the same night at nine, but she tells him that it is five past nine and that he has not honoured the agreement. Despite his complaint and disagreement about what the time really is, she does not open the door. The same happens with the second son of the king, who has paid five hundred (500) zecchini and arrives five minutes earlier the next day. Dolcetta refuses to open the door because he is too early for the appointment.

Fiorentinos is the third son of the king, and he also wants an appointment with the new courtesan, because he admires her beauty—but he does not recognise who the woman is. He prepays nine hundred (900) zecchini for an appointment with her, making her promise him that she will open the door and will not cheat him like she did with his brothers. She promises to open the door if he manages to step on the third step of the staircase without him falling. But she spreads honey and rovi/ρόβι (vicia fava beans) on the steps and Fiorentinos is unable to reach her door because he falls on the stairs.

When the royal youth reaches the courtesan's door, the storyteller details the negotiations and the agreements. First, we learn the fees the new courtesan charges: 100 for the first son, 500 for the second and 900 for the third son of the king. There is no explanation in the tale for the disparities in the prices, but the audience/readership who knows how Fiorentinos has treated Dolcetta, even if he is not to blame, may think that the fee he is charged is more than fair. It is also interesting to see how the courtesan insists on absolute implementation of the rules she imposes and how she uses the rules and the strictness of them to avoid providing the services to the royal clients. She refuses to sleep with her lover, most of all, who nevertheless abides by her rules.

In late medieval but mostly in renaissance Venice, it was very common for the first-born sons of nobility to get married (usually at middle age, making a socially and financially profitable marriage with a noble woman) and for the other male children of the family to remain unmarried in order to avoid division of the (patriarchal) family wealth. Many of the unmarried sons of nobility created affairs with courtesans or slave women, ranging from permanent relationships to concubinage. In many of those relationships, there were offspring too, who in some cases were recognised by their fathers, but in most cases they were not recognised (several Venetian courtesans were unrecognised daughters of nobility). In reality, the work of courtesans and prostitutes were not only a way out of poverty for the women involved, but also a way out of imposed celibacy for the men who could not get married for economic reasons (Clarke 2015; Ferraro 2001, Chapters 1, 2, 4, 6; Scippa Bhasin 2014; Rossiaud 2013, Chapters 1–3, 5, 6; Scully 1995; McKee 2004; Chojnacki 2000, 115–150, 227–256; Ruggiero 1985: 163).

In other words, courtesanship and prostitution were a way to discipline women and place them in well-defined (or confined) positions in a society in which the obligations towards the survival and social existence of those women were not taken over by anyone (Ruggiero 1985: 153–163). Exactly because the way out for men was offered at the expense of women, especially the poor ones, one may assume that the abruptly escalating prices that the princes must pay reflect the need of them to access a woman's body and affective labour. Fiorentinos is the third born son, so he will never be a king—Dolcetta knows that already. In Venetian terms (Venice did not have a king but an elected Doge), he is among the noble young men who will not be allowed to marry. Also in Venetian terms, the only way for Fiorentinos and Dolcetta to be together would be for them to have an affair through her courtesanship business, making Fiorentinos provide for her through money fees, instead of him provisioning as a husband.

Courtesanship and prostitution were some of the few solutions available to women who could not marry or had separated from their husbands or were married but their income was too low to live as working housewives.[3] Although there is a strong class distinction between the two words (courtesan-prostitute, cortigiana-meretrice/puttana) both nowadays and during Renaissance, in social terms most people did not see many differences among the women who provided sexual services or were living out of charging for their company. This was happening even for

[3] In many cases, the husbands had a strong role in pushing their wives to absolute poverty or violent lifestyle (which made them vulnerable to pimps/ruffiani) or they were themselves who started prostituting them (Rossiaud 2013).

(educated and usually middle- or high-class courtesan) women who were charging for a discussion or for spending a dancing evening with the client, without any sexual work necessarily involved in the agreement. That in the story the courtesan Dolcetta is fifteen years old and none of the prospective clients finds this problematic is very representative of the reality of courtesans and also of wives, who might have been forced to marry at even earlier ages (Scully 1995; Cohen 1991; Ferraro 2001, Chapter 4; Clarke 2015, Rossiaud 2013, Chapters 1, 4–6; Chojnacki 1992, 2000, 115–182). The story of the tale could be more based on the social or community awareness side of the dangers concerning young people rather than on practical institutional protection (Ferraro 2016) in a dominant culture that had normalised the exploitation of poor women in order for men and women of nobility to continue being part of that dominant culture (Ruggiero 1985: 11).

4.8 The Courtesan's Trial

The three princes complain to the king, who decides to open a judiciary procedure to take back the zecchini that the three princes paid to Dolcetta without receiving her services.

"At that time the court hearings were held in the palace. The king himself had the role of the judge and for the decisions to be made, some wise old men were giving him advice". The folktale says that in this case the queen is also present, attending to her sons asking for their money back from the courtesan.

Dolcetta is brought to the big hall of the palace where the trial is taking place. The charges are stated: "because she cheated the three princes and took the zecchini from them". The king-judge and the council "then they asked her what she herself has to say –to defend herself".

The narrative style changes at this point, and Dolcetta starts talking with rhyme. Dolcetta first addresses the king:

"You made me sit on the little stool to try me,
On the small stool of the thieves you made me, too, sit,
That I am an honest maiden and a king's child
Your sons with their gifts came to seduce me
To take my honour, to travel with it!"

She then addresses the queen asking her whether she kissed her son, and she reveals the curse of her own mother to separate from Fiorentinos if his mother kisses him.

Finally, she addresses Fiorentinos:

"Remember, my Fiorentino, my love, remember!
To our house the pirates brought you
I was washing you and combing your hair,
I was sprinkling you with blossom water!".

Fiorentinos remembers what has happened and he declares (in rhyme) that he wants to kill himself with his sword.

The folktale ends at that moment, after Fiorentinos is prevented from killing himself. "Love won over the curse" says the storyteller, and the young couple is married. "And those lived well and we lived even better".

It is unclear why this change of style happens: perhaps to put emphasis on the dramatic situation or to incorporate lyrical elements that a storyteller can use with melody? There is no information in Mavredaki's collection whether this part of the folktale is sung or what the melody could be. It might also indicate that the folktale was initially a poem or song, or a folk epic, or that we also need to see folk tales as epic forms of art (Meraklis 1991: 178–203). In such case, most of the lyrics have been forgotten and replaced with prose apart from the final part which has been preserved with its dialogues in rhyme. Another explanation could be to represent the royal courtesan as able enough to express ideas and arguments through poetry, a skill that was highly praised in courtesans of Italian Renaissance and was used for defence by the courtesans themselves (Rosenthal 1989). Or, maybe the folktale was at some point a theatrical play like the ones played in convents by the nuns, including ex-prostitutes. This might also explain the long dialogues saved not only in rhyme during the last episode, but also in prose in previous episodes of the tale (Bassanese 1988; Scippa Bhasin 2014).

In this episode, the courtesan-prostitute is literally tried for fraud. Technically, she has committed it, because she was receiving payments in advance while she knew that she was not going to provide the services she had agreed to provide. Nevertheless, the story, by describing the procedure with details, represents the point of view of the accused because she is the one who takes the lead in speaking the most and standing for her innocence.

The first thing that one observes is that the framework of bringing a foreign poor woman and officially prostitute at the court because she does not want to have sex with some rich people who paid her is exposing the entire status of the woman. It also exposes the values of the patriarchal exploitative legal system or polity she must live in. The folktale audience already knows that she is a refugee woman, abandoned by her lover in a foreign country, despite her forfeiting everything she had to save his life. She is also extremely poor, just like the old woman who took care of her. She is also very young (15 years old) in a society where senility, in particular that one of men, is associated with wisdom and political power (Chojacki 2000, 185–356; Finlay 1978). The royal judge perceives it as normal that a poor teenage woman must either starve or provide sexual services to his sons although they are rich and socially prominent enough to seek sexual partners, paid or unpaid, elsewhere if this woman does not like them. The power imbalance and the legal entitlement are made clearer with the presence of the queen mother who does not see any brutality or abusive righteousness in the case brought before her king husband. She does not intervene in the trial procedure until Dolcetta talks to her.

Dolcetta is not denying that she took the money nor that she did not provide her royal clients with her services. She self-defines as honest ("onesta" was also the title of courtesans who were providing company and services to the aristocracy, see Cohen 1991; Clarke 2015) and a "king's offspring" (just like many courtesans who have been legally unrecognised daughters of aristocrats) but she puts the blame on the clients. She claims that the clients with their money wanted to take her honour "to travel with it".

The statements of Dolcetta concerning who is to blame may have at least two readings: one is that she abides with the patriarchal values where an honourable woman is not having sex with men while unmarried, much less gets she paid for it by them—hence, if she does not provide sexual services her honour is well protected. The other reading is that the honour is not linked to sex as such but to her choice to refuse services even if the receiver of the refusal is her loved one. What she denies is not sex but mostly the entitlement of the royal clients to demand her sexual services because they had enough money to pay her. By putting the blame on them she claims her right to the money she received and her right not to provide services to the men who have given the money. The attack to her honour comes from their demand and claim and not from the contract she was forced to conclude in order to provide for herself and the other poor woman.

Dolcetta's statements take the perception of the need for full consent by the prostitute a step further. She knows that in theory she is a recognised legal subject with full power to enter into a contract and she also knows that she can refuse to provide her services and she can choose clients and the conditions on which she will agree with them (Rossiaud 2013; Chapters 4, 5, 7; Scully 1995; Ferraro 2001; Chapters 1, 4). Yet, she knows that practice is not what legal constructions prescribe because "The contract obscures the historical constraints on the freedom to choose" as Agathangelou (2004, 61) points out. The apology of Dolcetta is refuting not only her fraud or her obligation to give back the fees but also the entire legal structure that keeps her sitting on the "stool of the thieves". The respect and honouring of a contract are not more important than Dolcetta's need to survive and her decision to choose whom she will have sex with. The entire judiciary procedure is challenged and literally brought to a dead-end. The accusers-princes have no say in the story and the storyteller does not even allow the king-judge to reply to Dolcetta.

Dolcetta leads the discussion now, she de facto becomes the judge of everyone else. First, she turns to the queen mother and they have a (rhyme) dialogue where the queen's kiss is revealed as the reason that Fiorentinos forgot his loved one. Then, Dolcetta speaks to her lover, this time trying to make him remember her (something she did not try when he approached her as a client) by reminding him of her care work when he was a slave boy in her father's palace. The queen mother and Fiorentinos have no choice but to reply to Dolcetta as if they themselves were witnesses or defendants in the trial.

The storyteller says that Fiorentinos first remembered Dolcetta's voice and then everything else they had together been through. The tension of the story is resolved by Fiorentinos decision to kill himself immediately after all this injustice has been revealed in the court. We cannot know whether this decision was made out of his shame because he accused her to the court for something he was quite responsible of or for some other reason. His attempt reminds the moralist use of suicide in fiction and the contradicting statistics in history that Henry (2009) analyses about the nineteenth- to early twentieth-century men in finance.

5 Centuries-Long Persistent Anti-Patriarchal Critique?

That the couple survive all hardships and gets married at the end is very typical in folktales. This patriarchal ending has various meanings when the female protagonist is a courtesan and the male protagonist is a demanding client. An atypical couple for folktales has a very typical folktale ending in the story. It was not very common in historical reality for this type of couples, but it was often the hoped-for outcome by the woman who had to make a living under harsh economic and social conditions. It is also a claim by the women to a part of the wealth that the patriarchal family concentrates and channels to the first-born son, who, according to Venetian nobility practices, was the only one allowed to marry. The practice of leaving the younger sons practically disinherited dumped their lack of resources onto their partners (McKee 2004; Rossiaud 2013, Chapters 1–3, 5, 6; Clarke 2015; Ferraro 2001, Chapters 1, 2, 4, 6; Scippa Bhasin 2014).

The story of Dolcetta shows it is also very difficult to survive in patriarchy if you do not break at least some rules of it. She first must get into conflict with her family to make sure that slavery is not achieving its goal, i.e. to kill a slave. Then she has to become a courtesan to make a living in a foreign country. She abides with the rules of courtesanship but she also makes her own rules. She claims to be honest and a king's daughter, but she uses fraud to avoid demanding clients who just want their contract to be honoured. As a consequence, keeping her honour the way she perceives it requires not to honour her contracts if necessary. She is accused of a crime that we all know she committed, but she fires back showing that the biggest crime proven in the procedure is the demand of the princes to receive either her sex services or their money back. She uses patriarchal procedures of (in)justice to expose the injustice and patriarchy as a system that keeps women in a disadvantaged position and to make her lover remember her by exposing him in public.

What this story focuses on is not that Fiorentinos forgot his lover. The story in reality acquits him of his forgetfulness by linking the oblivion to acts that are beyond his control (a mother's curse and a mother's kiss). The focus is on the woman who tried so hard to abide by laws and norms to establish a relationship with a man she loves and ends up in distress and abandoned, forced to do things she might not like in order to survive. The biggest shame of Fiorentinos is his abusive claims, not that he forgot his lover. He was Dolcetta's lover anyway and we may assume that Dolcetta would also like to have sex with him, but not under the prerogative of a contract obligation, nor because she is poor, nor because he is rich enough to buy and demand her services.

Literally, she uses the judiciary system to have a public narrative of her story, instead of going directly to the palace and trying to negotiate in private with the oblivious Fiorentinos from the very beginning. She creates herself as a full person through her business practice and the contract she did not honour because it was unfair to begin with. She uses the public narrative not only to constitute herself as smart, articulate, innocent, honourable and wronged (Connor 2004) but also to debunk the collective legality that harmed her. She does not expose Fiorentinos only, but also the royal family, their money, their power to do justice (which is injustice) and she exposes the queen's secret superseding of her son's volition. The economic and/or sexual rights of the courtesan's clients are challenged as abusive and against a woman's honour, even if she agreed with them in the first place. She could not have done this without cheating them. But it would not be possible either if the judiciary system did not ignore all economic and social context or did not demand the honouring of the agreed contracts.

The misogynist stereotype of the sex worker not honouring her agreements and scheming to rip off her clients, whom she despises and sees only as sources of income, is turned upside down in this story. It is her clients who want to rip off the courtesan's honour and she rightfully demands to keep their money. In that respect, we can read Pietro Aretino (1536) under a new light and reflect whether the indignation or anger of Dolcetta as expressed towards her clients and then accusers is closer to the anger of courtesan Nanna against her own clients than we would like to admit. Female protagonists and "good women" in patriarchy are demanded not to express anger in public, while people take as normal that the Cretan elite member Sahlikis (1385–1390) wrote violent poems raging against the sex workers of Heraklion city of his era (he also ended up in prison because, as it seems, a courtesan reported him but he never mentions the reason).

The folktale was chosen as an example of grassroots economic thought but also of economic education from the point of view of a social group (women) who are disadvantaged in the economic system of patriarchy, and even more in capitalist patriarchy. The comparison is enlightening:

formal economic education has missed important aspects of gender, injustice, systemic violence and hierarchy while claiming to promote individual free will and freedom of contract. Mainstream economics also miss the role of the powerful, particularly of the state authorities, that set the rules of economic activity and participate actively in it to their own advantage and to the advantage of the people of their class (Agathangelou 2004).

The tale is also an example of how economic education that is done through informal pathways may allow the discriminated or exploited social groups to state publicly and, at the same time, understand what the powerful do to them. The take of the storyteller concerning perceptions about sex work is astounding: she shows that the economy is something that everyone needs to deal with somehow, but possibly not in the way the powerful ones want people to become economically active. As one of the anonymous reviewers commented: "This isn't really about courtesanship—it's about the way something seemingly amoral allows for a profoundly critical stance to take shape about a larger system of injustice. And this critique is possible through embracing exchange (and even cultivating a sort of economic literacy) as a form of self-empowerment".

It is very interesting that the economic information concerning the courtesan-prostitute's job is very much like what we know from research concerning the Venetian system of courtesanship. The names of the protagonists, the courtesan system described in detail and especially the name of the coins offered to the courtesan, just like the description of the courtesan sitting at the balcony to show her beauty and the old woman being the "matrona-madre" (the woman who was hosting the prostitute, running the business in terms of promotion and informing prospective clients), are all elements that show how this type of work was usually done. That the prostitutes could be judiciary subjects and speak before a court of law also shows that prostitution and courtesanship were completely legal within this setting (Rossiaud 2013).

It is also interesting to see that the hearing takes place not to force Dolcetta to have sex with the clients but to make her give back the money, which means that the consent of the prostitute about the sexual act was an absolute right of hers. However, it functioned as a relative right if the prostitute was very poor and relied only on prostitution to survive. Dolcetta challenges this relativeness by exposing the unfair demands of the rich clients. She reclaims her absolute right not to have sex with clients if she does not want to, and yet have access to money to live on. Her use of time precision as a framework and rule to allow her to protect herself and even avoid doing what she does not want to do reminds of the time frames collectively used by women to organise their societies and also have access to resources in an equitable manner with men (Knight 1991; Power 2022).

Various questions still remain, such as how this specific folktale arrived to be remembered in Crete, and what this survival of the story implies for women's formal and informal struggles but also for a truly critical economic education. The first part of the story is more generic, in the sense that it contains information about slavery and apprenticeship-career of poor children in the powerful households. The details were constitutive parts of a system of labour exploitation that was quite common for many centuries among various regions, whether in continental Europe, Italy or Ottoman Empire (Inalcik 2001; McKee 2004). To the contrary, the second part with the Dolcetta-as-courtesan is very much specific, showing clear Venetian influences on the story.

As mentioned before, it was not possible to find other versions of this story or similar folktales until now. It is unclear whether folktales based on such themes were not numerous anyway or whether the narrators and/or the collectors refrained from transcribing them and the publishers from publishing them, because they were touching upon very difficult issues like prostitution, women's poverty, men's entitlements and unfair legal and judiciary systems. If we take as a hypothesis that this story was unique or very rare anyway, we still need to question how this survived with all these details, plus the rhyme dialogues and trial procedure information. It seems that despite the tough topics this tale deals with, the preservation of the folktale was covering social needs that the successive storytellers wanted to address.

From the lecture paper and sources that Ms Liana Starida generously shared with me, it seems that the known sources about prostitution in Venetian Crete are representing a patriarchal and quite misogynist point of view constructed by men, in particular the powerful men of Venetian Cretan society, like nobility, prominent artists and priesthood (Starida 2017; Lyubarsky 1960; Mavromatis and Van Gemert 2017; Vassilaki 1986; Voulgaridou 2012; Kaplanis 2011; McKee 2004; Pettas 2020; Sahlikis 1385–1390; Van Gemert 1980). To that one should also add that Venetians were occupying and colonising Crete and the locals had to host, feed and appease the soldiers and Venetian authorities, with everything this meant for local women (McKee 2004; Voltarakia.gr 2019).

This folktale is, seemingly, a source coming from the women of the island, representing their own point of view and setting the framework of prostitution from the point of view of the prostitute. It is also a story that depicts in a critical way the hostile stance of privileged women, like the two queen mothers, who have no economic or social risk to face in their everyday lives, towards the women who belong to lower status social classes or defy the rules of patriarchy. If this analysis is correct, then this folktale might be the only source we have so far from Cretan women of the Venetian era dealing with the issue of sex work and courtesanship.

6 Conclusions

The tale raises the huge issue of who is making history, especially economic history. We are forced to question who is narrating and who is setting the rules of economic critique. In order to answer those questions, we also have to investigate who is creating the written and/or official sources about the way of life of the deprived social groups. It also shows that the economic information and economic thought that exist in folk literature are not sources to keep outside economic research. It might be the only source capable of giving us information concerning the economic activity and views of the people who belong to discriminated or disadvantaged groups with no chance to write or publish their views in more formal ways. Official documents or sources originating with the privileged groups of society are not necessarily more accurate or reliable than folk sources concerning everyday life and economic activity. In that sense, folk literature seems to be not only a complement but also a challenge to the dominant groups' perceptions and records concerning economic life.

This study showed that important economic thought, and indeed critical and subversive understandings, may exist in collective artistic creations and narratives. Those same creations might have accuracy in terms of describing a system or sub-system of economic life, although they might not be able (n)or willing to locate the events they are describing in terms of exact time and space. This resembles economic modelling very much, but it also embarrasses it: through narrative one can explain, discuss, criticise and propose possible resolutions for an economic phenomenon or issue without erasing important characteristics of economic actors, like gender, economic and political power, class or origin/ethnicity. Just like a truly good economic model, the folktale uses reductionism only when it is necessary and does not obscure economic conditions that directly affect the economy and the people who live in it.

The analysis of the folktale also showed that the perception of folk culture as pre-capitalist and somehow ignorant about the economy is inaccurate if not ahistorical. However, many questions of the historicity of this folktale and its economic ideas remain. Folktales may contain economic knowledge that may simultaneously refer to non-capitalist and capitalist economic structures that are coeval in time and geography. This might also explain why the folktales are so far away from contemporary economic discourse, much more from discourse of critical economic theories which see capitalism only. The historicity of the Venetian empire and its exploitation of slaves and poor women is a material context which the folktale educates about with amazing detail, raising questions about how several academic economic histories miss and why some story tellers from Crete Island focus on those aspects.

A final question that has not been answered is whether Cretan people remember this or similar folktales and narrate them today in their social gatherings and not to collectors or researchers only, because I have not conducted any such field research yet. I hope that this research is done in the future. There is huge need for exploring grassroots economic thought in various countries and communities and this study has been one only contribution to that direction of research.

Acknowledgements I am grateful to: Prof. Michalis Meraklis (Prof. Emeritus, University of Athens) for his encouragement and his precious advice on literature; Dr Maria Hnaraki (Drexel University) for her advice on Cretan culture; Dr Ferda Dönmez Atbaşı (University of Ankara) for the inspiration and the common research on Bacilar/Grassroots economics project; and Dr Willow Mullins (Washington University St Louis) for her collegiality to advise on literature related to Critical Folklore Studies. This paper has vastly benefited from the advice, support and generous encouragement by Ms Liana Starida, archaeologist, who has done research on prostitution during the Venetian and Ottoman eras in Crete and shared with me her lecture as an unpublished manuscript and other literature and photographic material related to the topic and to Ms Androniki Ntoussaki, scholar, who introduced me to Pietro Aretino's work. Finally, I am grateful to the librarians of the Municipal Library of Chania City for their generous assistance, to four anonymous reviewers for their insightful comments and advice, to Dr Justine Dombrowski for her comments on a previous version of this study and to the Editors of this volume for their support, comments and feedback. All deficiencies of this chapter are sole responsibility of the author.

References

Agathangelou, Anna M. 2004. *The Global Political Economy of Sex—Desire, Violence and Insecurity in Mediterranean Nation-States*. New York: Palgrave Macmillan.

Antoniou, Antonis A. 2010. Economic Realities and Modern Greek Folk Literature [in Greek]. *The Historicals [τα Ιστορικά]* 53(December):463–478.

Aretino, Pietro. 1536, 2006. *The School of Whoredom* [in Greek], Translated by G. Barouxis. Athens: To Pontiki.

Barker, Drucilla K., and Edith Kuiper, ed. 2003. *Toward a Feminist Philosophy of Economics*. London: Routledge.

Bassanese, Fiora A. 1988. Private Lives and Public Lies: Texts by Courtesans of the Italian Renaissance. *Texas Studies in Literature and Language* 30(3):295–319.

Bennholdt-Thomsen, Veronika. 1988. *Mies, Maria and Von Werlhof, Claudia*. Women: The last colony. Zed Books.

Beverley, John. 2004. The Subaltern and the Limits of Academic Knowledge [in Spanish]. *Revista Aktuel Marx* 2 (August), Translated by Marlene Beiza and Sergio Villalobos-Ruminott.

Bottigheimer, Ruth B. 2009. *Fairy Tales—A New History*. Albany NY: State University of New York.

Briggs, Charles L. 2012. What We Should Have Learned from Americo Paredes: The Politics of Communicability and the Making of Folkloristics. *The Journal of American Folklore* 125(495):91–110.

Chojnacki, Stanley. 1992. Measuring Adulthood: Adolescence and Gender in Renaissance Venice. *Journal of Family History* 17(4):371–375.

Chojnacki, Stanley. 2000. *Women and Men in Renaissance Venice—Twelve Essays on Patrician Society*. Baltimore: The Johns Hopkins University Press.

Clarke, Paula C. 2015. The Business of Prostitution in Early Renaissance Venice. *Renaissance Quarterly* 68(2):419–464.

Cohen, Elizabeth S. 1991. 'Courtesans' and 'Whores': Words and Behavior in Roman Streets. *Women's Studies: An Inter-Disciplinary Journal* 19(2):201–208.

Connor, Rebecca Elisabeth. 2004. *Women, Accounting, and Narrative—Keeping Books in Eighteenth-Century England*. London: Routledge.

Detorakis, Theocharis E. 1994. *History of Crete*. Translated by John C. Davis, Herakleion.

Ehrenreich, Barbara and Deirdre English. 1978, 2005. *For Her Own Good*. New York: Anchor books.

Eisenstein, Zillah. 1979. *Capitalist Patriarchy and the Case for Socialist Feminism*. New York: Monthly Review Press.

Federici, Silvia. 2013. *Revolution at Point Zero: Domestic Work, Reproduction and Feminist Struggles* [in Spanish]. Traficantes de Suenos-Mapas, trans. Scriptorium (Fernandez-Cuervos, C. & Martin-Ponz, P.).

Ferraro, Joanne M. 2001. *Marriage Wars in Late Renaissance Venice*. New York and Oxford: Oxford University Press.

Ferraro, Joanne M. 2016. Youth in Peril in Early Modern Venice. *Journal of Social History* 49(4):761–783.

Finlay, Robert. 1978. The Venetian Republic as a Gerontocracy: Age and Politics in the Renaissance. *Journal of Medieval and Renaissance Studies* 8(1):157–178.

Fraser, Nancy. 2013a. *Fortunes of Feminism—From State-Managed Capitalism to Neoliberal Crisis*. London: Verso Books.

Fraser, Nancy. 2013b. How Feminism Became Capitalism's Handmaiden—And How to Reclaim It. *The Guardian* 14(10):2013. http://www.theguardian.com/commentisfree/2013/oct/14/feminism-capitalist-handmaiden-neoliberal.

Gencarella, S. O. 2009. Constituting Folklore: A Case for Critical Folklore Studies. *The Journal of American Folklore* 122–484(Spring):172–196.

Gencarella, Stephen O. 2010a. Gramsci, Good Sense and Critical Folklore Studies. *Journal of Folklore Studies* 47(3):221–252.

Gencarella, Stephen O. 2010b. Gramsci, Good Sense and Critical Folklore Studies. *Journal of Folklore Studies* 47(3):259–264.

Gencarella, Stephen O. 2011. Folk Criticism and the Art of Critical Folklore Studies. *The Journal of American Folklore* 124/494(Fall):251–271.

Henry, Nancy. 2009. "Rushing into Eternity": Suicide and Finance in Victorian Fiction. In *Victorian Investments—New Perspectives in Finance and Culture*, ed. N. Hentry and C. Schmitt, 161–181. Indianapolis: Indiana University Press.

Henry, Nancy. 2018. *Women, Literature and Finance in Victorian Britain—Cultures of Investment*. Palgrave Macmillan.

Inalcik, Halil. 2001. *The Ottoman Empire—The Classical Age 1300–1600*. London: Orion Publishing.

Kaplanis, Tassos. 2011. New Literature, New Identity: Stefanos Sahlikis (14th cent.), The First Eponymous Author of Modern Greek Literature [In Greek]. In *Identities in Greek world (From 1204 till today)—Proceedings of 4th European Conference of Modern Greek Studies*, vol. 2, ed K. A. Dimadis, pp. 491–511. Athens: European Association of Modern Greek Studies.

Kapsomenos, Eratosthenis, and Kleio Papaderou. 2014. Features of Cultural Localisation in Cretan Folktale [in Greek]. In *The Cretan Folktale (tribute to Pavlos Vlastos) Conference Proceedings*, ed. Kostas Moutzouris, 127–142. Herakleion: Centre of Cretan Literature & Municipality of Minoa Pediadas.

Knight, Chris. 1991. *Blood Relations—Menstruation and The Origins of Culture*. London: Yale University Press.
Kousaleos, Nicole. 1999. Feminist Theory and Folklore. *Folklore Forum* 30(1–2):19–34.
Limon, Jose E. 1979. Western Marxism and Folklore: A Critical Introduction. *The Journal of American Folklore* 96(279): 34–52.
Limon, Jose E. 1984. Western Marxism and Folklore: A Critical Reintroduction. *The Journal of American Folklore* 97(385):337–344.
Limon, Jose E. 2010. Breaking with Gramsci: Gencarella on Good Sense and Critical Folklore Studies. *Journal of Folklore Research* 47(3):253–257.
Lipsitz, George, and Russell Rodriguez. 2012. Turning Hegemony on Its Head: The Insurgent Knowledge of Americo Paredes. *The Journal of American Folklore* 125(495):111–125.
Morin, Lopez, and R. Jose. 2006. *The Legacy of Americo Paredes*. Texas: Texas A & M University Press.
Lyubarsky, G. N. 1960. The Cretan poet Stefanos Sahlikis [in Greek]. *In Kritika Hronika/κρητικά Χρονικά* 14:308–334.
Mantioni, Susanna. 2016. *Courtesans and Prostitutes in Rome of 16th Century* [in Italian]. Ariccia: Aracne Editrice.
Mavromatis, Yannis, and Arnold Van Gemert. 2017. The Concise and Annotated Publication of the Poems by Stefanos Sahlikis—Observations on the Working Method of the Poet [in Greek]. In *Mapping Popular Literature (12th-17th cent.)—Conference Proceedings of the International Conference Neograeca Mediaevi*, ed. Stefanos Kaklamanis, and Alexis Kalokairinos, pp. 217–228. Herakleion: Society of Cretan Historical Studies.
McKee, Sally. 2004. Inherited Status and Slavery in Late Medieval Italy and Venetian Crete. *Past & Present* 182:31–54.
Mejia, Marco Raul J. 2015. *The Popular Education in 21st Century—An Intercultural Resistance From the South and From Below* [in Spanish]. Seminario Mitos e Imaginarios—Paradigmas de Education Popular en America Latina y el mundo. Guadalajara, Mexico. 7–9.5.2015.
Meraklis, Michalis. 1984. *Greek Folklore Ethnography—Social Formation* [in Greek]. Athens: Odysseas Publishing.
Meraklis, Michalis. 1986. *Greek Folklore Ethnography—Mores and Customs* [in Greek]. Athens: Odysseas Publishing.
Meraklis, Michalis. 1988. *What is Folk Literature* [in Greek]. Athens: Centre of Marxist Studies and Modern Era Publishing.
Meraklis, M. 1991. Our Folktales [Τα παραμύθια μας]. Thessalonike, Constantinidis Publishing [Εκδόσεις Κωνσταντινίδη].
Paredes, Americo. 1963. *The North-American Cowboy in Folklore and Literature* [in Spanish]. *Cuadernos del Instituto Nacional de Antropologia* 4, Buenos

Aires, Instituto Nacional de Antropologia—Ministerio de Educacion y Justicia, pp. 227–240.

Pettas, Constantinos. 2020. *Stefanos Sahlikis: The Derelict Life, the Innovation in Poetry* [in Greek]. 6.8.2020 MaxMag.gr. https://www.maxmag.gr/book/stefanos-sachlikis-i-asoti-zoi-i-kainotomia-stin-poiisi. Accessed 3 Sept 2020.

Power, Camilla. 2022. How to Breath. *Journal of Global Faultlines* 9(2):126–137.

Rosenthal, Margaret F. 1989. Veronica Franco's Terze Rime: The Venetian Courtesan's Defense. *Renaissance Quarterly* 42(2):227–257.

Rossiaud, Jacques. 2013. *Commercial Loves: Prostitution in Medieval Europe* [in Italian]. Roma-Bari: Editori Laterza.

Ruggiero, Guido. 1985. *The Boundaries of Eros—Sex Crime and Sexuality in Renaissance Venice*. Oxford: Oxford University Press.

Rutterford, Jannette, and Josephine Maltby. 2009. Women and Wealth in Fiction in the Long Nineteenth Century 1800–1914. In *Women and Their Money 1700–1950—Essays on Women and Finance*, ed. A. Laurence, J. Maltby, and J. Rutterford, 151–160. New York: Routledge.

Sahlikis, Stefanos. 1385–1390 [2015]. *Weird Narration of Humble Sahlikis* [in Greek]. Centre of Greek Language. online

Scippa Bhasin, Christine. 2014. Prostitutes, Nuns, Actresses: Breaking the Convent Wall in Seventeenth-Century Venice. *Theatre Journal* 66(1):19–35.

Scully, Sally. 1995. Marriage or a Career?: Witchcraft as an Alternative in Seventeenth-Century Venice. *Journal of Social History* 28(4):857–876.

Sotiropoulou, Irene. 2013. Terms of the Cretan Dialect for Non-monetary Transactions. In *Hellenic Language and Terminology, Conference Proceedings*, ed. Costas Valeontis, 81–293. Athens: ELETO.

Sotiropoulou, Irene. 2016. Cooking Struggles in Cretan Folktales: Undermining Patriarchy and Forging Solidarity Among Women. *Conference Proceedings of the 3rd Greek Gastronomy Symposium "Over a Hot Stove: Women in the Kitchen"*. Karanou of Chania, Greece, 25–26.7.2015.

Sotiropoulou, Irene. 2019. 'Why the Sea is Salty': Folktales as Sources of Grassroots Economics. In *The Folklorist in the Marketplace: The Economics of Folklore and the Folklore of Economics*, ed. Willow G. Mullins and Puja Batra-Wells. Colorado: Utah State University Press-University Press of Colorado.

Sperling, Jutta. 1999. The Paradox of Perfection: Reproducing the Body Politic in Late Renaissance Venice. *Comparative Studies in Society and History* 41(1):3–32.

Starida, Liana. 2017. *Intertemporal Tour in the Prostitution Houses (politikareia) of Kastro/Herakleion* [in Greek]. Lecture delivered on 12.05.2017 at Youth Multicentre in Herakleion, Greece. Unpublished manuscript.

Taussig, Michael. 1980. *The Devil and Commodity Fetishism in Latina America*. Chapel Hill: The University of North Carolina Press.

Van Gemert, Arnold F. 1980. *Sahlikis and His Era* [in Greek]. *Thesaurismata—Θησαυρίσματαα* 17:37–130.

Vargas, Carlos. 2018. Presentation: Popular Education: New Challenges. *Saberes Andantes* 2(4):5–8.

Vassilaki, Maria. 1986. The Representations of Sinned Women on Wall-Painted Churches of Crete [in Greek]. *Archeology/αρχαιολογία* 21:41–46.

Voltarakia.gr. 2019. *Prostitution in the Castle* [in Greek] (historical trail in Heraklion city with Liana Starida). May 30, 2019. www.voltarakia.gr/index.php/pigame-ki-itan-oraia/item/880-i-porneia-sto-kastro.

Voulgaridou, Despoina. 2012. *Images of Women in Early Cretan Poetry (12th–14th Centuries)* [in Greek]. MA thesis, Literature Department, School of Philosophy, Aristotle University of Thessalonike.

Zipes, Jack. 1993. Spinning with Fate: Rumpelstiltskin and the Decline of Female Productivity. *Western Folklore* 521:43–60.

Zipes, Jack. 2001. *Breaking the Spell—Radical Theories of Folk and Fairy Tales* [in Spanish], Translated by Vanina Cuccaro, Grupo Editorial Lumen. Buenos Aires & Mexico.

Zipes, Jack. 2006. *Fairy Tales and the Art of Subversion—The Classical Genre for Children and the Process of Civilization*, 2nd ed. London: Routledge.

Conclusion

Teresa Perry

The leaky pipeline in economics has persisted despite efforts to address it (Bayer and Rouse 2016; Sarsons et al. 2021). Is economics different from other social sciences in its treatment of and outcomes for women? The female share of bachelor's degrees has increased across most undergraduate and graduate majors since the 1980s, reflecting progress in representation (National Center for Science and Engineering Statistics [NCSES] 2019). Table 1, created using data from the NCSES (2019), illustrates how the percentage of degrees awarded in the social sciences and economics has changed from 1997 to 2016.

The percentage of women receiving bachelor's, master's, and doctorate degrees in economics and the social sciences has increased over time. However, at the undergraduate level, the percentage of women majoring in economics has increased by less than one percentage point over nearly twenty years. When comparing the percentage of degrees awarded by gender in the social sciences versus economics, economics lags behind by at least fourteen percentage points for each degree type.

T. Perry (✉)
Department of Economics, California State University San Bernardino, San Bernardino, CA, USA
e-mail: teresa.perry@csusb.edu

© The Author(s), under exclusive license to Springer Nature Switzerland AG 2026

V. Dolar and T. Perry (eds.), *Missing Voices in Economics*,
https://doi.org/10.1007/978-3-031-97180-8_12

Table 1 Degrees awarded to women by year and discipline

Degree and year	*Percent women- Economics*	*Percent women- Social Sciences*
Doctorate		
1997	23.6	39.2
2006	30.7	46
2016	34.7	48.8
Master's		
1997	34	51.1
2006	39.6	56.4
2016	41.2	57.2
Bachelor's		
1997	30.8	51.8
2006	31	53.7
2016	31.7	54.8

For decades, researchers have argued that the mathematical and quantitative nature of economics is one primary reason for why gender differences in majors exists in economics but not in other social sciences (Dynan and Rouse 1997; Ahlstrom and Asarta 2019). This is why economics is often compared to STEM, which are some of the only fields that have lower levels of gender equity than economics. Of the nine most male-dominated disciplines at top U.S. universities, all nine fell within STEM (Kruus et al. 2024). Unlike economics, eight of those nine disciplines have experienced increases in gender diversity between 2010 and 2021 and some fields have experienced a convergence in gender representation (Kruus et al. 2024). In 2022, the share of economics majors at PhD granting institutions increased to 36 percent, but it decreased to 37 percent at non-PhD-granting institutions (Chari 2023). While this represents an increase from 2016, economics has not made the same gains in women's representation as most STEM majors. The disparity in the progress in gender equity between STEM and economics majors suggests that mathematics is not the primary driver of gender inequity in economics.

Why then has economics made such little progress over time in achieving more equal gender representation, particularly at the undergraduate level? This lack of progress is not due to a lack of effort. For instance, in 2023, Claudia Goldin became the first woman to win the Nobel Prize in economics on her own. The American Economic

Association, the largest economics organization in the profession, has remained steadfast in devoting resources to eliminating the discrimination that women economists experience. For instance, since 1974, the American Economic Association has sponsored a Summer Training Program aimed at enhancing diversity in the discipline (Bayer and Rouse 2016). Additional programs, such as the Diversity Initiative for Tenure in Economics (DITE) and CSMGEP's Mentoring Program, support underrepresented minorities at later stages of the pipeline (Bayer and Rouse 2016). However, as shown above, economics has made less progress in achieving gender equality among undergraduate majors compared to other historically male-dominated fields such as math, engineering, and the natural sciences (American Academy of Arts & Sciences, n.d.). The persistence of gender inequity at every level of the profession suggests that researchers must continue investigating why gender disparities persist in economics despite ongoing efforts to improve representation and equity, an objective that *Missing Voices in Economics* aligns with.

This book analyzes the reasons for these gender disparities across many different levels, using various methodologies and data sources, and across different geographic regions. It presents evidence across three spheres in which women are underrepresented and excluded in economics, highlighting the gender disparities that exist, and exploring why they persist.

Missing Voices in Economics opens with personal anecdotes and stories from one of the editors that illustrate the unfair treatment of women economists. It then outlines the third sphere of analysis, which explores the leaky pipeline effect, or the persistent gender gaps that exist at every level of the profession. Chapter 1 features interviews with female economists, discussing sources of gender inequality including disparities in faculty representation, hiring, promotions, teaching evaluations, research opportunities, and networking. Chapters 4 and 5 further investigate the challenges women face in the field, revealing discrimination, differing expectations for their research, and exclusion from economic theory. Chapter 3 demonstrates that gender influences field specialization, with women underrepresented in high-prestige subfields. Chapter 9 critiques economists' view of gender itself, which is often defined within a narrow, cis-heteronormative framework, arguing that this limitation undermines economic research.

Several chapters explore the first sphere of analysis, which focuses on the exclusion of women and gender from economic theory and models.

Chapter 7 discusses the struggles feminist economists face in hiring and promotion due to their research focus, highlighting the undervaluation of gender-related economic theories. Chapter 3 finds that feminist and gender economic studies receive limited attention from economists of all genders compared to more mainstream topics. Despite this resistance, Chapter 8 shows that gender economics courses and theories resonate with undergraduate students.

While the first sphere of analysis focuses on exclusion from economic theory, the second sphere examines how historical and institutional forces have reinforced this exclusion. These chapters not only illustrate how the profession has excluded women, but they also examine how institutions and patriarchal norms have reinforced this exclusion. Chapter 10 examines the overlooked contributions of Florence Edler De Roover, shedding light on her intellectual partnership with economic historian Raymond De Roover. Chapter 11 closes the book with a folk tale that emphasizes the interconnection between gender and economics at the institutional, individual, structural, and social levels.

The qualitative and quantitative research presented throughout the book provides overwhelming evidence that gender disparities persist in economics, contributing to a leaky pipeline effect. What can be done to address this issue? Key avenues for closing these gaps include increasing female leadership, strengthening DEI initiatives, rethinking how economics is presented and taught, and expanding course offerings.

Diversity, equity, and inclusion (DEI) policies provide an approach to addressing the leaky pipeline. Chapter 6 analyzes the impact of DEI policies on reducing the underrepresentation of women in economics and concludes that current efforts remain insufficient. The authors recommend that, in addition to recruiting and retaining underrepresented students, classrooms, departments, and university-wide administrators must work together to address inequality. In the classroom, educators can adopt more inclusive teaching strategies and assessment methods. This includes incorporating gender-inclusive readings and examples, promoting active learning, and diversifying assessment methods to include low-stakes assignments in addition to high-stakes exams and research papers (Chapter 6).

Departments can increase female representation by ensuring that faculty composition reflects gender diversity. Chapter 2 highlights that institutions in Democratic-leaning states, public universities, and those with female department chairs tend to exhibit greater gender equity.

These findings emphasize the role of female leadership and institutional factors in promoting equal representation in economics, aligning with other research that supports the importance of representation (Carrell et al. 2010; Fairlie et al. 2014; Paredes et al. 2020). Departments can also promote gender equality by offering courses on gender and feminist economics. Chapter 8 shows that gender economics courses increase student interest in taking more economics courses. Additionally, departments should reevaluate hiring and admissions practices by moving away from traditional but biased approaches, such as exclusively hiring from elite PhD programs, using test score cutoffs, or relying on network recommendations (Bayer and Rouse 2016).

University-wide administrators can help address the leaky pipeline by promoting and enhancing diversity, equity, and inclusion in tenure promotions and research. Research on DEI in economics is critical for identifying and overcoming the barriers that persist in the field. As discussed in Chapter 3, women are less likely to publish in subfields perceived as rigorous, meaning administrators need to value research across methodology and subfield to foster equality in promotion and tenure decisions. Administrators can also establish mentoring programs to support faculty of all genders in research and grant proposals (Blau et al. 2010). Furthermore, university administrators shape institutional attitudes toward gender equity. A strong commitment to inclusivity at the university level can influence departmental and classroom practices.

Outside of universities and academic settings, attention to gender discrimination as a result of institutional, structural, and social structures is also important to consider. For example, social and institutional factors impact occupation choice in the paid labor market, undergraduate major choice at the university level, and research fields at the professional level (Blau et al. 2013). Broader social structures indirectly shape decision-making and outcomes by gender, leading to gender inequality at many levels. Future research must also investigate not only the direct causes of gender discrimination in economics but also the extent of these indirect influences. Both qualitative and quantitative methods, as well as various economic schools of thought, can add depth to this conversation.

These underlying social factors can also lead to discrimination and gender biases, which further contribute to the leaky pipeline in economics (Bayer and Rouse 2016). For example, an analysis of 12,000 reference letters and 3,700 candidates for entry-level faculty positions in the economics job market for entry-level faculty jobs showed that the attributes used to explain candidates who were women differed compared to the attributes that were used to explain candidates who were men (Eberhardt et al. 2022). A different study found that editorial boards that had a low level of representation of women harmed the success of female authors (Bransch and Kvasnicka 2022). These differences, which are often driven by implicit biases, still impact gender-based outcomes in economics. Hiring more female faculty and editors and educating and creating awareness about gender biases in the economics profession can help address the systemic roots of gender inequality in economics.

The book also outlines various directions for future research to further enhance gender representation in economics. Importantly, gender in economics is still largely framed as binary, excluding many individuals based on their gender identity. Future research should explore inclusive pedagogies that accommodate all genders. Additionally, economic surveys need to adopt more inclusive definitions of gender to foster better and more comprehensive research.

Another critical yet often understudied element of the leaky pipeline is how economics is introduced at the high school level. In 2009, about 58 percent of high school students had completed at least one economics course (Walstad and Rebeck 2012). Since most students take economics before they enter college, it is crucial to understand how high school curricula and pedagogy might influence gender differences in undergraduate economics courses and how these classes shape students' decisions to major or not major in economics. This may be another contributing factor to the persistent gender inequality that is present within economics.

Missing Voices in Economics sheds light on the persistent exclusion of women in economics and emphasizes the urgent need for structural change within the profession. Economics as a discipline has significant ground to make up before it is representative of the world for which it studies. Diversity strengthens any profession, leading to more balanced policy recommendations, a greater variety of research and methodologies, more impactful teaching and scholarship, and better decision-making overall (Bayer and Rouse 2016). Including the voices of women will only improve economics as a field, ultimately leading to better outcomes for everyone.

Now is the time to act. By addressing these disparities at every level, we can move toward a more equitable and inclusive field. The future of economics depends on the voices we amplify. Let us ensure that no voice is missing.

References

Ahlstrom, L. J., and C. J. Asarta. 2019. The Gender Gap in Undergraduate Economics Course Persistence and Degree Selection. *AEA Papers and Proceedings* 109:255–260.

American Academy of Arts & Sciences. n.d. *Gender Distribution of Bachelor's Degrees in the Humanities*. Humanities Indicators. Retrieved from https://www.amacad.org/humanities-indicators/higher-education/gender-distribution-bachelors-degrees-humanities.

Bayer, A., and C. E. Rouse. 2016. Diversity in the Economics Profession: A New Attack on an Old Problem. *Journal of Economic Perspectives* 30(4):221–242. https://doi.org/10.1257/jep.30.4.221.

Blau, F. D., J. M. Currie, R. T. A. Croson, and D. K. Ginther. 2010. Can Mentoring Help Female Assistant Professors? Interim Results from a Randomized Trial. *American Economic Review* 100(2):348–352. https://doi.org/10.1257/aer.100.2.348.

Blau, F. D., P. Brummund, and A. Y. H. Liu. 2013. Trends in Occupational Segregation by Gender 1970–2009: Adjusting for the Impact of Changes in the Occupational Coding System. *Demography* 50(2):471–492. https://doi.org/10.1007/s13524-012-0151-7.

Bransch, F., and M. Kvasnicka. 2022. Male Gatekeepers: Gender Bias in the Publishing Process? *Journal of Economic Behavior & Organization* 202:714–732. https://doi.org/10.1016/j.jebo.2022.07.031.

Carrell, S. E., M. E. Page, and J. E. West. 2010. Sex and Science: How Professor Gender Perpetuates the Gender Gap. *The Quarterly Journal of Economics* 125(3):1101–1144. https://doi.org/10.1162/qjec.2010.125.3.1101.

Chari, Anusha. 2023. Report of the Committee on the Status of Women in the Economics Profession. *AEA Papers and Proceedings* 113:815–839.

Dynan, K. E., and C. E. Rouse. 1997. The Underrepresentation of Women in Economics: A Study of Undergraduate Economics Students. *The Journal of Economic Education* 28(4):350–368. https://doi.org/10.1080/00220489709597939.

Eberhardt, M., G. Facchini, and V. Rueda. 2022. Gender Differences in Reference Letters: Evidence from the Economics Job Market. CEPR Discussion Paper No. 16960. CEPR Press. Retrieved from https://cepr.org/publications/dp16960.

Fairlie, R. W., F. Hoffmann, and P. Oreopoulos. 2014. A Community College Instructor Like Me: Race and Ethnicity Interactions in the Classroom. *American Economic Review* 104(8):2567–2591. https://doi.org/10.1257/aer.104.8.2567.

Kruus, N., I. Grigoryeva, and J. Kruus. 2024. The Gender Gap in STEM at Top U.S. Universities: Change over Time and Relationship with Ranking. *Journal of Emerging Investigators*. https://doi.org/10.59720/23-31.

National Center for Science and Engineering Statistics (NCSES). 2019. *Field of Degree: Women*. In *Women, Minorities, and Persons with Disabilities in Science and Engineering*. National Science Foundation. Retrieved from https://ncses.nsf.gov/pubs/nsf19304/digest/field-of-degree-women#figtblpanewmpd19-sr-fig02a.

Paredes, V. A., M. D. Paserman, and F. Pino. 2020. Does Economics Make You Sexist? National Bureau of Economic Research Working Paper No. 27070. https://doi.org/10.3386/w27070.

Sarsons, H., K. Gërxhani, E. Reuben, and A. Schram. 2021. Gender Differences in Recognition for Group Work. *Journal of Political Economy* 129(1):101–147. https://doi.org/10.1086/711401.

Walstad, W. B., and K. Rebeck. 2012. Economics Course Enrollments in U.S. High Schools. *The Journal of Economic Education* 43(3):339–347. https://doi.org/10.1080/00220485.2012.686394.

Index

A
AEA, 29
age/age group, 79, 89
American Economic Association's (AEA's) survey, 1
American Economic Association's Committee on the Status of Women in the Economics Profession, 139
an academe dominated by sexism, 208
anti-DEI legislation, 119
apprenticeship, 223
ASSA meetings, 29
Assistant Professor, 3
Associate Professor, 3
associations, 77
average proportion of female economists, 100

B
Bergmann, Barbara, 150
Binary trans, 176
biographical sketch of her life, 198
building community, 150

C
Cisnormativity, 181, 187
co-authored, 85
co-authorship, 85
Colorado State University, 156, 159
conferences, 8
conservative societies, 104
correct methodology, 21
course evaluations, 9
Courtesanship, 231
Crenshaw, Kimberlee, 174
Cretan communities, 217
Cretan storytellers, 218
Crete island, 221
cultural stereotypes and biases, 52

D
deficit-based approach, 178
demographic data, 28
De Roover, Florence Edler, 198, 207, 210
de Roover, Raymond, 197
difficult to survive in patriarchy, 236
discrimination, 21, 90

© The Editor(s) (if applicable) and The Author(s), under exclusive license to Springer Nature Switzerland AG 2026

V. Dolar and T. Perry (eds.), *Missing Voices in Economics*, https://doi.org/10.1007/978-3-031-97180-8

dissertation, 199
distribution of working time, 87
diversity, equity, and inclusion (DEI) initiatives, 42, 113, 114, 117, 250
doctoral attainment, 80
domestic work, 86
double burden on women, 110
Dr Ferda Dönmez-Atbaşı, 217
Duncan segregation index, 82, 89

E
economic education, 237
Economic seminars, 20
Economics Jobs Market Rumors (EJMR), 115
EDI initiatives, 114, 115, 117, 123, 125, 129
educational backgrounds, 80
Elite schools, 4
Elsevier's SCOPUS database, 43
Elson, Diane, 140
external factors, 53
external funding, 151

F
family issues, 103
family status, 79
female-dominated field, 64
female economics majors, 107
female economists heading in the top 25% of economics departments, 101
female representation, 250
feminism, 138
feminist and activist groups, 139
feminist economics, 61, 66, 68, 135, 139, 151, 152
feminist economics in the graduate degrees/feminist economists in master's programs and in PhD programs, 143
feminist economists have faced getting tenure, 141
fields of concentration/fields of specialisation/fields of study, 45, 61, 88
financial economics, 64
Finding community, 138
folk culture, 241
folk literature, 215
folktales, 220
Full Professorship, 3

G
gender as an "add in" variable, 177
gender-aware economics, 124
gender binary, 177
gender differences in academic production by field, 59
gender distribution, 46, 51
gender distribution of the field of research, 62
Gender economics, 68
gender economics, 61, 66, 146
Gender Equality and Economy Program at The Levy Economics Institute at Bard College, 140
gender equity training, 27
Gender in the Economy, 159
gender segregation, 65, 66, 69
gender studies programs, 139
geography in history, 205
global south, 102
Glossary, 206
graduate
  graduate level, 137
  graduate programs, 137
  graduate student pipeline, 26
  graduate students, 5
  graduate training, 136

grassroots economics thought, 216, 237
Grown, Caren, 140

H
Health and Labor, 53
health, education, and welfare, 64
high school economics, 252
hiring, 27
historical and institutional forces, 250
history of banking, 202
holistic approach, 130

I
index of dissimilarity, 66
indispensable collaborator, 197, 210
institution type- private vs. public, 50, 52
Interdisciplinarity, 128
International Association for Feminist Economics, 138
International Working Group on Gender, Macroeconomics, and International Economics, 140
intersectional approach, 165
Intersectionality, 106
introductory class focused on economics and gender, 155
Italian Economic Society, 77, 78
Italian universities, 76
Italian women economists, 78

J
JEL code, 59, 61, 67

L
leaky pipeline/pipeline problems, 115, 148, 168, 247, 249, 251
leave the profession, 23
legal codes and concerns, 205
LGBTQ+, 183
love for her son, 226

M
macroeconomics, 64
main field of research, 62
Mainstream economics, 238
male-dominated fields, 64
Maria Mavredaki, 220
Mariyam Zia Baloch, 104
masculine experience, 136
mathematical and quantitative methods, 64
Medici Bank, 200
medieval economy, 203
mentoring and recruiting/mentoring programs, 24, 26, 151
microeconomics, 64
Mobility, 105
monetary economics, 64
mother and daughter, 224

N
National Center for Science and Engineering Statistics [NCSES] 2019, 247
network, 8
New Economic Papers (NEP), 99, 102
Nil, 140
non-academic jobs, 13
non-binary trans, 176
non-tenure-track positions, 3
novel dataset, 38

O
oral history(ies) collection, 137
our own identity, 176

P

patriarchy, 217, 240
  patriarchal ending, 236
  patriarchal norms, 105
Perceptions of Women, 13
PhD degrees, 5
PhD dissertation, 80
Political affiliation/political leaning, 41, 52
political and cultural factors, 46
problems women face in the profession of economics, 1
Program on Gender Analysis in Economics, 140
prostitute/prostitution, 231, 234
publications/publishing, 11, 84

Q

qualitative analysis/qualitative and mixed methods, 76, 128
queer and trans topics, 187

R

Race, Inequality, and Discrimination, 167
rate of acceptance of their publications, 85
registrar data, 156
relationship with their advisor, 185
religious affiliation, 42
research interests/research topics, 51, 61
Research Papers in Economics (RePEc), 59, 60, 99
Role models, 25

S

semi-structured interviews, 100
sexual harassment, 15
SGM (Sexual and Gender Minority)/ SM (Sexual Minority)., 174
slave trade, 223
socially excluded, 17
social provisioning approach, 124, 125
South Asia/South Asian context, 99
Sponsorship, 106
state political affiliation, 50
STEM, 248
student's preferences to take future economic courses, 159
systematic survey, 77

T

teaching and assessment methods, 126
tenure decisions, 12
TGD faculty, 190
TGD identities, 182
TGD people of color, 180
the continued underrepresentation of women, 113
the exclusion of women and gender from economic theory and models, 249
the exercise of power on, 226
the field of specialization, 100
the history of marine insurance, 200
the index of dissimilarity, 66
the low presence of women in the economic discipline, 75
the main research fields of both women and men top economists, 64
The Medici Bank, 207
Theories, 21
The Rise and Decline of the Medici Bank, 207
the role of gender in the economics profession, 58
Title VI of the Civil Rights Act of 1964, 117
top 10% of authors, 60

top 240 economics departments, 44
top five economic journals, 116
top of the organization, 24
top women and men economists' publications, 61
Trans and Gender Diverse (TGD), 174
trans-celebratory, 190
trans experience in higher education, 184
transing, 179
Transing economics, 191
transmit economic information, 215
treatment strategy, 161

U
UK universities, 118
undergraduate gender economics courses, 144
Undergraduate men, 164
undergraduate students, 5, 108
undergraduate women, 164
Union for Radical Political Economy's (URPE's) Women's Caucus, 139
university funding and budget models, 148
US Supreme Court, 119
US universities, 118
usury, 203

W
web-scraping, 38, 43
woman chairman, 42
women, 216
women and men's top economists, 62

FSC
www.fsc.org
MIX
Papier | Fördert gute Waldnutzung
FSC® C083411

Kolibri 360 GmbH
Ferdinand-Jühlke-Straße 7
99095 Erfurt, Deutschland
produktsicherheit@kolibri360.de